Dr. BBQ's Big-Time Barbecue Road Trip!

Also by Ray Lampe

Dr. BBQ's Big-Time Barbecue Cookbook

Dr. BBQ's "Barbecue All Year Long!" Cookbook

Dr. BBQ's Big-Time Barbecue

Road Trip!

Ray Lampe
a.k.a. Dr. BBQ

Foreword by Chris Lilly

St. Martin's Griffin ❧ New York

www.stmartins.com

Library of Congress Cataloging-in-Publication Data
Lampe, Ray.
    Dr. BBQ's big-time barbecue road trip! / Ray Lampe a.k.a. Dr. BBQ; foreword by Chris
Lilly.
        p. cm.
    ISBN-13: 978-0-312-34958-5
    ISBN-10: 0-312-34958-0
  1. Barbecue cookery. I. Title.
TX840.B3L37 2007
641.7'6–dc22

        2007008999

Design by Ralph Fowler / rlf design

First Edition: June 2007
10 9 8 7 6 5 4 3 2 1

This book is dedicated to
John Beadle,
my friend and mentor.

Contents

Acknowledgments

This book sure was fun to write. It was simply a reliving of about ten years of my own wonderful road trips. If I wrote down all the names from all around the country it would be another whole book, so let me just say thanks to all the men and women who are out there living the barbecue life. If it wasn't for you there would be no reason for anyone to make a barbecue road trip.

I've also got to thank all the folks who take my writings about my wonderful journeys and turn them into a book. I sure couldn't do it without them. My good friend Dave DeWitt is the one I turn to when I'm stuck, and he always has a good idea. Michael Flamini is always a great inspiration to me, and on this book he's been as good as ever. Thanks to Vicki Lame for keeping Michael and me in synch all the time. Thanks to Scott Mendel, my great agent, for keeping the i's dotted and the t's crossed so I can just write the books. Thanks to John Karle for all he does to get me in the places I need to be to promote my books, and thanks also to his assistant, Kelly Spann. They are always a pleasure to work with. Thanks to all the great folks at St. Martin's who do all the behind-the-scenes work to make us all look good on the shelf: Amelie Littell, James Sinclair, Cheryl Mamaril, Ralph Fowler, Pete Garceau, and especially Matthew Shear, the St. Martin's Griffin publisher.

Because of all these great folks I'm living my dream of promoting barbecue every day.

Foreword

Folks, I have traveled the country and spent many days barbecuing with Ray from Seattle to New York City. I have faced this imposing barbecue icon at cookoffs and burnt the same wood with him as a team member of Worst Kept Secret. Competitions, caterings, and cooking classes have given us the opportunity to both teach and learn this splendid art of cooking.

I am here to tell you there is no better barbecue companion, no better barbecue guide than Ray Lampe. From salmon to satays, brine to brisket, foie gras to frog legs, Ray gives you a new perspective on food and a fresh understanding of why the cultish popularity of barbecue has enthralled the nation. His no-nonsense, straightforward, and in-your-face style translates into fun times and great Q on the road!

With this book you can travel the same path and speak with the same people Ray did on his journey. Take his suggestions, follow his cross-country route, devour the food, and meet some of the fantastic people of barbecue. Be careful mentioning his name. The result could be as tricky as tenderizing a free-range brisket. Good times often leave a path of smiles; great times leave a path of people wondering "What the #%$#%$* just happened?" Ray's path is bigger than most.

—Chris Lilly,
Big Bob Gibson Bar-B-Q

Introduction

The Start of the Barbecue Road Trip

This has been a fun book to research and write. Many of us have dreamed of the chance to travel the country eating and learning about barbecue, and now many of us do it. Seeking out the legendary old barbecue haunts has become a common vacation activity. I think it's because we all travel so freely now and we have the ability to find interesting new things to do while we're traveling. But it's also the magic of barbecue that draws us to it. There's just something about an old barbecue restaurant that can't be matched by a seafood shack or a famous old diner. I think it's all about the preparation of the barbecue. A great seafood shack is mainly built on the freshness of the fish and the waterfront tables. A famous diner is often about the flakiness of the piecrust and the sweetness of the waitress, or is it the other way around? At a barbecue joint it's about that pitmaster's own version of the greatest American cuisine. The surroundings can be anything and anywhere. If the food is good it works. How many of us spend our whole lives in search of the ultimate rib? I know I do. Anytime I drive past a barbecue joint I haven't been to I can't help but think that this might just be the place with the best rib anywhere so I'd better stop. I wouldn't want to make my life's decision about the best rib ever and be unsure because I've skipped this place. Sound familiar? Okay, maybe it's brisket for you or pork, but you know you have your favorite barbecue specialty.

In my travels I've found consistencies and surprises. The most consistent thing about a barbecue restaurant is the passion for the food. It's always the top priority. Whether I was talking to Mr. Powdrell, the weathered old barbecue restaurant man in Albuquerque, or to Dave Klose, the legendary pit builder in Houston, or to Adam Perry Lang, the French chef turned barbecue man in New York City, it's all about the food. The culture and patina just seem to happen around barbecue, and it's often taken for granted. That could be because they are all so focused on the food that painting the walls or getting a new sign just takes a backseat. Sometimes it takes a seat and never gets back up. Louie Mueller's in Taylor, Texas, couldn't be funkier if they tried, but it's one of the best barbecue joints I've ever been to. Every person, place, or thing in this book is completely focused on the quality of the food. Now that doesn't mean there aren't some places that are a little better kept. The new Oklahoma Joe's in Olathe, Kansas, is quite nice, while the original in Kansas City, Kansas, is in a funky gas station. I'm happy at either one, though, because the food is always good. It's their top priority.

As for the differences in barbecue around the country, some are obvious. They cook almost all pork in North Carolina and mostly beef in Texas. No surprise there, they grow hogs in North Carolina and cattle in Texas. The sauces are generally sweeter as you head north and there are always regional specialties like the barbecued mutton in Kentucky. But I found that many of the legends that are written about just don't seem to be true. When I go somewhere and eat the barbecue I've often wondered if some of the people who write about regional barbecue have ever been to these places. Trust me: If you're reading about smoky-tasting barbecue in North Carolina the writer hasn't been there, if you're reading about all the white barbecue sauce in Alabama the writer hasn't been there, and if you think you won't get slaw on your sandwich outside of North Carolina, you haven't been to Memphis. I had a brisket sandwich at House Park Bar-B-Que in Austin, Texas. It's been there since 1943. They served sauce on my sandwich. Wait a minute. I thought there wasn't any sauce in Texas, so I asked. The guy said, "Sure we put it on, our sauce is homemade and it's good." It was. On the contrary, the barbecue up north doesn't all get a bath of sauce as some think.

What about beer with barbecue? It seems like a natural, but I ate in twenty-two restaurants in North Carolina and couldn't get a beer at any of them. In Texas many of the barbecue joints were primarily beer joints that served barbecue. Beer certainly goes well with barbecue and it's very popular, but it's not the chosen drink in the world of barbecue. What is? Sweet tea. Sweet tea is a staple in the South but I don't think I've ever been to a barbecue joint anywhere that didn't serve it. Sometimes up north you'll get "iced tea," which southerners would recognize as unsweet tea, but they've always got some of those little sugar packets so you can make do. Here's the first recipe in the book and it goes here because it's universal to all the regions of barbecue.

Sweet Tea

Yes, there is a recipe for sweet tea. Making sweet tea is a serious thing to southerners, and northerners are catching on thanks to the spread of real barbecue. Good tea can make or break a restaurant in the South. That premixed stuff just doesn't cut it. It needs to be fresh brewed with lots of sugar. Here's how I like mine. You may want to up the sugar to 2 full cups. • **Yield: 1 gallon**

1 gallon water

4 family-size tea bags
(designed to make 1 quart each)

1½ cups sugar

In a medium saucepan, bring 1 quart of water to a full boil. Remove from the heat and drop in the tea bags. Let the tea steep for 6 minutes, tumbling the tea bags a couple times. Remove the tea bags and stir in the sugar. Let rest for 1 minute and stir again until the sugar is all dissolved. Pour into a 1-gallon pitcher and add 1 quart of water. Stir well. Add one or two trays of ice and stir again. Add enough water to fill the pitcher and stir again. Keep in the refrigerator and serve over ice.

If you know me or you've read my other books, you know that I've spent a lot more years driving a truck than I have writing books. So this book, like my others, is kind of free-form. Some of the places in the book I've been going to for many years and know well. Some of the people are old friends. Others are new friends that I sought out just to learn about for the book. Same with the places, I stumbled across some of the new ones but also made specific trips to some new places to learn about them for this book. That's why you'll read twelve restaurant reviews written by me in Texas. I wrote those immediately after I'd eaten at the places with the intention of blending them later. When I got done it seemed a shame to break them up

so I've left them intact. The North Carolina trip was with my friend, The Pope of Peppers, Dave DeWitt. Dave wanted to score the restaurants so we'd have a favorite when we got done. Sounded good to me and that's how you'll read it. Kansas City is a place I've gone for many years, and the barbecue joints and people are so much a part of my life that it was hard to write about as a road trip. So please enjoy each chapter in its own way. I begin each chapter with a rub recipe and a sauce recipe. These are by no means meant to be the end-all regional rub and sauce for that area. If I found anything on this trip it was that there usually isn't a specific taste that fits the whole region, despite what you might have heard. These are just my recipes inspired by the regions. I call for the rubs and sauces in recipes within the chapters, but you should feel free to mix and match them. Speaking of the recipes, you're going to find some great recipes in this book from some famous barbecue people. I generally don't ask them for one of their signature recipes; I know those are usually confidential. Besides, one book can only have so many rib or brisket recipes. The good news is these folks all gave me something interesting and it has made for a great collection of recipes. I highly recommend every person, place, and thing in this book as a stop on your barbecue road trip. Tell them all Dr. BBQ says hi.

Ray Lampe

Kansas City

Dr. BBQ's Kansas City Barbecue Rub

Dr. BBQ's Kansas City Barbecue Sauce

Arthur Bryant's, Gates, and Arthur Pinkard

Kansas City–Style Brisket and Burnt Ends

The American Royal Barbecue

Party Chick's Sweet Potatoes

Smokin' Guns Broccoli Casserole

Sausage-Fest Barbecue Beans

The Kansas City Barbeque Society

Twin Oaks Friday Night Jalapeño Peppers

Twin Oaks Pepper Rub

Ray Basso/The BBQ Forum

Best Ribs in the Universe

Bichelmeyer's Meats

Barbecue Sausage

Oklahoma Joe's

Jeff Stehney's Smoked and Braised Beef Short Ribs

Jones Bar-B-Q

Smoked Ham Kansas City Style

Smokin' Guns BBQ

Linda's Coffee Cake

Rosedale Barbeque

K.C. Red Rose BBQ Sauce

Fiorella's Jack Stack

Easy Cheesy Corn Casserole

Culinary Center of Kansas City

Chef McPeake's Honey Maple Salmon

It's fitting for me to start this book in Kansas City, because that is where my barbecue roots are. After attending my first sanctioned barbecue cookoff near Chicago in 1991, I wanted to learn more about this magical thing we call barbecue. The sanctioning group that day was the Kansas City Barbeque Society. Soon after that cookoff, I joined KCBS and began to hear about how things were done in Kansas City. There were the old restaurants, the legendary pitmasters, lots of cookoffs, and the icing on the cake, the American Royal. All of these things made this place sound like barbecue Disney Land. It was only an eight-hour ride to Kansas City from Chicago, so I began making weekend trips every chance I had. I would cook in a contest or judge one or attend the year-end banquet or just drive down to eat in the restaurants. Remember, I was new to all this and I was starving to learn more. In those days barbecue wasn't very popular in Chicago and barbecued brisket just wasn't available. But in Kansas City there were dozens of places that had it, and it was their number-one menu item. So I have a strong affection for the barbecue in Kansas City, and I still enjoy going there any time I can. There is no experience quite like lunch at Arthur Bryant's. Then you can swing by Ambrosi Brothers Cutlery and get your knives sharpened while you wait. Ambrosi is one of those places that the folks from K.C. take for granted, but would be hard to find in

any other city. It's a sharpening service with a storefront where you can buy some nice gourmet kitchen stuff, but they're really all about sharpening knives. Many a good barbecue man has cut himself with the razors you leave there with. Then you should head over to see Matt Bichelmeyer for some great meat in an amazing old-fashioned butcher shop setting, and, last but not least, head to Smoke N Fire to see big smokers and tons of sauce, cooking wood, and rub right on the showroom floor. Only in Kansas City!

Kansas City is beef country. In years past, it was the site of the big stockyard auction in the middle of the country and cattle were plentiful, so that's what the people ate. In the barbecue joints it's always brisket, but Kansas City is also very fond of their steaks, boasting some of the oldest and finest steak houses in the country. Things have changed a little now, but it wasn't very long ago that most of the barbecue joints in K.C. didn't even have pork on the menu. When I say that I mean pork loin or shoulder. Pork ribs somehow have transcended all boundaries of barbecue. They show up on barbecue menus everywhere. I think that's because they're just that good.

So, if you walk into a restaurant in Kansas City and order a barbecue sandwich, it will be brisket, either dry or with a little bit of interesting sauce on top. Contrary to popular belief, you will not receive a sandwich drowned in thick, sticky sauce with a bunch of molasses in it. There is that famous sauce that Dr. Rich Davis brought to the market called KC Masterpiece, and it sells very well in the stores in K.C. as well as the rest of the country, but that's just not what you'll get when you dine in Kansas City. When I eat at Gates, I get a delicious barbecue sauce that is like no other I have had. It's a tangy red tomato-based sauce with a distinct celery seed flavor. It's not overly sweet or sticky and has no taste of molasses. I don't personally eat much barbecue sauce at home, but if I do it's usually Gates Original.

Then there's Arthur Bryant's. Their original barbecue sauce is also like nothing else I've ever had, but you won't find this one in my fridge at home. I do, however, eat it and enjoy it on my sandwich when I'm eating at Bryant's. It's a grainy sauce, seemingly loaded with paprika. I won't even guess what else is in it, but there is a legend about an ingredient that is allowed to ferment in the front window. You'll see it there, in a large glass bottle, but I've never asked. I don't think I want to know. There are plenty of other interesting original sauces at the barbecue houses of K.C. Be sure to try Rosedale, LC's, Danny Edwards, Jones, and Zarda. But without a doubt Bryant's and Gates are the biggest names in K.C. barbecue. They both have very successful flagship restaurants with a few satellite locations as well as successful rub and sauce businesses. Unfortunately, that also means they have been written about over and over, and even though the stories are great, I'm going to be quick with them so I can bring up some new places for you to see when you're in K.C.

I asked Ardie Davis, a.k.a. Remus Powers, local barbecue historian and host of the world's largest barbecue sauce contest (www.thinkbbq.com), what he thought of my suspicion that most of America misunderstood what K.C. barbecue sauce was. He wholeheartedly agreed with me that K.C. barbecue sauce is a series of interesting originals and not any one type of sauce. It's amazing what you can find when you go to a place and experience the real things. I love Kansas City barbecue and I think you will, too.

Dr. BBQ's Kansas City Barbecue Rub

⅓ cup salt

¼ cup brown sugar

¼ cup turbinado sugar (Sugar in the Raw)

2 tablespoons paprika

1 tablespoon chili powder

1 teaspoon granulated garlic

1 teaspoon onion powder

1 teaspoon lemon pepper

1 teaspoon finely ground black pepper

½ teaspoon cayenne pepper

⅛ teaspoon ground allspice

½ teaspoon ground nutmeg

- Yield: About 1¼ cups

Combine all the ingredients and store in an airtight container.

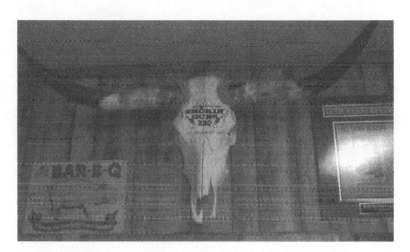

Dr. BBQ's Kansas City Barbecue Sauce

2 tablespoons butter

1 medium onion, chopped fine

One 12-ounce can of beer

1 cup brown sugar

1 cup ketchup

½ cup cider vinegar

1 teaspoon celery seed

1 teaspoon hot sauce

1 teaspoon salt

- Yield: About 2½ cups

Heat the butter in a medium saucepan, add the onion, and sauté over medium heat, stirring often, until the onion is soft, about 4 minutes.

Add the rest of the ingredients and bring to a boil. Reduce to a simmer and cook uncovered, stirring occasionally, for about 20 minutes, or until thickened.

Arthur Bryant's, Gates, and Arthur Pinkard

Kansas City, Missouri:

www.arthurbryantsbbq.com

www.gatesbbq.com

▼▼

According to Doug Worgul, K.C. barbecue historian extraordinaire and author of a great book about it called *The Grand Barbecue*, a fellow named Henry Perry started it all in Kansas City in 1907. An interesting twist to the story is that Henry Perry was born near Memphis, Tennessee, another great barbecue city. At some point Henry Perry had three restaurants and one of them was being run by Charlie Bryant, Arthur Bryant's older brother. Arthur Bryant also worked for Mr. Perry, and so did a man named Arthur Pinkard. More about him later. When Henry Perry died in 1940, one of his restaurants became Charlie Bryant's. In 1946, when Charlie Bryant retired, it became Arthur Bryant's. It has since become a treasured landmark in K.C., once called "The Best Damn Restaurant in the World" by Calvin Trillin and frequented by American presidents and countless celebs. An interesting story about Bryant's is that the famous K.C. burnt ends were created there. When you were in line you could just scoop up some of the crumbled stuff that fell off the slicer and put it on your plate. It's now a very popular dish in Kansas City and is usually made up of the point muscle, cubed and cooked a little longer than the flat muscle, which is sliced.

About that same time, in 1946, a man named George Gates bought a K.C. restaurant named Ol' Kentuck Bar-B-Q. The pitmaster at Ol' Kentuck was Arthur Pinkard, who had previously worked the pit for Henry Perry. The Gates family say they learned about barbecue from Mr. Pinkard, and that's why his picture hangs in all of their restaurants. The story sometimes gets mixed up to say that George Gates and Arthur Bryant both worked for Henry Perry, but that's just not true. The connection is Arthur Pinkard, who is largely unknown but a very important man in the history of Kansas City barbecue. In 1960, George Gates died, and the business has been headed by Ollie Gates ever since. Ollie Gates is a K.C. legend in his own right and has even appeared on *The Martha Stewart Show*, where he showed Martha how to cook real Kansas City barbecue. Gates has grown to be the bigger of the two K.C. legends, if not the most famous, and their sauce business is huge. They have six full-service restaurants in the Kansas City area and all are doing very well. When you walk in the door of a Gates restaurant, you will immediately hear a server yell, "Hi, may I help you?" They don't necessarily expect you to order right away, it's just how they like to greet you at Gates. It's a warm welcome to hear, and I usually respond by saying "I'll have a slab, no pickle, and a red soda." By the way, there are no burnt ends at Gates. Mr. Gates says, "We try not to burn our meat."

Kansas City–Style Brisket and Burnt Ends

1 choice-grade whole packer-cut brisket, about 12 pounds

¹/₂ cup Worcestershire sauce

Dr. BBQ's Kansas City Barbecue Rub (page 5)

1 cup Dr. BBQ's Kansas City Barbecue Sauce (page 5)

¹/₂ cup beef broth

This is how many great cooks in Kansas City treat their beloved brisket. • **Yield: About 12 servings**

Trim the fat around the brisket down to about ¹/₂ inch all over. In a big pan, rub the Worcestershire all over the brisket. Season liberally with the rub. Cover and return to the refrigerator for at least an hour and up to overnight. Prepare the cooker for indirect cooking at 235°F, using oak and hickory wood for flavor. Put the brisket in the cooker fat side down and cook for 4 hours. Flip the brisket and cook until the center of the flat muscle reaches an internal temp of 195°F. This should take 7 to 10 more hours, depending on your cooker. Remove the brisket to a cutting board. Using a long, sharp knife, separate the two muscles of the brisket. Trim the fat off the flat muscle and wrap it tightly in a double layer of aluminum foil. Place the flat in an empty ice chest. Fill the ice chest with crumpled newspaper and close the lid. Trim the fat from the point muscle and add a little more seasoning. Put the point back in the cooker for 2 more hours. Remove the point to a cutting board. Cut it into cubes about 1¹/₂ inches square. Put the cubes in a pan. Combine the sauce and the broth and pour the mixture over the cubed point. You may not want to use it all. Toss to coat. Return to the cooker for 30 minutes, tossing once during that time. Remove the flat from the cooler and slice it. Transfer to a platter and drizzle a little sauce over it. Spoon the cubes, which are now burnt ends, onto the same platter.

The American Royal Barbecue

Kansas City, Missouri

www.americanroyal.com

▼▼

The American Royal is a 100-plus-year-old livestock show and a month-long festival that surrounds it. It's held at the American Royal Complex in an area of Kansas City called The Bottoms, and it's right where the old stockyards were. One of the events is the American Royal Barbecue cookoff, and it's a doozie. It all started in 1980, which was clearly the early days of barbecue cookoffs. The first one was held in the parking lot of the legendary K.C. steak house The Golden Ox, but the cookoff moved over to the big parking lots outside the American Royal building long ago. These days, when the first weekend in October rolls around, all the big names in competitive barbecue load up their cookers and head for Kansas City. The team count is over five hundred, the prize money is over $80,000, and the party is herculean. It's often called "The World Series of Barbecue" and it boasts the largest field of competitors anywhere. The amount of beer and barbecue that is consumed that weekend is outrageous. There are bands set up to play in many of the booths, and because of the random nature of the placement, you may see two bands standing next to each other playing in different booths. Now that's a party! They even have an award for the Best Party of the Year. I've never quite figured out how they judge this category, but they always have a winner. Aside from the typical KCBS categories, they have sausage, dessert, and a big side dish contest. The side dish contest involves three categories and is taken very seriously by the cooks. The categories are Potatoes, Beans, and Vegetables. There are also awards for the overall of the three, a Grand Champion of barbecue side dishes.

I once had the pleasure of the Rub Me Tender team from Detroit joining me at the Royal to cook my side dishes. They did very well with a perfect score in the potato category, and I'm pleased to include their recipe here. I've also included a winning vegetable recipe from Linda at Smokin' Guns and a first-place bean recipe from 2005 from Sausage-Fest BBQ.

Party Chick's Sweet Potatoes

1½ cups light brown sugar

1½ cup coarsely chopped pecans

¾ stick butter, cut in small pieces and softened

5 pounds sweet potatoes

4 large eggs

3 tablespoons pure maple syrup

2 tablespoons vanilla

1 tablespoon fresh lemon juice

2 teaspoons salt

This is the recipe that the girls from the Rub Me Tender team cooked for me at the American Royal in 2000. It got a perfect score! • **Yield: 12 servings**

Preheat the oven or smoker to 350°F.

Mix together the brown sugar, pecans, and butter. Chill until ready to use.

Wrap the potatoes individually in foil and roast until done, about 1 hour. Let cool, then unwrap. Remove skins. Place the potatoes in a large bowl. Using a hand mixer, beat until smooth.

In a separate bowl, beat eggs, syrup, vanilla, lemon juice, and salt together. Add to the sweet potatoes. Mix well. Spread the mixture evenly into a buttered 9×3-inch baking pan. Cut the pecan-butter mixture into small pieces and sprinkle evenly over the potatoes.

Bake until the topping bubbles, about 1 hour. Let stand 15 minutes.

Smokin' Guns Broccoli Casserole

2 bags frozen broccoli florets

1 stick butter

1 small onion, chopped

2 cups cooked white rice

2 cans cream of celery soup

One 15-ounce jar Cheese Whiz

1 cup french-fried onions (the kind sold in the can)

This recipe took first place in the Vegetable Side Dish category at the 2004 American Royal Barbecue Contest. • **Yield: 8 servings**

Preheat the oven to 350°F. This can also be done on the cooker at indirect heat, 350°F. Cook the broccoli in the butter until just thawed. Combine broccoli mixture and remaining ingredients. Mix well. Pour into a 9×13-inch pan. Bake for 30 minutes. Top with the french-fried onions and bake for 10 more minutes, watching closely so that the onion rings don't burn.

Myself and some young barbecue fans at World Pork Expo 2006.

Sausage-Fest Barbecue Beans

1½ cups chopped smoked pork or brisket or a combination

Three 28-ounce cans Bush's Baked Beans

½ cup brown sugar, plus more for sprinkling

½ cup molasses

1 medium onion, chopped

3 tablespoons beef or pork rub (I'd suggest Dr. BBQ's Kansas City Barbecue Rub, page 5)

This recipe came to me from Troy Boehm, the head cook for Sausage-Fest BBQ. The American Royal is known for the creative team names, and Sausage-Fest sure fits the bill. This team is also famous for their first-place beans at the 2005 American Royal, and Troy has generously shared the recipe with me. • **Yield: About 12 servings**

Prepare the cooker for indirect cooking at 225°F, using cherry wood for flavor. Place all ingredients in an aluminum foil baking pan, add ½ cup water, and mix well. Sprinkle a little additional brown sugar on top. Put the pan in the cooker for about 5 hours.

Take the pan out of the cooker. Wrap the pan in foil and let it sit for 15 to 30 minutes before serving.

The Kansas City Barbeque Society

Kansas City, Missouri

www.kcbs.us

▼▼

The Kansas City Barbeque Society has had a huge influence on the growth of competitive barbecue. Certainly Food TV and the Internet have given a big push in recent years, but KCBS was promoting cookoffs before most of us had ever heard of them. Carolyn Wells tells me that she was working for Wicker's, a barbecue sauce company, when she first encountered the Memphis in May cookoff in the early eighties. It was and still is an extravaganza. Meanwhile, some other folks from Kansas City had also heard about MIM and they decided to have their own cookoff, now fondly known as the American Royal. One day in 1985 Carolyn, her husband, Gary, and a friend named Rick Welch decided there was so much interest in this that they needed to start a barbecue club. They named it the Kansas City Barbeque Society and declared that the number one rule would be that nothing would be taken too seriously. That would be grounds for disqualification. They started their own cookoff in 1986 called Spring Training, and because this was all in fun they charged $69 to enter. Everyone got meat to cook and a cooler and there were small trophies. I was lucky enough to attend one of the last Spring Training cookoffs.

According to Carolyn, it ended after ten years because it just wasn't needed anymore. You see, things grew up all around KCBS.

Lots of people were organizing cookoffs, and KCBS had become the premier barbecue cookoff–sanctioning body. By the mid-nineties things were growing way past the boundaries of Kansas City, with cookoffs in Illinois, Tennessee, Washington State, and even California. The word was spreading fast. By about 2001 KCBS was sanctioning 100 cookoffs a year and boasted 3,000 members from all over the world. But it wasn't slowing down. Five years later those numbers were double, with 200 cookoffs and 6,000 members, and it's still not slowing down. Gary and Carolyn Wells have put many years of time and effort into KCBS, and we all owe them a lot of thanks. Carolyn told me a story today while we were talking about a friend of ours named Buddy Babb. Seems recently someone asked Buddy about KCBS and he replied that it had changed his life. Buddy and his son Charlie won the World Barbecue Association Championship in 2000 and now run a successful barbecue restaurant in Nashville. KCBS has changed my life, too. Without KCBS I seriously doubt that I could make my living writing about and cooking barbecue. There are many others on the list of people who have had their lives changed by KCBS, too. The world of competition barbecue is very healthy thanks to the Kansas City Barbeque Society.

Twin Oaks Friday Night Jalapeño Peppers

12 jalapeño peppers

12 small raw shrimp

½ cup cream cheese

12 slices bacon

Twin Oaks Pepper Rub
(recipe follows)

Twin Oaks Smoking Crew is one of the best KCBS cooking teams of all time, so who better to include here. Bart Clarke and his dad, Dick, have won the Jack Daniel's World Championship and they've been the KCBS Team of the Year twice. On Friday night if you stop to see Bart he'll probably be cooking "Peppers," and he was nice enough to share his recipe with me. • **Yield: 12 peppers**

Prepare the cooker for indirect cooking at 350°F. Cut the tops off the peppers. Use an apple corer to scrape out the seeds and veins. If you want them hotter, leave some of this in. Rinse them out with water. Stuff each of the peppers half-full with the cream cheese, then one of the shrimp. Wrap a piece of bacon around the tip and open end of the pepper, to keep the cream cheese from leaking out. Secure with a toothpick.

Place on the grill and cook the peppers for 30 minutes, turning every once in a while. Sprinkle liberally with the rub. Continue cooking until the bacon is done and crisp, about another 30 minutes. Remove to a platter and let cool for at least 10 minutes. Enjoy with good friends and a cold drink.

Twin Oaks Pepper Rub

2 tablespoons white sugar

1 tablespoon salt

1 teaspoon finely ground black pepper

1 teaspoon granulated garlic

½ teaspoon ground sage

Combine and mix well.

Ray Basso/The BBQ Forum

www.bbqforum.com

▼▼▼

Ray Basso is an Internet pioneer. He's also a great fan of barbecue and he lives in suburban Kansas City. I've written about Ray before, but he deserves another look because he has had a huge influence on barbecue in Kansas City, as well as around the country. The way Ray tells the story, he was driving to an appointment to sell some term life insurance and listening to the radio when he heard an interview with Carolyn Wells. When Carolyn said she'd send a free copy of *The Bullsheet* (a barbecue newsletter) to anyone who called, Ray's lightbulb went off. If he put together a Web page where you could request a free *Bullsheet*, everyone would come there, and while they were there he would get them to buy some Kansas City barbecue sauce. This was in 1995, and thus was born the first-ever Web page about barbecue. It still exists as The K.C. BBQ Connection, at http://www.rbjb.com/rbjb/bbq.htm, but, sadly, Ray never got rich selling barbecue sauce. His Web site did get popular enough that Carolyn called one day and said that she couldn't keep giving all those *Bullsheets* away. Ray Basso has helped facilitate the beginning of many great barbecue ideas by giving us a wonderful home base where we can communicate. Barbecuers from all over the world now meet on The BBQ Forum every day, and that has had a major influence on the industry. I'm proud to count him as a friend. The following recipe is probably the most famous recipe that has been posted on The BBQ Forum. Mike Scrutchfield was one of the best cooks ever and he shared this recipe with Ray Basso.

It is still used today by many cooks who got it on The BBQ Forum.

Best Ribs in the Universe
a.k.a. BRITU

1 cup sugar

1 cup noniodized table salt

½ cup brown sugar (dried out lightly by exposing on a cookie sheet for several hours at room temperature, or slightly warmed)

5 tablespoons plus 1 teaspoon chili powder

2 tablespoons plus 2 teaspoons ground cumin

4 teaspoons MSG (Accent)

4 teaspoons cayenne pepper

4 teaspoons black pepper, freshly ground (important)

4 teaspoons garlic powder

4 teaspoons onion powder

1 rack of IBP brand loin baby back ribs (1¾ to 2 pounds), membrane on the inner side removed and all excess fat trimmed

From Ray Basso: Mike Scrutchfield gave this recipe to me in 1996 and told me to keep it to myself. I didn't tell anyone about it until 1999, when I called him one night and asked his permission to post it on The BBQ Forum. That is when it went all over the Internet and a lot of people then claimed credit for it.

This recipe and cooking procedure won the prestigious title "Best Ribs in the Universe" at the 1993 American Royal Barbecue contest as the Overall Grand Champion. They also took Reserve Grand Champion at the 1994 American Royal, the largest barbecue contest in the world. Enjoy!

Mix all the dry ingredients thoroughly to make the rub. Store in an airtight container.

Two hours before cooking, sprinkle the ribs with the rub and allow the meat to come to room temperature. Do not overseason. A good overall dusting of the spices is all that's needed. The spices will become a nice red liquid coating after sitting for about an hour, if you used the proper amount.

The ribs should be smoked in a "water pan" smoker—i.e., a Brinkman cooker or a Weber "Smoky Mountain Cooker" (the best). Start the charcoal (7 to 10 pounds) and 4 chunks of white oak and 2 chunks of cherry wood (about the size of a tennis ball) at least 1 hour before cooking the meat. All fuel should be started in a chimney-style starter (no starter fluid), and all the charcoal must be gray/white hot. Remove all bark from the wood chunks and do not soak them. Very little smoke will be visible. Don't worry about that, you'll get the flavor. Use straight water in the water pan and keep it full during the entire cooking process. Control the temperature of the cooker by regulating the bottom vents only. Never, ever, completely close the top vent! If you don't have one, put a thermometer on your cooker. Cook the ribs for 3 hours fairly cool at 225°F on rib racks. After 3 hours lift the lid for the first time, flip the slabs end for end and upside down, and open all the vents on the smoker wide. The temperature of the cooker should rise into the 250 to 275°F range. Peek every half hour to monitor doneness. The ribs will be finished when fairly brown in color, and when the meat has pulled down on the long bones at least three-quarters of an inch (usually another 1 or 2 hours). Remove the ribs from the cooker and sauce both sides before cutting individual ribs. I like KC Masterpiece barbecue sauce sweetened even more (5 parts sauce, 1 part honey), and so do the judges! This basic cooking procedure is probably the most important of all, and works very well with other meats as well. Forget about how much smoke is coming out of the cooker; if you've got the wood you like in there burning up cleanly, the flavor will be in the meat. Smoke is nothing more than a smoke screen, and any coming out of the top of the cooker is flavor lost!

Bichelmeyer's Meats

Kansas City, Kansas

▼▼

Bichelmeyer's is a big old-fashioned butcher shop, like the places that many of us remember from long ago. Now I mean a real butcher shop, where they have hanging sides of beef in the back and hogs and lambs. They cut these into retail cuts, some of which are rarely seen anymore. You see, most meat these days is broken down into large primal cuts at the big processing plants and then shipped to the local stores to be cut into steaks, chops, etc. I understand the need for this and they do a very good job, but one of my "beefs" with it is that they leave most of the bones behind. They just make it harder for the local meat cutter. Unfortunately, most folks don't really care. That's why you'll rarely see a bone-in pot roast, sirloin steak, or round steak anymore. I don't like that! The bones are an important part in some cooking techniques and I miss them. So when I go to Bichelmeyer's I buy a sirloin steak that has the bone in, or a bone-in pot roast, and most definitely some sausage. That's another great thing about an old-fashioned butcher shop. They make their own sausage, and Bichelmeyer's even has a smokehouse to finish some of them up. I'm not talking about some wimpy little smoker like they have in the grocery stores. I'm talking about a whole room where you roll in big carts of sausage to smoke. It's very cool.

Bichelmeyer's Meats is not very far from the old stockyards and right near the location of the American Royal, so I visit Matt Bichelmeyer about every time I get to Kansas City. They'll cut you any kind of special trim you want, and are happy to do it. That's why so many of the top cookoff guys in Kansas City stop there. I live in Florida now, where they grow lots of beef, but I can't find a butcher like Bichelmeyer's anywhere. On a recent visit I met Matt's dad, Joe, and his uncle Jim, all working in the market. When I asked them to get together for a picture they immediately posed under a picture of their father/grandfather that hangs proudly in the shop. The shop has been there since 1946. This is another classic K.C. place that would be hard to find anywhere else.

Barbecue Sausage

1 1/4 pounds ground pork

1 tablespoon granulated garlic

1 tablespoon chili powder

1/2 tablespoon onion powder

1/2 tablespoon salt

1/4 teaspoon ground nutmeg

1/4 teaspoon celery seeds

Bichelmeyer's makes some amazing sausages, both fresh and smoked. At home I like to make my sausage into loaves instead of stuffing it into cases. It's a simple and tasty way to make homemade sausage.

• **Yield: 4 servings**

In a big bowl mix, all the ingredients well with your hands. Cover and refrigerate for at least a couple hours and up to 12 hours.

Prepare the cooker for indirect cooking at 300°F, using cherry wood for flavor.

Mix the sausage mixture again. Poke a bunch of holes in a disposable loaf pan. Put the meat in the pan, packing it tight. Place the loaf in the cooker for 30 minutes. Turn the loaf out onto the grate. Cook another 30 minutes, or until it reaches an internal temp of 160°F. Remove the loaf from the cooker and wrap it tightly in foil. Let it rest for 15 minutes. Slice and serve with barbecue sauce on the side.

Two generations of the Bichelmeyer family. They have been selling fresh meat in Kansas City since 1946.

Oklahoma Joe's

(The Restaurants)

Kansas City, Kansas

Or

Olathe, Kansas

www.oklahomajoesbbq.com

▼▼

Jeff and Joy Stehney have built two wonderful barbecue restaurants in the Kansas City area, but I have to start by explaining why they are named Oklahoma Joe's. There really is an Oklahoma Joe; he's Joe Davidson and he started a cooking team that grew to become a cooker-building company and a sauce and rub business, and Joe was even part of the original restaurant. It's a long story, but the name lives on in a few different incarnations that Joe is no longer involved with. The good news is the restaurant end of things ended up in the very capable hands of Jeff and Joy.

The concept of opening a new barbecue joint in Kansas City is like opening a brothel near the Chicken Ranch. It's gonna be an uphill battle. But Jeff had made a name for himself cooking in contests under the name Slaughterhouse Five, even winning the American Royal. He'd also been doing a little catering on the side, so he had a built-in clientele in K.C. To help with his catering, he'd rented some space in a gas station that included the use of a walk-in cooler. So one day Jeff decided that this location was a viable spot for a restaurant. He and Joe were partners in a restaurant in Oklahoma at the

time, but he wanted something closer to home. So Oklahoma Joe's in the gas station next to the liquor store on 47th and Mission was born. This is now and forever going to be a famous barbecue address, because long ago it joined the old joints on the list of legendary places to eat barbecue at in Kansas City. I recently had dinner at the second Oklahoma Joe's in Olathe, Kansas, and the food is just as good as in the original, with a little nicer and roomier atmosphere. I think in this newer place the Stehneys have found the perfect combination of real barbecue joint funky mixed with nice restaurant savvy. Jeff knows about the sauce and seasoning business as well. His Cowtown brand products are very good and available in specialty and grocery stores throughout the country. Jeff has also dabbled in the cookoff organizing business, primarily for fun and as a tool to promote his restaurants. He hosted the cookoff at the Kansas Speedway for a few years, all well-run and well-attended events, but has now turned his sights on the Oklahoma Joe's World Brisket Championship. The story is that Jeff went to a cookoff in Texas in 1992 and was crowned the World Brisket Champion. He was also given the second-place trophy because the rules allowed the cooks to turn in more than one entry. Yes, you understood that correctly. A guy from Kansas went to Texas and took the top two places in the World Brisket Championship. I think those Texans were so disappointed that they never had their cookoff again. (Here's a tip: When you go to Oklahoma Joe's try the brisket!)

Fast-forward to 2006 and Jeff has resurrected the idea and it will now be held in Kansas with him as the host. You can find info on all of this at www.oklahomajoesbbq.com.

Jeff Stehney's Smoked and Braised Beef Short Ribs

5 pounds beef short ribs, cut into 4-inch pieces

4 tablespoons olive oil, as needed

Barbecue rub, as needed (I'd suggest Dr. BBQ's Kansas City Barbecue Rub, page 5)

1 tablespoon minced fresh garlic

1 cup diced onions

1/2 cup diced carrots

1/2 cup diced celery

2 bay leaves

1 teaspoon dried thyme leaves

3 cups beef stock

One (14-ounce) can diced tomatoes with juice

1 cup dry red wine

1/4 cup Worcestershire sauce

2 tablespoons diced canned chipotles in adobo

• Serves 4 to 6

Prepare the cooker for direct searing, and then for indirect cooking at 250°F, using oak wood for flavor. Brush the meaty side of the ribs with 2 tablespoons of the olive oil and season liberally with the rub.

Sear the ribs over a hot direct fire for 3 to 4 minutes and then switch to indirect cooking.

Cook the ribs over an indirect fire for 1 1/2 hours, maintaining a 250°F cooking temp. While the ribs are smoking, sauté the garlic, onions, carrots, and celery in the remaining olive oil for 10 minutes over medium-high heat in a 6-quart Dutch oven. Add the bay leaves and thyme during the last 5 minutes. Add the remaining ingredients and bring to a slow boil, then turn off the heat and leave the mixture on the stove until the ribs are off the grill/smoker.

After 1 1/2 hours on the smoker/grill, remove the ribs and cut into single-bone portions. Preheat the oven to 350°F. Place the ribs into the Dutch oven with the broth and vegetables and cover. Put in the oven and braise for 1 1/2 to 2 hours, or until the ribs are very tender and falling off the bone. Remove the ribs from the Dutch oven and keep warm. Skim any fat off the top of the braising broth and reduce the broth over high heat for 5 minutes.

Ladle the braising broth over the ribs and serve.

Jones Bar-B-Q

Kansas City, Kansas

It's pretty hard to find a barbecue joint in Kansas City that no one has heard of, but that's what Jones Bar-B-Q is. I predict it won't be that way for long, though. My old buddy Fast Eddy was bugging me that we had to go to this place. It's not that hard to get me to a new barbecue joint, so off we went. It's a great-looking barbecue joint with a built-in brick pit and a few hardworking cooks right in plain view. There is a nice patio on the side with a live keyboard player out there for lunch when the weather is right. The pitmaster is a lady, Deborah Jones, and her sister, Mary, is the nicest waitress in the world. These girls can cook for me anytime. Jones serves real homemade food. They serve the barbecue straight from the pit and slice it to order. There are no holding cabinets or microwaves here. I didn't ask, but it was obvious that their sauce is homemade, too. It's yet another K.C. original with the distinct taste of celery seed and it's delicious. They even make their own sausage daily. They also have rib tips, which is unusual for a Kansas City place. The plate of food they give you is huge, but I manage to finish it every time I go there. In typical Kansas City fashion, combinations are very popular here. I like that because I can never decide which one thing I want, especially at Jones. I recommend the ham, pork, brisket, and ribs. You'll have to narrow it down from there. Mary will bring you a wet nap, a toothpick, and a couple pieces of candy to complete your wonderful meal.

Smoked Ham
Kansas City Style

1 boneless ham, 3 to 4 pounds

¼ cup brown sugar

1 teaspoon cayenne pepper, or to taste

Dr. BBQ's Kansas City Barbecue Sauce (page 5)

Jones Bar-B-Q serves a very good version of smoked ham. This is a popular item in Kansas City. It's just a grocery store ham cooked again in the smoker.

• Yield: 8 to 10 servings

Prepare the cooker for indirect cooking at 225°F, using oak wood for flavor. Mix the brown sugar and the cayenne and rub it all over the ham. Put the ham in the cooker and cook until it reaches an internal temp of 160°F. Remove the ham to a plate, tent with foil, and let rest for 10 minutes. Slice and serve with Dr. BBQ's Kansas City Barbecue Sauce.

Mary Jones serves up some of the best barbecue in Kansas City.

Smokin' Guns BBQ

North Kansas City, Missouri
www.smokingunsbbq.com

▼▼

Smokin' Guns BBQ Restaurant and Catering Company is a new barbecue joint by Kansas City standards, but they've already made their mark in a big way. The Smokin' Guns barbecue team was started in 1997 by Linda and Phil Hopkins, a very nice couple from Kansas City. They became very good soon after and in 1999 they competed in and won the Jack Daniel's World Championship, which is arguably the most coveted of all barbecue awards. (I know it's my most coveted.) Then they began to sell their incredibly popular barbecue rub and, last but certainly not least, came the restaurant. Smokin' Guns BBQ opened on January 27, 2003. It's a no-frills kind of place with limited hours, but the food is world-class Kansas City barbecue. They are most proud of their "burnt ends," as well they should be, but the ribs, brisket, and side dishes are all pretty good, too. Linda is the side dish queen. Her potato casserole was selected as the Best Side Dish by the *Kansas City Star* in 2003, and the restaurant recently started serving her broccoli casserole, which was the first-place vegetable at the American Royal in 2004. She was nice enough to share that one with me, and it's on page 10 with a couple other American Royal winners. Smokin' Guns has also kindly shared the coffee cake recipe here. Many a barbecue man has enjoyed this coffee cake on a Saturday morning.

Linda and Phil Hopkins of Smokin' Guns with their World Championship trophy

Linda's Coffee Cake

2/3 cup sugar

4 cups Bisquick mix

2 eggs

1 cup milk

Cinnamon-Sugar Topping
(recipe follows)

3/4 cup powdered sugar

1/2 teaspoon vanilla

Milk

This recipe took fourth place in the dessert category at the 1999 Jack Daniel's World Championship Barbecue contest. • **Yield: 1 coffee cake**

Preheat the oven to 375°F. Stir the sugar into the Bisquick. Beat the eggs and add them to the milk. Add egg and milk to the Bisquick. Stir until ingredients are thoroughly blended. Do not beat.

Grease a 9×13-inch pan. Spoon half of the batter into the pan and spread it out. Sprinkle with half of the Cinnamon-Sugar Topping recipe (below). Spoon the remaining batter on topping. Spread it out as best you can. Top with the remaining topping.

Bake for 20 minutes, or until a toothpick inserted comes out clean.

Make the glaze: Stir together the powdered sugar, vanilla, and enough milk to make it thin enough to drizzle. Drizzle it over the warm cake.

Cinnamon-Sugar Topping

1 cup white sugar

1 cup brown sugar

8 tablespoons Bisquick or
Jiffy mix

4 teaspoons ground
cinnamon

12 tablespoons butter

• **Yield: 2½ cups**

Combine the dry ingredients. Cut in the butter with a pastry blender.

Rosedale Barbeque

Kansas City, Kansas

▼▼▼

I really like this place. It doesn't get the attention that some of the K.C. joints get, but it's not because they don't have an old tradition. It's been around since 1934, although they did build a new building a while back. The new building is in the same location, so Rosedale is actually the longest-running, same-family-owned, same-location barbecue joint in Kansas City. It's not flashy, unless you count the young lady I encountered behind the bar with the gigantic tattoo of Elvis on her bicep. The barbecue is straightforward and authentic Kansas City. You'll get brisket, ham, turkey, or ribs, with the traditional barbecue sides and white bread, but it's all very well done. The sauce is another K.C. original, with a distinctive taste that I'd say has some relation to cloves or allspice. Good stuff! I've reprinted a recipe here from my first book that accidentally came out tasting kind of like theirs, although theirs is smooth. Some kitchen accidents are good ones.

K.C. Red Rose BBQ Sauce

2 tablespoons vegetable oil

1 cup chopped onion

1/4 cup chopped green bell pepper

2 cloves garlic, crushed

1 1/4 cups commercial chili sauce

1 1/4 cups ketchup

1/2 cup cider vinegar

1 teaspoon ground allspice

1/2 teaspoon cayenne pepper

1 cup brown sugar

• Yield: About 1 quart

In a saucepan, heat the oil. Add the onion and bell pepper and sauté for a few minutes, stirring occasionally. Add the garlic and continue to sauté until the vegetables are all soft. Add all the other ingredients except the brown sugar and slowly bring to a simmer. Then add the brown sugar and blend well. Remove from the heat and cool, stirring occasionally. Store in a plastic or glass container in the refrigerator.

Fiorella's Jack Stack

Kansas City, Missouri

www.jackstackbbq.com

▼▼

I've always heard great things about Jack Stack but hadn't been there until recently. Now I see why everyone likes it so much. It's a little bit fancy for a barbecue joint, but it works. You'll get a nice bakery bun and real plates and silverware here, in a cool old steakhouse kind of atmosphere. That's the way they want it. The story goes that the Fiorella family, who started Jack Stack in 1957, decided they wanted to be more than a typical barbecue joint. So they added steaks, seafood, and upscale side dishes to the menu to set themselves apart from the rest. It worked. The Fiorellas now have three busy restaurants and a big catering business, and like many of the big barbecue houses, they now ship their food all over the world. The side dishes are a big attraction at Jack Stack. The beans are very famous, and they're good, but I like the Cheesy Corn Bake and the Cheesy Potato Bake.

Easy Cheesy
Corn Casserole

1 tablespoon butter

1 tablespoon flour

$1/4$ teaspoon salt

1 cup milk

1 cup grated sharp
Cheddar cheese

One 16-ounce can whole
corn kernels or $1^1/4$ cups
frozen corn, defrosted

$1/4$ cup crumbled cooked
bacon

$1/2$ teaspoon paprika (or
red chile powder)

This is the closest approximation to Jack Stack's famous side dish that I could come up with, short of breaking into their offices and stealing the recipe.

• **Yield: 4 to 5 servings**

Preheat oven to 350°F.

Melt the butter in a saucepan and add the flour and salt, stirring with a whisk for about 15 seconds. Add the milk all at once, stirring constantly to keep the mixture from lumping and the milk from burning. When it is thick (3 to 5 minutes), remove from the burner and add the cheese, stirring until it melts, and then stir in the corn. Sprinkle the bacon on the bottom of a 1-quart casserole dish, and then pour the corn mixture over the bacon. Sprinkle with paprika or red chile powder and bake for 15 to 20 minutes, or until the casserole is hot.

Culinary Center of Kansas City

Overland Park, Kansas

www.kcculinary.com

▼▼

Just a little south of Kansas City in Overland Park is a great place called the Culinary Center of Kansas City. My first reaction when I walked in the door was "Why isn't there one of these in every town?" It's a cool-looking place with kitchens kind of spread out through the rooms. There is one primary podium-type counter and they arrange the tables and chairs according to the event. They host many cooking classes, both using their in-house staff and also using local and visiting chefs. It's a real fun place, and if I lived nearby I'd go there often. Laura O'Rourke is the owner and driving force and she does an incredible job. Laura practiced law for eighteen years before changing careers and opening the CCKC in 1998. She says she just needed to spread her wings and feed her entrepreneurial hunger, so she moved on. I love people like that. We should all be glad she did. There's got to be a barbecue tie-in to this story, so here it is. Laura renewed her acquaintance with Chef Richard McPeake, whom she had actually worked with in a restaurant many years earlier. Richard was interested in doing some barbecue classes and Laura wanted to have some barbecue classes, so they got together on this idea. Richard is currently the vice president and culinary director for a very successful restaurant group in K.C. as well as a very good barbecue competitor with his team Rib Stars, so needless to say this worked very well with Richard's first classes in Barbecue 101. Kansas City is a big barbecue town, so the interest continued to grow. Richard is now teaching eleven unique classes at the CCKC and does a total of about thirty a year. As a matter of fact, Richard and Laura have even teamed up to start the Midwest Barbecue Institute within CCKC. If you attend a certain number of Richard's classes you get a personalized apron and are anointed a graduate. Very nice. I am proud to have been the first outside instructor to teach a class in this series. CCKC is a great place and I still wish there was one in every town. If you're in the area and have a chance to attend a class at the Culinary Center of Kansas City, you'll be glad you did.

This wonderful salmon recipe comes from Chef Richard McPeake. It's from his book *The Art of Smokology*, available at www.ribstars.com.

Chef McPeake's
Honey Maple Salmon

Two 3-pound salmon fillets, boned, skinless

1 batch Honey Maple Brine for Salmon, cold (recipe follows)

The sweetness of this brine matches well with the moist texture of the salmon fillets.

• Yield: 10 to 12 servings

Place the boneless fillets with the now skinless side down into a shallow pan or dish. Pour the brine over the salmon fillets and marinate in the brine for 8 hours.

Remove the fillets from the brine and pat them dry with a clean cloth or towel. Air-dry the fillets for 1 hour under refrigeration. Prepare the smoker for indirect cooking at 200°F, using maple or apple wood for flavor. Place the fillets on the racks in the smoker with the now skinless side down. Smoke until just done. Seafood is cooked properly when it reaches an internal temperature of 145°F, so test with a temperature probe! Salmon should have a firm touch to it when done. Approximate cooking time is about 2 hours.

Honey Maple Brine for Salmon

1 cup kosher salt

1 cup honey

1 cup real maple syrup

½ cup fresh lemon juice

2 tablespoons garlic juice

1 tablespoon ground allspice

1 tablespoon fresh cracked black pepper

This brine gives you an outstanding sweet smoked salmon.

• Yield: Makes enough brine for two 3-pound sides of salmon

Carefully measure out 2 quarts of hot water and place it into a plastic container. Add all the ingredients to the hot water and stir to completely dissolve. Cool to room temperature before using.

North Carolina

Dr. BBQ's North Carolina Barbecue Rub

Dr. BBQ's Western North Carolina Barbecue Dip

Dr. BBQ's Eastern North Carolina Barbecue Dip

Bubba's Barbecue (Charlotte)

Smokey Joe's Barbecue (Lexington)

Barbecue Center (Lexington)

Lexington BBQ (Lexington)

Jimmy's BBQ (Lexington)

Southern Barbecue Too (Lexington)

Pig-N-Out (Winston-Salem)

Clark's Bar-B-Q (Kernersville)

Stamey's Old Fashioned (Greensboro)

BBQ & Ribs Co. (Burlington)

Hursey's Bar-B-Q (Burlington)

Parker's (Wilson)

Bill's Barbecue (Wilson)

B's Barbecue (Greenville)

The Skylight Inn (Ayden)

King's Barbecue (Kinston)

McCall's Barbecue (Goldsboro)

Wilber's Barbecue (Goldsboro)

Smithfield's (Raleigh)

Blue Mist (Asheboro)

Whispering Pines (Albemarle)

Log Cabin Bar-B-Que (Albemarle)

Chopped Wood-Cooked North Carolina–Style Pork Shoulder

North Carolina Slaw

North Carolina–Style Hush Puppies

Chocolate Pound Cake

Kings Mountain Firehouse BBQ Cookoff (Kings Mountain)

Cheesy Cabbage

Carolina Whole Hog

Alamo Pies

Nahunta Pork Center (Pikeville)

Grilled Pork Meatball Hoagies

▼▼▼▼

By any and all accounts, North Carolina is an important location in the history of American barbecue. They have been cooking hogs and pork shoulders over open pits around there for a long time. My barbecue travels hadn't taken me there, though, with the exception of the big Blue Ridge Barbecue Festival in Tryon, where I was one of the vendors and competitors for a few years. Tryon is pure North Carolina barbecue and a major attraction for any barbecue enthusiast, but for this book I needed to expand my horizons on the subject at hand. So I called my friend Dave DeWitt and invited him on a tour of the state's famous barbecue landmarks. The best I could tell was that they are mostly restaurants, so a lot of eating was going to be involved. Dave's always up for a good adventure, and traveling with him makes me feel like I'm in a Hunter Thompson novel traveling with my swami-like attorney, without the LSD, of course. Dave DeWitt, a.k.a. The Pope of Peppers, is a serious foodie with a knowledge of hot and spicy foods that is unmatched. The problem with Dave is he's kind of skinny and I was worried if he'd be able to eat five heavy meals a day. But his eyes were bigger than his stomach, so he said yes.

We met in Charlotte and hit the ground running with a meal at Bubba's Barbecue. As you'll read in my travelogue, Dave did have a breakdown one evening at the fifth restaurant of the day, but he learned to pace himself after that and got the job done. Dave also acted as the official scorer for the event, so that we could ultimately name the best barbecue in North Carolina. Hey, he runs the Scovie awards so he is surely qualified. We had a wonderful time and saw an amazing number of beautiful little churches. We also really learned a lot. For instance, after dining in twenty-two restaurants in five days, we hadn't been able to have a single beer with our barbecue. I think much of this has to do with the conservative Bible Belt nature of the area. The liquor stores are state-run. Not a bad thing, but quite different from the barbecue joints of Texas, which are often just taverns that sell barbecue.

The North Carolina places are typically diners that serve barbecue. Many serve breakfast and have a menu that has burgers, daily specials, and other typical diner fare. Don't misunderstand this to mean that they don't take the barbecue seriously, because they do. Most of these diners have a pit house out back where the barbecue is cooked in a very traditional manner. They burn the wood down to coals and spread the coals under the meat to cook it in a nice, slow, direct fashion. This process is excruciatingly labor-intensive, as it requires almost constant tending. I'm not a big fan of this style of cooking, because I really don't think the food gets much of a smoke flavor this way. They burn all the good stuff out of the wood before they put it under the meat. I'd throw a log in there once in a while for flavor.

But there's no denying how much North Carolina natives love their slow-cooked pork. As a matter of fact, they simply call it "barbecue." Ribs, beef, chicken, or anything else cooked on the pit goes by its own name.

"Barbecue" is chopped pork. Period. So all you need to do is order a barbecue sandwich and you'll get a chopped pork sandwich with cole slaw on it. If you are like me and don't want slaw, you'd better be sure to order it without. We learned a few other things about custom ordering as we worked our way through the state. Most places chop the meat pretty fine, but you can order coarse chopped if you want it a little chunkier. You can also ask for some dark, brown, or outside meat if you like the crusty bark. Some places just chop it all together, but most will serve you the light inside meat if you don't ask for the dark. So for me it's a coarse chopped barbecue sandwich, brown meat and no slaw. The sauce will be lightly added to the meat and a bottle of it will be on the table.

I like this barbecue, but it's not at all like the smoky barbecue in other parts of the country. That was probably the most surprising thing to me. Of course, that's why we went to all those places, to seek the truth. As for the Lexington style versus the Eastern style being a distinctive regional standoff, I'd have to report that as true. We were told that Greensboro sat on a line that divided east from west and the sauce would turn to vinegar as we went east from there. I was skeptical, but I'm not anymore. We found that to be accurate. I didn't think I'd like the hard-core vinegar sauces, but I must tell you that they work very well on the pork. I liked the Lexington-style sauces, too. They're different but equally good. They seem to be a simple combination of vinegar and ketchup. Simple but good. By the way, they call it dip, not sauce. (It looked like sauce to me and nobody was dipping anything.)

The trip wasn't all about restaurants, though, and since we didn't find any bars, we managed to see some other interesting things. You'll learn about the museum in Lexington, the Nahunta Pork Center, and everything else we learned about the history of barbecue in North Carolina in this chapter, too. Since we found the food to be very similar throughout North Carolina with the exception of the two sauces and the difference between whole hog and shoulder, I decided that rather than repeat the same recipes it would be better to have a typical North Carolina barbecue joint menu at the end of the restaurant reviews on page 48. It uses a pork shoulder since I figure most folks don't cook whole hogs at home, but there's a whole hog recipe from Charles Fretwell on page 54 in case you want to give it a try.

Dr. BBQ's North Carolina Barbecue Rub

Salt and pepper

We visited twenty-two restaurants and never saw anyone use anything more than salt and pepper. Some skipped the pepper and some skipped seasoning the meat at all. If you want it authentic use salt and pepper. If you want a little more flavor, borrow one of the rub recipes from the other chapters.

Dr. BBQ's Western North Carolina Barbecue Dip

1 cup vinegar

²/₃ cup ketchup

2 teaspoons sugar

1 teaspoon salt

¹/₂ teaspoon red pepper flakes

1 teaspoon Worcestershire sauce

• **Yield: About 2 cups**

Combine all the ingredients in a saucepan. Cook over low heat for about 4 minutes, stirring to blend.

Dr. BBQ's Eastern North Carolina Barbecue Dip

1 cup vinegar

1 teaspoon salt

1 teaspoon sugar

½ teaspoon red pepper flakes

½ teaspoon paprika

• Yield: 1 cup

Combine all the ingredients in a saucepan. Cook over low heat for about 4 minutes, stirring to blend.

Dave DeWitt, a.k.a. The Pope of Peppers, poses in front of the famous dome at the Skylight Inn.

The Restaurants of North Carolina

As long as there were two of us and since we were guys, we decided to make a game out of this by rating the restaurants. The results are in and here they are.

Our Scoring System

BBQ Taste and Texture: 10–50 points
Sides: 5–10 points
Ambience: 5–10 points

Dave and I decided that we would each vote independently and then our scores would be averaged. At the end of the trip, we would know by the scores the Best Barbecue, Best Sides, Best Ambience, and Best Overall of all the 'cue we tasted in North Carolina.

Charlotte

▼▼

Dave had flown into the Charlotte airport, so that's where we started the BBQuest, as we called our tour. It began with a trip to **Bubba's** on Sunday. Call it a "warm-up." We didn't know much about it but we wanted to get started. The ribs were okay, the pork was uneventful, and the beans were straight from a can. It was bound to get better.

Lexington
"The Barbecue Capital of the World"

▼▼

The Barbecue Capital of the World, that's what the natives of Lexington call their town, so we decided to make it our first road stop. The North Carolina Legislature has designated Lexington as "The Hickory-Smoked Barbecue Capital of North Carolina," which is quite a mouthful. There are about twenty barbecue restaurants in this town of 20,000 people, so you know how popular barbecue is there. We couldn't eat at every single restaurant there, but we gave it a good shot. Childress Vineyards makes Fine Swine Wine, but we never got a chance to drink any of it because none of the restaurants served beer or wine! Lexington is so into pork barbecue that when a couple of restaurants began serving brisket, that fact was headline news in *The Dispatch*, Lexington's newspaper.

We spent the entire day Monday in Lexington and even took an hour to visit the Davidson County Historical Museum, which is located in the former courthouse. It had a very interesting display based around local citizens who had fought in World War II, complete with uniforms and memorabilia. It also had the worst (or the best) barbecue joke of the entire BBQuest, told to us by one of the curators. Ralph, an insurance rep, is visiting his customer Homer, who is a farmer. While pulling into Homer's long driveway, Ralph notices in the yard a pig with a wooden right front leg. After Homer greets him, Ralph asks, "What's with the pig with the peg leg?"

"Oh, that's Swine Flew," replied Homer. "He used to live with Aunt Polly. Polly's house caught on fire and that pig flew into the house and pulled Polly and three other ladies out of the fire. He's a hero of a pig."

"Did he lose the leg in the fire?"

"Hell no," said Homer, "but you can't kill a hero pig like that, so we only barbecued one of his shoulders for Easter dinner."

Lexington is justly famous for the Barbecue Festival, now in its twenty-fourth year. It's held on the town square in Lexington, and we were told that 150,000 people come to Lexington (is that possible?) for the one-day event in late October. Only seven local restaurants are selected to sell just the signature pork shoulder barbecue at the festival, but each one serves 1,600 to 1,800 pounds during the event.

October, "Barbecue Month in Lexington," features a bicycle race called the "Tour de Pig," a marathon called "Hawg Run," the Pepsi "Pig Tales" Creative Writing Competition, and, of course, the BBQ Festival High School Air Rifle Match. One of the sponsors is Fine Swine Wine from Childress Vineyards! Besides the barbecue, the country music, and the Alabama Blues Brothers, the 2005 festival featured a pig sand sculpture, the barbecue carnival, a car show, racing pigs at the Hogway Speedway, the Festival Chop Shop (with lumberjacks competing in "traditional chopping and sawing events"), and bicycle stunt shows. For more information, go to www.barbecuefestival.com.

Monday

A town that's called the Barbecue Capital of the World seemed like a good place to start the serious eating. I had a sandwich, no slaw, and some beans at **Smokey Joe's**. It was good, all white meat dressed with the dip. The beans were plain old canned beans. The hush puppies were good but probably frozen. Dave had his sandwich with slaw and really liked it. Our waitress had been working there for forty-two years. Nice posters from the annual barbecue festival and a couple of sidewalk painted pigs were on display. The sugar-sweet waitress took us into the kitchen, where the pitmaster showed us the typical wood-burning North Carolina pits. Very nice folks and a very nice place.

the pit—very traditional with whole shoulders cooking over hickory and some oak burned to coals in a separate burn box. This was all in the kitchen. They are also famous for their banana splits, but we had to pass.

At **Lexington BBQ** we got the same type of sandwich, but now I knew how to order. It was good and very similar to the others. They had a hot sauce–size bottle of an intense barbecue sauce. It was spicy, vinegary, dark in color and good. They also had pig skins available as a side dish. They were fried very well, crispy and tasty. Extra points for those. I wasn't sure of the boundaries, but I put some on my sandwich and liked it.

I must tell you that at this point we were feeling a little underwhelmed. The food was almost identical and the legendary stories were few. We regrouped at the hotel before heading out for a double dinner.

At **Jimmy's BBQ** I noticed that these barbecue joints all had the same broken tile inlaid floor. What's up with that? They also all had these really chintzy cardboard plates just barely big enough to hold the food. There was a menu item everywhere called a tray. It was a really little cardboard tray filled to the point of the food falling out, with pork, slaw, and maybe a couple of hush puppies. Anyway, we each had a sandwich. It was kind of dry and crunchy on the brown. A little character finally, but not much. I looked over at Dave. He was getting very full and I worried about him holding up.

By the time we got to **Southern Barbecue Too** Dave was maxed out and wouldn't even order. I made him eat the slaw because I hate slaw. I had a barbecue plate, mainly because the fries sounded so good after eating

At the **Barbecue Center**, which has existed since 1955, we met Stephanie Saintsing-Gryder from the Barbecue Festival, the city manager, a councilman, and Cecil, the son of the family that owns the place. We were immediately given samples of outside dark meat with and without the dip/sauce. It was very good and I learned how to order dark, lean, coarse chopped. It's good stuff. The sauce was a ketchup/vinegar concoction that they are very proud of. It's tasty, maybe with a touch of Worcestershire added. The slaw looked great, the hush puppies were good. We were shown barbecue at five restaurants in one day. Turned out the pork was really good and the dip was the best I'd had. It actually had some seasoning in it and the pork had a little fat in it. It was my favorite so far. Dave was amazed at how much I had eaten that day. The place closed within a week of my writing and they moved to a new location. Unfortunately that probably means the demise of their wood-burning pits, but I gotta tell you that there was no smoke flavor in the food anyway, so I'm not sure anyone will notice. I can't believe I'm about to say this, but Lexington barbecue was very much about the sauce.

Tuesday

I skipped breakfast Tuesday. We drove to Winston-Salem to have lunch at Wild Hogs. We were using Bob Garner's book, *Guide to North Carolina Barbecue*, as our bible and he recommended the place. We arrived to find that the name had changed . . . to Fantasies. A "gentleman's club." They were selling somethin' there, but it sure wasn't barbecue. We considered going in and blowing off barbecue for the day, but we regained our composure and headed down the street to **Pig-N-Out**.

Well, it was a good move because the place was real nice and Gus, the owner, came out to say hi. He fixed us up with a custom sampler of chopped chicken, chopped brisket, chopped barbecue (pork), ribs, beans, and slaw. It was all very good and had more all-around flavor than anything we'd eaten so far. I think I'll skip the brisket from now on. Gus had cooked it just like he did the pork, and it just didn't work for me. (We had a line on a place in Lexington that served brisket, Smilies, but

Two friendly servers, myself, Gus, and a peach cobbler at Pig-N-Out

when we asked, the waitress said they used to serve it but that it wasn't very popular so now it only showed up as an occasional Sunday special.) The banana pudding at Pig-N-Out looked great, but we still had four more places to eat at that day so I had to pass. Dave was back up to eating speed and was inspired by the newfound variety.

Our next stop was **Clark's** Kernersville for a second lunch. So far they have my vote for the best side dishes. I had the same old barbecue sandwich and some hush puppies. Hush puppies are a staple in North Carolina but they aren't the little round ones I'm used to being served with catfish. They are little turd-shaped things that are probably either spit out of a hush puppy pooping machine, or bought shaped and frozen. My guess is we've had both and it's hard to tell the difference. They were all pretty decent but nothing more. Clark's, on the other hand, had hush puppies

that looked just like onion rings. It was a little strange eating something that your mind thinks is an onion ring but tastes like a hush puppy. They were crunchy and crispy and really good. Stop here just for these babies. Dave had a good-looking barbecue salad. He was holding up well and the roughage would only help. The salad was mostly lettuce topped with a pile of chopped pork (what a surprise) and "Italian-style" salad dressing.

From Clark's we drove to Greensboro to eat at **Stamey's**. It was a nice wood-decorated place with decent food, right across from the big basketball arena, but it wasn't in the top ten places we dined at.

The last stop for the day was Burlington. We checked into our hotel and planned a double dinner at 5:30. We started at **BBQ & Ribs Co.** It's a small chain and the name is very telling about North Carolina barbecue. Barbecue is pork. Period. Ribs, chicken, and beef are tolerated, but when you ask for some barbecue there is no question what you'll be getting: pork. So I had the pork and Dave had the ribs and some greens. My pork was good but it was my first taste of true vinegar sauce this trip. Seemed we'd crossed over the line to eastern North Carolina barbecue. I must admit that vinegar is not something I like much, but I can eat it on my barbecue. I expect it to taste better as we proceed. Dave, on the other hand, really liked his ribs, and so did I. They were pink and a little smoky. It was the first hint of smoke we'd tasted on the trip. He also loved the greens. I don't generally eat green food so I passed.

Our second dinner was at **Hursey's** and it was a winner. It's a nice little place with a big pig on the sign and another group of three pigs in a car painted high on an indoor wall in mural form, with actual tires on their car. Very nice. The food was pretty good and there were options. Dave had the Tuesday special barbecue chicken and I had the beef ribs. Everything here was excellent. We told the waitress what we were up to and she sent out Chris Hursey, the grandson of the original Mr. Hursey who sold barbecue in Burlington. Seems his grandfather and a few friends were drinking one night and stole a hog. They prepped the hog and were cooking it the next day when people kept stopping and asking to buy some barbecue. A business was born that day that is flourishing some fifty years later.

Wednesday

First thing today we headed for Wilson, a famous barbecue town. We started at **Parker's**, a very nice country-type place with well-dressed young men as the waitstaff. They wear white shirts with the Parker's logo on them and paper butcher-type hats. It was a window into the past, circa 1949. The menu is simple and the food is good. As usual, chopped pork is the main focus, but around here it's all about whole hog. I was surprised to find that the whole hog was much tastier than the shoulders we'd been eating. I would have expected the opposite. I guess it's the mix of all the different cuts. They clearly use a vinegar/pepper sauce to dress it, but the vinegar doesn't overwhelm. It's subtle and works very well. We also discovered corn sticks there. In Dave's words, not recommended. I'm not sure what they are about, seems they might be baked but they're not very good. They also have hush puppies

and they were better, although they were the same as everywhere else.

Across town is **Bill's**. It's a barbecue complex with huge catering rigs in the parking lot and a burned-out restaurant still standing next to a buffet restaurant that is open. The buffet was a real treat for us. It was a chance to try some different things while still tasting the core of North Carolina barbecue. They had a whole hog on the buffet that you could pull from, as well as some chopped barbecue, also from a whole hog. Both were very good. They also had chicken and pastry (dumplings), wonderful fried chicken, some great sausage, and the Wednesday special of meat loaf. What a treat this was. Dave was getting much better at pacing himself, so he went kind of easy on the buffet, but I worked it over pretty good. I liked this place very much. It's funky and good and has the obligatory picture of Bill with Richard Petty. I'm pretty sure this is a requirement to open a barbecue restaurant in North Carolina.

Third today is **B's** in Greenville. This is one extra-funky little place. It looks like an old house or store and it seems most of the business is done out the walk-up window. Judy was our friendly-as-can-be counter girl, and she told me they cook between eight and twelve hogs every day at this little place. I believed her. She also told me to have the sweet tea, which was good advice. I love sweet tea, but on this trip I'm having it about half the time, offset by some Diet Pepsi. The sugar buzz would be too much. The food was good and the sauce was on the table in a recycled Crown Royal bottle. How very upscale of them. In my opinion a barbecue joint can be extra funky and that's a good thing. This place wasn't trying to be extra funky, it just came naturally. I'd call it patina. The trashed-out Coca-Cola sign out front didn't come from a yuppie restaurant theme designer, it just happened to be hanging there when they moved in and nobody had ever bothered to take it down or paint it. I like B's and hope to go back some day.

While traveling in the east, one day Dave wore the golf shirt that Stephanie Saintsing-Gryder, the Barbecue Festival organizer, had given him. Three waitresses noticed the logo on the front of the shirt and asked him where the festival was held. He answered, "Lexington," and one of the waitresses commented, "I didn't know that they had barbecue in Kentucky." He corrected her and informed her that Lexington, North Carolina, claimed to be the "Barbecue Capital of the World," and she laughed. "Sure they are," she said sarcastically.

We only had one dinner that night

This nice lady served us some great sandwiches at B's Barbecue.

and it was at one of the most famous of all North Carolina barbecue joints, **Skylight Inn** in Ayden. Of course, it's not an inn in the classic sense of the word, but just a barbecue joint. There is a ridiculous capitol dome structure on the roof that seems so out of place that it's in place. It's painted a bad silver color and seems to be calling in aliens. This would be an excellent place for the aliens to start, though. It's as basic as it gets. There are three items on the menu: pork, slaw, and the worst cornbread on the planet. I don't think the aliens will like that stuff. It could easily be the worst polenta on the planet because it's kind of thin, flat, and really dense, but they call it bread. While I don't recommend that, I do recommend the pork because it was very good. Not much different than the others but our "pound" had a little more pepper taste to it. When I asked Dave about the slaw he accused me of carrying a giant vat of slaw in the van and having them serve the same stuff to him at every stop. Not bad but nothing special. The good pork and great ambience make this place a special one, though, and I could easily see why it's become famous. There is no cash register. The money is in a few big piles on the back counter. In between the back counters is a big chopping block with a huge pile of pork on it and a heat lamp over it. The guy in the kitchen chops the pork and pushes it from his block to the front one. It's as basic here as it gets and it's wonderful.

Thursday

First stop, **King's** in Kinston. There's a Piggly Wiggly next door, so the King's sign has a pig sign right below it. No surprise about what

Chopped whole hog ready to be served at the Skylight Inn. Notice the cash on the counters.

the feature would be, but a pleasant surprise was what sits next to the pork here. We were greeted by a nice guy who asked if we'd be having the buffet. I asked if we'd miss anything from the menu, and he replied that the chopped barbecue wasn't on there but a big pan of whole hog meat freshly pulled was. He immediately offered to bring us some of the chopped pork anyway so we could try it all, and we took him up on it. That turned out to be a good thing. The chopped barbecue was juicy and tasty, while the hog meat on the buffet was in big chunks that were kind of dry and not very flavorful. In addition to the pork I sampled fried chicken, fried trout, mashed potatoes and gravy, southern chicken (fried chicken covered in a brown gravy), shrimp stew, and the regular sides. What a feast! I wish I lived near this restaurant.

Our second lunch was at **McCall's** in Greensboro. It's a nice southern-looking room with a small buffet, but we opted to order there. I had the barbecue plate with sides of barbecue boiled potatoes and Brunswick stew. The potatoes were simply boiled halves tossed with a tomato and vinegar sauce and the stew was pretty good. Brunswick stew is a common menu item in the Southeast that originated in Brunswick, Georgia. It's a tomato-based stew that uses leftover barbecue meats along with onion, corn, and lima beans. They used baby lima beans, which I liked because the big ones can be overwhelming to the dish. I used that idea for my version of burgoo on page 179. The pork was good.

The third lunch got us to another famous place, **Wilber's** in Goldsboro. This is a country-looking place with really friendly and quick waitresses and a knotty pine feel all around. They cook a lot of hogs out back at this place and it's good stuff. The meat was seasoned a little spicier, and we liked it.

Only one dinner on Thursday for us. We were in Raleigh and decided to visit a local chain called **Smithfield's** to see how they compared to all the authentic joints we'd been to. We heard there would be no smokiness to the meat, but since we hadn't tasted any smoke on the meat all week, we weren't concerned about it. So we went and had the fried chicken and pork combo and it was all pretty darn good. The Brunswick stew and the slaw were the best we'd had and the pork and chicken were worthy of an independent place. I applaud them for holding the tradition well in a chain situation but have one complaint. The banana pudding had no bananas in it. I know fresh bananas create problems with shelf life, but you just can't have banana pudding without bananas. They owe me one for that.

Friday

Lunch one on our final day took us to **Blue Mist** in Asheboro. It's very much a diner with barbecue as the featured item. We sat at the counter and enjoyed a typical North Carolina lunch of pork and slaw. The owner happened by, so I said hi to him and told him what we were doing. He's a really nice guy and talked with us for a while. Seemed he'd recently started serving St. Louis–cut ribs, and we went out to see his pit man getting them started. The pit house is very typical and very efficient. The pit man was cooking some shoulders and the St. Louis–cut ribs, and also some big meaty beef ribs covered in rub. We hadn't seen any food with a heavy rub on it all week, so I asked him about it. He told us that the boss didn't like to put any seasoning on the food before cooking it, but he'd given him some freedom with the beef ribs. The guy said he was using a recipe out of a book by Steven Raichlen and the guests were loving them. I told him that sounded like a good plan. I find it interesting that ribs are moving into North Carolina. I think it's definitely a result of the popularity of ribs in the barbecue joints up north. Imagine that!

Our next stop was in Albemarle, where we had an average lunch at a diner-style place called **Whispering Pines**. Our last restaurant was the **Log Cabin Bar-B-Que** in the same town. It's a cool-looking little place with wonderful grandma-type waitresses. I had a good feeling about this place. Dave did, too, but I thought it was because he wouldn't have to eat any more barbecue. I ordered a barbecue plate with onion rings. These were my first onion rings of the week, and it was a good choice. They were crispy and golden and obviously homemade. High points for these, but the big story for me was the pork. It had a little more flavor and a little more crunch than just about any I'd tasted all week. They seemed to have intentionally mixed in some of the crunchy stuff, but it was chopped fine so it was still a nice, tender combination. I really liked it. Log Cabin had the best display of NASCAR photos of any place we'd been and some great desserts. I opted for a wonderful chocolate pound cake but had to skip the cherry pound cake and some great-sounding lemon cake. Above all of that the waitress recommended the pecan pie! Dave skipped dessert.

The Ratings

Best Barbecue: Bill's Barbecue, Wilson

Best Sides: Clark's Barbecue, Kernersville

Best Ambience: Hursey's Bar-B-Q, Burlington

Best Overall: The Top Five—Total Points Available: 70

Restaurant	Location	Total Score
1. Bill's Barbecue	Wilson	63
2. Barbecue Center	Lexington	62
3. Hursey's Bar-B-Q	Burlington	60.5
4. Parker's	Wilson	60.25
5. Log Cabin Bar-B-Que	Albemarle	60

Rest of the Pack

Restaurant	Location	Total Score
King's Barbecue	Kinston	59.7
Wilber's Barbecue	Goldsboro	59
The Skylight Inn	Ayden	59
Southern Barbecue Too	Lexington	59
B's Barbecue	Greenville	58.5
Pig-N-Out	Winston-Salem	58.5
Blue Mist	Asheboro	57.5
Smithfield's	Raleigh	56.5
McCall's Barbecue	Goldsboro	56
Smokey Joe's Barbecue	Lexington	56
Jimmy's BBQ	Lexington	55
Lexington Barbecue	Lexington	54
BBQ & Ribs Co.	Burlingon	54
Stamey's Old Fashioned	Greensboro	51.5
Whispering Pines	Albemarle	51.5
Clark's Bar-B-Q	Kernersville	51.5
Bubba's Barbecue	Charlotte	35

Chopped Wood-Cooked North Carolina–Style Pork Shoulder

1 whole pork shoulder, about 15 pounds

Salt as needed

Dr. BBQ's Western or Eastern Carolina Barbecue Dip (pages 36–37)

20 hamburger buns

North Carolina Slaw recipe follows)

In North Carolina this is simply known as "barbecue."
- **Yield: About 20 servings**

To do this in a traditional fashion you'll need the ability to burn logs of hickory and oak down to coals and then shovel them into the cooking area under the meat. You'll need to have the meat on a grate 18 to 24 inches above the coals and you'll need to cover the meat. This can all be done by stacking cinder blocks three or four high, creating a four-sided pit. You'll need to create a couple openings on the bottom for access to shovel the hot coals. Top the blocks with a grate made out of uncoated steel. Then you add another layer of blocks and top it all with a sheet of plywood or corrugated steel. Do not do this on your asphalt driveway! I'd also advise against doing it on the concrete or paver stone driveway or the lawn if you're married. If you're living at a frat house, go for it. For most of us it's best to find a spot behind the shed and make a nice gravel base before you build your pit. You'll also need to build a second pit for burning the wood down to coals. This is usually done on a grate a foot above the ground with big spaces in the grate. Look for a piece of scrap rebar grate at the local concrete guy's yard. You burn the logs on the grate and when they get cooked enough the coals will fall to the ground so you can shovel them into the cooking pit. Sound like a hassle? Now you understand why many of the restaurants in North Carolina have switched to automated electric cookers.

You'll also need a remote thermometer with the wire and a little readout station to monitor the grate temp. I'd suggest cooking at a grate temp of 275°F.

Once you have the pit all stoked up, salt the shoulder liberally and put it on the pit directly over the coals, skin side down, and cook until the internal temp of the meat reaches 190°F. This will take a long time, probably 10 to 12 hours. Be sure to have a lot of wood and a comfy chair because you can't get very far away from the pit during the whole time.

When the shoulder reaches an internal temp of 190°F, take it off the pit, tent it with foil, and let it rest for an hour. Next remove all the fat, skin, and bones with your hands—wear a big pair of rubber gloves. Now chop the meat with a cleaver or two until it's the consistency you like. In North Carolina they seem to like it pretty finely chopped. I prefer it a little chunkier. Add 1 or 2 cups of one of my North Carolina sauces (pages 36–37) and toss the meat with it. You don't want it to be very wet, just coated.

This is typically served on a bun with a scoop of slaw.

North Carolina Slaw

1 cup mayonnaise

2 tablespoons cider vinegar

1 tablespoon clover or other mild honey

1 teaspoon celery seeds

½ teaspoon salt, or to taste

¼ teaspoon freshly ground black pepper

1 head (about 1½ pounds) green cabbage, finely shredded

1 small onion, shredded

Here's my version of what North Carolina barbecue fanatics serve with their pulled pork sandwiches.

• Yield: 8 servings

In a large mixing bowl, mix together the mayonnaise, vinegar, honey, celery seeds, salt, and pepper. Add the cabbage and onion and stir until coated with the dressing. Cover and chill before serving.

North Carolina-Style Hush Puppies

Vegetable oil for frying

1 cup yellow cornmeal

½ cup flour

1 teaspoon baking powder

1 teaspoon sugar

½ teaspoon baking soda

½ teaspoon salt

½ teaspoon finely ground black pepper

1 egg

½ cup buttermilk

• Yield: About 12 servings

Fill a Dutch oven with about 3 inches of vegetable oil and bring the temp up to 350°F.

In a large mixing bowl, combine the cornmeal, flour, baking powder, sugar, baking soda, salt, and pepper.

In a small bowl, mix together the egg and buttermilk, beating with a fork to combine. Add the buttermilk mixture to the dry ingredients and stir together to make a thick batter.

Put the batter in a large zip-lock bag. Cut one corner off and squeeze out the hush puppies like you would from a pastry bag. Clip them with a butter knife to a size of about 2 inches long. Don't overcrowd them in the oil and try to keep them separated.

Fry about 1 minute on each side, or until golden brown. Drain on paper towels before serving.

Chocolate Pound Cake

1 cup butter

⅓ cup vegetable shortening

2½ cups sugar

5 eggs

3 cups flour

½ cup cocoa powder, plus extra for dusting the cake pan

½ teaspoon baking powder

½ teaspoon salt

1 cup milk

2 teaspoons vanilla extract

Pam oil spray

Well, maybe this isn't typical but I sure did like the one I tried at Log Cabin Bar-B-Que in Albemarle.

• **Yield: 12 servings**

Preheat the oven to 325°F.

Using an electric mixer, beat together the butter, vegetable shortening, and sugar until smooth and creamy. With the mixer running, add the eggs one at a time.

In a mixing bowl, sift together the flour, cocoa powder, baking powder, and salt so that they are well blended.

In a small bowl, combine the milk and vanilla extract.

With the electric mixer running, add one-third of the dry ingredients, then one-third of the milk, and repeat two more times, mixing until thoroughly combined.

Spray a Bundt pan with Pam and dust with cocoa. Pour the batter into the prepared pan and bake for 1 hour to 1 hour and 15 minutes, until a toothpick inserted in the middle of the cake comes out clean.

Remove the cake from the oven and cool on a wire rack for 15 minutes before inverting on a serving plate.

Dave and I in front of the NASCAR photos at Log Cabin Bar-B-Que

Kings Mountain Firehouse BBQ Cookoff

Kings Mountain, North Carolina

www.kcbs.us

After we booked our trip to visit all the restaurants I realized that there was a KCBS cookoff scheduled to start the Friday we were finishing up, so we decided to add a visit there to our trip. It was the tenth annual Kings Mountain Firehouse cookoff. When we

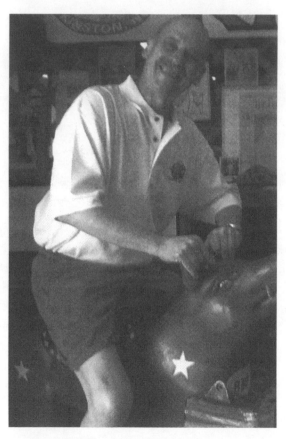

Dave DeWitt riding a hog in the lobby at the Kings Mountain barbecue.

got there, we found some old friends and had a nice visit with them. My good friend Marsha Russell was there and had made me a buttermilk pie just because she knows I like them. (That recipe is in *Barbecue All Year Long!*). She'd also made some grilled steaks, mashed potatoes, grilled vegetables, and a big trifle bowl full of banana pudding. She had to let a few judges sample it first, but we got to join in eating the leftovers. Dave proclaimed it some of the best food he'd ever eaten, but I suspect it had to do with the fact that it wasn't pork barbecue and hush puppies. I stayed around to judge on Saturday. They held the judging in a cool old fireman's museum. This is a really nice cookoff and it was a great way to end a terrific barbecue trip to North Carolina. I'm pretty sure Dave went home and ate some enchiladas.

The Grand Champion that day was another old barbecue friend named Charles Fretwell. Charles uses the team name B.S. Pitmeister. He claims it's because he hails from Boiling Springs, South Carolina, but his friends have other ideas. I called Charles to congratulate him and ask him for a recipe to include in this story, and he was generous enough to offer a whole hog recipe, a side dish, and even a dessert. You'll have plenty of time while the hog is cooking so you might as well make all three on the same day.

Cheesy Cabbage

Courtesy of Charles Fretwell

3 cups coarsely chopped cabbage

1 pound spicy sausage, precooked and sliced thinly

1 tablespoon whole peppercorns

1 cup grated Swiss cheese

1 cup grated Cheddar cheese

1 cup cubed cream cheese

½ cup grated Parmesan cheese

Half a squeeze bottle of Parkay

1 teaspoon garlic salt

This is an easy side dish that you can cook in your smoker. With the foil kind of loose, the cheese topping will pick up some nice smoke flavor. • **Yield: 6 servings**

Fill a 9×13-inch glass baking dish about two-thirds full with the cabbage. Add the sausage slices on top of the cabbage. Sprinkle the peppercorns over all. Add all of the cheeses to the top of the mixture. Squeeze the margarine over the top and sprinkle the garlic salt on top. Loosely cover with aluminum foil and put it in the smoker at 225°F for about 4 hours. The cheeses should be completely melted and the cabbage tender.

Carolina Whole Hog

Courtesy of Charles Fretwell

Here in the Carolinas when you mention barbecue, most people's minds go to whole hog, and from a cookoff standpoint there are a bunch of nonsanctioned whole hog cookoffs around this area. That is the way I started and here is what I do. My technique differs from most people's because I skin the hog before cooking. And I create ribs that are not dried out. Use hickory wood for smoke the first three hours and the last three hours. For the heat source I use lump charcoal because I am too lazy to use a burn barrel."

Charles doesn't mention what he cooks on so I'll add my directions for building a concrete block barbecue pit, which is very common in North Carolina.

Carolina Hog Cooking Barbecue Pit

• **Yield: Varies according to the weight of the hog**

To build the pit, lay 4 blocks lengthwise in a line to form one side of the pit. Then lay 1 block on a 90-degree angle to begin forming the end. Leave a 12-inch space to shovel coals in and lay another block. Now, on another 90-degree angle, lay 4 more blocks to form the other side and then two more to form the other end. If you've done it right, the outside dimension should be approximately 60 inches wide by 78 inches long, and you should be able to add coals at either end. Spread the sand evenly on the bottom of the pit. Now add two more layers of blocks on top of the first layer but don't leave any spaces on the ends. Some of the blocks will overhang a little but that's okay. Lay the

56 full-size concrete blocks

One 4 x 6-foot sheet of expanded steel

One 4 x 6-foot sheet of corrugated steel

100 pounds of sand

1 whole hog, at least 100 pounds, cleaned

The Injection

1 cup apple juice

1 cup Worcestershire sauce

1/2 cup apple cider vinegar

1/2 cup Parkay-type margarine, melted

Juice from 1 orange

1 teaspoon table salt

Olive oil as needed

Dr. BBQ's North Carolina Barbecue Rub, as needed (page 36)

expanded metal on top of the blocks and then add another layer of blocks. Lay the sheet of corrugated steel over the top and use the last two blocks to hold it in place.

Now build a big fire out of hickory logs. You're gonna need a lot of wood! Burn them down to coals and add the coals to the pit on both ends. Throw some to the middle now and then, but you'll want most of them in the corners for cooking a whole hog. To monitor the temp you'll have to use a remote thermometer with the cord and readout. For the best results you'll need to use two of these to monitor both sides of the pit. Add coals as needed to keep the pit at 225°F. This is going to require almost constant attention for about 16 hours.

Skin the hog from the base of its ears back and trim out most of the fat under the skin. With a Roto Zip–type tool, cut from the inside through the ribs. Make two cuts per side so that you are separating the baby backribs and spareribs from the backbone. When this is done, the ribs can be removed easily after the hog is cooked.

Make the injection: In a bowl, combine all the ingredients. Inject the hams and loins with the mixture.

Rub the hog all over with olive oil, then give it a good coating of the dry rub. Cover the rib and loin areas with aluminum foil to keep them from drying out.

Remove the metal lid from the cooker and place the hog on the grate. Replace the lid and the blocks to weight it down.

At about the 13-hour point, or when the shoulders have reached an internal temp of 170°F, remove the foil from the portion of the hog that was covered so it gets the smoke at the end of the cooking time.

Cook for about another 3 hours, or until the shoulders and hams are 195°F internal temp.

Alamo Pies

Courtesy of Charles Fretwell

4 flour tortillas

½ cup peanut butter

2 bananas, sliced

2 cups baby marshmallows

1 cup semisweet chocolate chips

1 tablespoon butter

Sugar, cinnamon, and powdered sugar for garnish

I call these Alamo Pies because the basics came from an ancestor of mine, Simoneus Equinox Fretwell, who is little known but was the sole survivor of the Alamo when Santa Anna's men stormed in and killed everyone but him. When the Mexicans came in with their weapons drawn, they found Simoneus, who was the cook, huddled under the table in the kitchen. He just knew he was a dead man, but when they spoke they said that they were hungry and for him to fix food. Well, old Simoneus heard this and he knew he might live if he made them something good enough, and he also knew that the Mexicans were not famous for their desserts, so he whipped up something called the Alamo Pie. (Note: By the way, this story was something I made up to tell some judges at an 'Anything But' judging.)"

• **Yield: 4 servings**

Starting with a soft flour tortilla, spread peanut butter on one side to within about 1 inch of the edge. On one half of the peanut butter put some ripe banana slices, baby marshmallows, and semisweet chocolate chips. (The amount of the ingredients can be varied to suit one's taste.) Then fold it in half like a taco.

On the grill, heat a cast-iron skillet until it's so hot that butter sizzles in it. Place the pie in the hot buttered pan for about a minute, then turn it over. Now sprinkle some sugar and cinnamon on the side that is up, and after it has been that side up for about a minute, turn it over again and sprinkle the currently up side with sugar, powdered sugar (for looks), and cinnamon. The time will vary with the pan temp and thickness of the filling, but what you want is melted gooey filling and a somewhat crispy shell.

Nahunta Pork Center

Pikeville, North Carolina

www.nahuntaporkcenter.com

▼▼

As we drove through North Carolina one day, we began seeing signs for the Nahunta Pork Center, kind of like we were coming up on Wall Drug or Ruby Falls. Needless to say, I was excited at the thought of a pork-themed attraction, and to my screwed-up way of thinking it was possible. The logo for the Nahunta Pork Center that was on all the billboards featured a happy pig wearing a king's crown. Watch your back, Mickey Mouse. So we followed the signs and made all the turns and arrived at the Nahunta Pork Center. It probably wouldn't be considered an attraction to most folks, but it was to me. It was a small processing plant and a pork retail store. I guess you could call it a big butcher shop, but there were pens across the road so the butchering started very early in the process, if you know what I mean. But that was handled nicely and out of view so that what you saw was a really nice series of meat cases like any grocery store would have, but the only product was pork. There were whole hogs, whole shoulders, pork chops, ribs, snouts, tails, ears, and whole heads. Any cut of pork you could possibly imagine was right there in front of you. I lost count, but the number of unique cuts was amazing. I've never seen anything like it in my life. As we walked through the place, we also saw that they had fresh country hams and racks of smoked sides and shoulders. They had many different sausages and even some old-fashioned processed things like souse and liver pudding. They had barbecue, too, what looked like smoked and chopped pork, probably tossed with some vinegar sauce. But it was all pork! Unfortunately we were living in hotels and unable to cook anything, so all I bought was a bottle of water with the Pork King's picture on it. I miss the Pork King, their cheerful-looking cartoon pig logo. This place is highly recommended if you love pork, and who doesn't?

Grilled Pork Meatball Hoagies

The Meatballs

1 pound ground pork

2 large eggs

$\frac{1}{2}$ teaspoon ground black pepper

$\frac{1}{2}$ teaspoon salt

$\frac{1}{2}$ teaspoon onion powder

$\frac{1}{2}$ teaspoon garlic powder

$\frac{1}{2}$ teaspoon paprika

$\frac{3}{8}$ cup dry bread crumbs

The Sauce

2 tablespoons olive oil

1 medium onion, halved and sliced thin

1 green bell pepper, halved and sliced thin

2 cloves garlic, crushed

One 15-ounce can petite diced tomatoes

$\frac{1}{2}$ teaspoon ground black pepper

1 teaspoon dried basil

4 hoagie rolls

Freshly grated Parmesan cheese

In honor of the Pork King.

• **Yield: 4 servings**

In a large bowl, combine the meatball ingredients and mix well. Form 16 meatballs about the size of a golf ball. Put them on a plate and set aside in the refrigerator.

In a medium saucepan, heat the oil over medium heat. Add the onion, bell pepper, and garlic and sauté until soft. Stir in the tomatoes, black pepper, and basil. Cover and cook until all the vegetables are soft. Add a bit of water if the mixture gets dry. When done, lower heat to keep warm.

Prepare the grill to a medium temp over direct heat. Gently transfer the meatballs to the grill. They will get firmer as they cook. Grill them for 10 to 12 minutes, turning occasionally. When the internal temp reaches 160°F, remove them to a large bowl. Spoon the tomato mixture over the meatballs and toss gently.

Place 4 of the meatballs on each roll. Spoon one-quarter of the tomato mixture over each roll. Grate some fresh Parmesan cheese over the top.

Tennessee

Dr. BBQ's Tennessee Barbecue Rub

Dr. BBQ's Tennessee Barbecue Sauce

Memphis in May

Apple City Barbecue

Smoked Stuffed Green Peppers on the Pit

Magic Dust

Big Bob Gibson Bar-B-Q

Pit-Fired Caribbean Pork Tenderloin with
Passion Fruit Butter Sauce

Corky's Bar-B-Q (Memphis)

Memphis St. Louis Dry Ribs

The Bar-B-Q Shop (Memphis)

Dr. BBQ's Smoked Bologna

Leonard's Pit Barbecue (Memphis)

Chopped Pork Memphis Style

Cozy Corner (Memphis)

Smoked Cornish Hens Cozy Corner Style

The Rendezvous (Memphis)

Rendezvous-Style Charcoal Ribs

Interstate Barbecue (Memphis)

Barbecue Spaghetti

Paradise Ridge Grille (Nashville)

Steaks with Paradise Ridge Grille Seasoning

Amazin' Blazin' BBQ Cookoff (Lebanon)

Fast Eddy's Championship Steak Recipe

Jack Daniel's World Championship Barbecue Cookoff (Lynchburg)

Sheri Gray's First-Place Caramel Apple Crunch

Marsha's Grits Pie

▼▼▼▼▼

This chapter was going to be just about Memphis, but there is some pretty great barbecue all across Tennessee, so I decided to include it here. My favorite barbecue cookoff of the year is in Lebanon, Tennessee, and the friends I've made there are as good as gold. Then there's Lynchburg, mostly known for making Jack Daniel's whiskey, but they take their barbecue real serious there, too. There's a barbecue joint right on the square with all the little Jack Daniel's souvenir shops. Stop by the Lynchburg General Store and you might even see an autographed copy of my first book for sale. Don't miss the barrel shop either, they make all sorts of things out of the surplus whiskey barrels. Keep an eye out as you drive around Lynchburg, because there might be somebody selling barbecue to make a few dollars for some project at the local high school. What a deal, you get some great barbecue and you help out the local kids. You should always look out for these kinds of opportunities when traveling in the South. It'll

probably be some good barbecue and you'll definitely meet some nice folks. The oldest KCBS cookoff east of the Mississippi is held every September in Cookville, Tennessee, and there's another good one in Sevierville. While you're there you can stop at the Lodge Cast Iron factory outlet for a chicken frying pan or a Dutch oven to cook smoky chili right in your barbecue pit. Don't forget Nashville—there's Jack's BBQ, which made my top five list a few years ago, and a fairly new place run by some old friends of mine, the Babb family The Babbs are some serious cooks; don't miss their place on the west end of Nashville.

As much as I like all of these other places, Memphis is the undisputed barbecue capital of Tennessee. The main party street in Memphis is the legendary Beale Street, and just about every one of the extravagant party bars serves up some barbecue along with their live blues. The party gets so big that they close Beale Street down at night and it becomes one big nightclub. Be sure to stop by Silky O'Sullivan's, he's a long-time Jack

Daniel's judge and supporter of barbecue. I also spent some time at a place called the Flying Saucer last time I was there. It was a block off Beale Street and they didn't have any barbecue, but they had cute little waitresses in skimpy outfits and hundreds of different kinds of beer. What a concept!

In Memphis there are barbecue joints everywhere in every part of town. If you read about Memphis you'll inevitably hear about the big controversy of wet ribs versus dry ribs. Seems some places like to put a little more rub on before serving and others like to put some sauce on. Is this really a big deal? I don't think it is. I asked Don McLemore at Big Bob Gibson Bar-B-Q in Decatur, Alabama, if he'd serve me my ribs dry with a little extra rub sprinkled on them, and he said that wouldn't be any problem at all. Any good barbecue joint in any town will serve you your ribs dry, and they'll be happy to sprinkle a little extra rub on them. Many have their rub on the table anyway. It makes for a good story,

but it really isn't a big deal to a true barbecue aficionado.

The barbecue sandwich of choice in Memphis is chopped pork shoulder, with bologna as a distant second. Both will be served with slaw on the sandwich. Yes, you read that right and this is the Memphis chapter. **Your barbecue sandwich in Memphis will be served topped with coleslaw.** Of course, everyone thinks this is an exclusively Carolina thing, but it's not. I've seen this many other places, too, but it's a must in Memphis. Some locals will tell you that the quality of the slaw is as important as the quality of the meat. Who knew?

The city of Memphis also plays host to the granddaddy of all the big barbecue cookoffs, Memphis in May. Technically it's just one event that's part of the month-long Memphis in May Festival, but to barbecue enthusiasts, MIM is all about the barbecue. A barbecue trip to Memphis is a must, but don't forget the rest of Tennessee.

Dr. BBQ's Tennessee Barbecue Rub

1/4 cup paprika

2 tablespoons salt

2 tablespoons brown sugar

1 tablespoon finely ground black pepper

1 teaspoon granulated garlic

1 teaspoon onion powder

1/2 teaspoon dry mustard

1/2 teaspoon cayenne pepper

• Yield: About 3/4 cup

Mix together and store in an airtight cointainer.

Dr. BBQ's Tennessee Barbecue Sauce

1 cup cane syrup (available in the South or online for the northerners)

1 cup tomato sauce

1 tablespoon cider vinegar

1/2 teaspoon allspice

1/2 teaspoon finely ground black pepper

1/4 teaspoon ground cloves

1/4 teaspoon ground cinnamon

1/4 teaspoon cayenne pepper

• Yield: 2 cups

In a medium saucepan, combine the ingredients. Cook over medium heat, stirring often, until the ingredients are all combined. This should take 4 to 5 minutes.

Memphis in May
World Championship Barbecue
Cooking Contest

www.memphisinmay.org

▼▼▼

At Memphis in May, the fatter you are, the hairier you are, the drunker you are, the more revered you are." So says Elizabeth Karmel in *Chile Pepper* magazine. I don't know about you, but that sounds like a party I want to go to. Now, technically Memphis in May (MIM) is a month-long festival that features the Beale Street Music Festival and the Sunset Symphony, but for me the main event is the World Championship Barbecue Cooking Contest (WCBCC). Besides, I'm pretty sure the fat drunk hairy guys are frowned upon at the Sunset Symphony. To barbecuers MIM means the barbecue championship, and the whole world of barbecue comes to Tom Lee Park on the shore of the Mississippi to see who's going to win. In 2006 there were 253 teams competing and Diane Hampton tells me that is a full house. Diane is the executive vice president of marketing for MIM and she does a great job. When you walk through Memphis in May you'll see film crews from all the networks. They've had celebrities like Martha Stewart, Paula Deen, and Al Roker host their shows from the event. Al Roker even competed in the contest. Another notable celeb who has cooked at MIM is former Tennessee senator and vice president Al Gore. Diane has done her job of promoting this event very well. They have guests from all fifty states in attendance and nine foreign countries. It's all about cooking

pork at Memphis in May. The championship categories are pork ribs, whole pork shoulder, and whole hog. They use a two-tiered system, and the finals judges eat the best three from each category and pick the one best entry for the day as Grand Champion. The list of past champions is a who's who of the barbecue world. Names like John Willingham, Paul Hood, and Bessie Lou Cathey. Bessie Lou was the first-ever MIM Grand Champion way back in 1978. Since then a handful of teams have won the contest two times, but only one team has won three Memphis in May Grand Championships and that team was Apple City Barbecue. Mike Mills and Pat Burke teamed up to win an incredible 32 Grand Championships out of 69 cookoffs during their short five-year run. They were arguably the best MIM team ever. Two other teams that deserve a mention here are Jack's Old South and Big Bob Gibson. They've each won two Grand Championships and are both still at the top of their game. Big Bob's has won the shoulder category six times and Jack's Old South has won the whole hog category four times. I'm proud to know all these guys, and they've all shared a recipe with me for the book. I wouldn't ask them for their barbecue secrets, just three great recipes from three great barbecue teams. (The Jack's Old South recipe is in the South chapter, on pages 165–66, with a story all about Myron.)

Memphis in May International Festival
World Championship Barbecue Cooking Contest

Grand Champions

Year	Grand Champion	Category
1978	Bessie Lou Cathey	Ribs
1979	Don Burdison	Ribs
1980	John Wills	Ribs
1981	John Wills	Ribs
1982	Martec Coaters	Shoulder
1983	Willingham's River City Rooters	Ribs
1984	Willingham's River City Rooters	Ribs
1985	Holy Smokers, Too	Whole Hog
1986	Pig Iron Porkers	Whole Hog
1987	Cajun Country Cookers	Whole Hog
1988	Holy Smokers, Too	Whole Hog
1989	Super Swine Sizzlers	Whole Hog
1990	Apple City Barbecue	Ribs
1991	David Cox Barbecue Team	Ribs
1992	Apple City Barbecue	Ribs
1993	The Other Side	Shoulder
1994	Apple City Barbecue	Ribs
1995	Rebel Roaster Revue	Shoulder
1996	Pyropigmaniacs	Ribs
1997	Wildfire Gourmet Cooking Team	Shoulder
1998	The Other Team	Ribs
1999	Custom Cookers	Whole Hog
2000	Big Bob Gibson Bar-B-Q	Shoulder
2001	Jack's Old South	Whole Hog
2002	Pyropigmaniacs	Ribs
2003	Big Bob Gibson Bar-B-Q	Shoulder
2004	Jack's Old South	Whole Hog
2005	Gwatney Championship BBQ Team	Whole Hog
2006	Red Hot Smokers	Shoulder

Apple City Barbecue

The three-time Memphis in May championship team has been retired for quite a while, but both former members are still very active in barbecue. Pat Burke has continued cooking under the name Tower Rock and is still winning contests on a regular basis. Mike Mills runs a series of successful barbecue restaurants (www.memphis-bbq.com) and has written a great book of his memoirs with his daughter, Amy Mills Tunnicliffe. The book is titled *Peace, Love, and Barbecue*, published by Rodale, Inc., and the authors have generously shared these two recipes with me.

Smoked Stuffed Green Peppers on the Pit

1 pound ground beef (chuck or hamburger)

½ medium onion, diced

1 teaspoon Magic Dust (recipe follows)

1½ cups cooked white rice

One 15-ounce can diced tomatoes, drained

6 green bell peppers, tops cut off and peppers seeded

½ cup bread crumbs

2 cups ketchup (I use Hunt's)

½ cup packed brown sugar

Mike Mills says, "We ate stuffed green peppers at least once a week for years when I was growing up. They were, and still are, economical, easy, and delicious—especially when you can pick the green peppers right out of your own garden. Cooking them on the pit instead of in the oven elevates the taste to a whole new level." • **Yield: 6 servings**

Brown the beef and onion in a medium skillet over medium heat. Stir in the Magic Dust while you're cooking. Remove from the heat and pour the meat into a sieve to drain the grease. Transfer the meat to a medium bowl and stir in the rice and tomatoes. Arrange the green peppers upright in a baking dish. Spoon the hamburger mixture into the peppers and top with the bread crumbs.

Smoke on the pit for 1½ hours at 210°F.

Meanwhile, combine the ketchup and brown sugar in a small saucepan and cook over medium heat until the sugar dissolves and the sauce is warm. Spoon the sauce over the peppers during the last 10 minutes of smoking.

Magic Dust

½ cup paprika

¼ cup kosher salt, finely ground

¼ cup sugar

2 tablespoons mustard powder

¼ cup chili powder

¼ cup ground cumin

2 tablespoons ground black pepper

¼ cup granulated garlic

2 tablespoons cayenne pepper

There's a big shaker of Magic Dust right next to the salt and pepper in my own kitchen and at all my restaurants. I wish I could figure out a way to attach the bottle to the restaurant tables because, at my restaurants, it's the most frequently stolen item! To make it a little more hot and spicy, increase the mustard powder and black pepper to 1/4 cup each. • **Yield: About 2½ cups**

Mix all the ingredients and store in a tightly covered container. You'll want to keep some in a shaker next to the grill or stove. Keeps indefinitely, but won't last long.

Memphis in May legends Pat Burke and Mike Mills,
a.k.a. Apple City Barbecue

Big Bob Gibson Bar-B-Q

The Big Bob Gibson cooking team is headed by Chris Lilly and always includes Don McLemore and Bill Bullen and often includes Carolyn (Don's wife), John Underwood, and John Markus. They've won the Memphis in May World Championship twice and have won the shoulder division an amazing six times in a row. Here's a great recipe from Chris. It's one that Don and I prepared with him at the James Beard House.

Pit-Fired Caribbean Pork Tenderloin with Passion Fruit Butter Sauce

Marinade

1/4 cup olive oil

1/4 cup lime juice

1 tablespoon Worcestershire sauce

1/4 cup apple juice

1/4 cup sugar

1/4 cup Big Bob Gibson Championship Red Sauce

1/4 cup soy sauce

1 tablespoon white vinegar

1 tablespoon oregano

1/2 teaspoon ground cumin

1/2 teaspoon ground black pepper

1/2 teaspoon cayenne pepper

2 whole pork tenderloins

Passion Fruit Butter Sauce (recipe follows)

• Yield: 6 servings

Mix the marinade ingredients. Place the pork tenderloins in the marinade and refrigerate for 6 to 8 hours.

Preheat the oven or an outdoor cooker to 250°F. Place the tenderloins in the cooker for 1 1/2 to 2 hours. The internal temperature of the tenderloins should be 150 to 160°F when removed from the cooker.

Increase the cooker temperature to 350°F. Coat the pork tenderloins with Passion Fruit Butter Sauce. Place tenderloins back on the cooker for 5 minutes and baste with the remaining sauce. Remove the tenderloins, cut into medallions, and serve.

Passion Fruit Butter Sauce

1 passion fruit

1½ cups water

¼ cup sugar

1 stick salted butter

Remove the pulp from the passion fruit and place it in a saucepan. Add water and sugar and bring the mixture to a boil. Reduce the heat and add the stick of butter. Simmer for 15 minutes. Pour the mixture through a strainer, removing the pulp from the sauce. The mixture is ready to baste the tenderloin.

Chris Lilly and John Markus tending to some ribs for the Big Bob Gibson team.

The Barbecue Joints of Memphis

There are many great barbecue joints in Memphis. The biggest names are the Rendezvous and Corky's. They're quite different from each other and I like them both. My favorite place is the Cozy Corner, again, completely different. The Bar-B-Q Shop is another unique place, but so are Leonard's and A&R and Interstate. To me the one outstanding feature about Memphis barbecue joints is that they all do their own thing. You can't lump them all together. Most of them have borrowed the barbecued bologna and spaghetti from each other, but I'm quite sure that's just because their customers were asking for those items. Same with the wet versus dry rib thing. They all play along, but I talked to a couple of pitmasters who think that it's kind of blown out of proportion. They'll be happy to serve your ribs however you'd like them. Here's a rundown of my favorite places to eat barbecue in Memphis, in no particular order.

Corky's Bar-B-Q

Memphis
www.corkysbbq.com

▼▼

Corky's original place is a nice-looking barbecue joint. It's been there since 1986 and has lots of celebrity pics on the walls along with too many newspaper clippings to count. I asked the bartender who was the most famous guest she'd seen and her answer was Jack Nicholson. Well, I'd say that is A-list all the way. Speaking of A-list, the ribs I was served there were too. They were St. Louis–cut, served with dry rub, and cooked just right. I had them as a combo with pork shoulder and the pork was good, too. Long strings pulled from whole shoulders with some excellent Corky's sauce on it. Corky's is well run, maybe a little too organized for my taste in barbecue joints, but it's a great place. They also have a mega mail-order business shipping ribs, pork, and sauce all over the world.

Memphis St. Louis Dry Ribs

2 slabs St. Louis–cut ribs, about 2½ pounds each

Dr. BBQ's Tennessee Barbecue Rub, as needed (page 63)

St. Louis is the name used for the sparerib cut with the cartilage removed. Memphis is where Corky's is and that's where I ate some ribs like these that were real good.

• Yield: 4 servings

Prepare the cooker for indirect cooking at 235°F, using hickory wood for flavor. Peel the membrane from the back of the ribs and trim off any excess fat. Season liberally with the rub. Place the ribs in the cooker bone side down for 1 hour. Flip the ribs and cook another hour. Remove the ribs and wrap each slab tightly in aluminum foil. Return to the cooker meaty side up for 1 hour. Unwrap the ribs and leave on the cooker meat side up. Cook for about 1 more hour, or until tender. Depending on your cooker this could take longer. To test for tenderness, push a toothpick down into the rib meat and feel for resistance. When the toothpick slides in like soft butter the ribs are done. Remove from the cooker and apply a light coat of rub to the meaty side. Let rest for 5 minutes. Cut the ribs apart and serve.

The Bar-B-Q Shop

Memphis

www.barbqshop.com

▼▼

The Bar-B-Q Shop is a very nice place. It's a clean and well-decorated diner kind of restaurant, and the employees are all friendly. They serve chopped pork on Texas toast that is as good as any you'll find. There's a shaker of rub on the table, common in Memphis, and I shook a little on my sandwich. They also serve ribs, wet or dry, rib tips (unusual for Memphis), barbecue spaghetti, and smoked bologna. They have some of the best sweet tea I've ever tasted here, too. I met the owner, Frank Vernon, after I had eaten, and I asked him about the whole wet versus dry rib thing. He said they'd be happy to serve the ribs anyway a customer liked them. He didn't seem to think this was a big deal. Now when I asked about the barbecue spaghetti, Mr. Vernon was very opinionated. He's very proud of the barbecue spaghetti they serve at The Bar-B-Q Shop, telling me that they make a base sauce specifically for theirs while other restaurants just use their regular barbecue sauce. He brought me a sample and it was delicious. Just the right amount of sweetness and just enough chopped pork. I'm already thinking about my return visit and will order a plate of that. He's also proud to have been one of the first places in Memphis to have barbecued bologna on the menu. Mr. Vernon has only owned the Bar-B-Q Shop for about twenty years, but it's been there a lot longer. It used to be known as Brady & Lil's Restaurant, but the name change hasn't affected the food or the service. It's all good at The Bar-B-Q Shop.

Dr. BBQ's Smoked Bologna

One 3-pound chub of bologna or a 3-pound piece cut off a larger chub

Dr. BBQ's Tennessee Barbecue Rub, as needed (page 63)

In honor of Mr. Vernon, here's a recipe for smoked bologna, Memphis style. The Bar-B-Q Shop serves it on thick white bread (untoasted Texas toast) with barbecue sauce and a scoop of coleslaw. • **Yield: Serves many, depending on how thinly you slice it.**

Prepare the cooker for indirect cooking at 235°F, using hickory wood for flavor.

Season the bologna liberally with the barbecue rub. Place it in the cooker for about 4 hours.

Remove and slice to serve. If you need to have it a little sooner or need to leave it in a little longer it will be fine.

My old buddy Blind Dog once asked our other buddy, Cubby, what temp he cooked his bologna to. Cubby replied that he never checked as it wasn't very critical. "It's done when you put it on!" So take John's advice and cook it until you need to eat it.

Leonard's Pit Barbecue

Memphis

www.leonardsbarbecue.com

▼▼▼

Leonard's has been serving barbecue in Memphis since 1922, and they are proud to tell you that they are still using the same recipe. You would expect that it's a heck of a recipe and you'd be right. When you walk into Leonard's, you'll see an refurbished old delivery van parked right in the restaurant. I mean right in the middle. You can't miss it. It's a neat old relic from the business and it helps make Leonard's a friendly place. I spoke with Janet Brown, who owns Leonard's with her husband, Dan, and she told me a great story about the van. It has a different vehicle number on each side. It seems the original owner thought that if his customers and competitors saw van #1 in the morning, van #2 at lunch, and van #3 at dinner they'd think he really had a big business. Of course they actually saw the left side in the morning, the right side at lunch, and the back at dinner, all on the same van. Leonard's serves pork loin back ribs, big meaty ones. I had those on a combo plate with some of their pulled pork shoulder. The shoulder was juicy and tasty and seemed to be pulled by hand with great care. They also have a buffet that is known far and wide. The buffet at Leonard's boasts their beautiful pork shoulder, barbecued chicken, fried catfish, and all the side dishes to go with it. It just doesn't get much better than that.

Chopped Pork Memphis Style

1 pork butt, 6 to 8 pounds, untrimmed

Dr. BBQ's Tennessee Barbecue Rub, as needed (page 63)

2 cups apple juice

2 ounces Tennessee whiskey

In Memphis pork shoulder is the main course. Wet and dry ribs make a good story, but the locals are eating pork shoulder. In barbecue terms the shoulder is a big piece of meat. It's described by Memphis in May as "The portion of the hog containing the arm bone, shank bone, and a portion of the blade bone." That's what most of the restaurants in Memphis cook, but it's pretty big for most home grills and they're also hard to find in most places. A pork butt will work as a pretty good substitute. In Memphis this is served on a white fluffy bun topped with coleslaw.

• **Yield: About 12 servings**

At least an hour before you plan to cook and as long as the night before, season the pork butt liberally with the rub.

Prepare the cooker for indirect cooking at 235°F, using hickory wood for flavor. Put the butt on the cooker with the fat cap down and cook for 6 hours before peeking.

Combine the apple juice and whiskey in a spray bottle or a bowl. After 6 hours, spray or mop the meat heavily with the apple juice mixture. Turn the butt over and spray again. Cook for another 4 hours. This time, check the internal temp of the butt. It should be getting close to the target temp of 190°F. If it's not done, turn it over and spray heavily again. Cook until the internal temp reaches 190°F.

Remove to a platter and tent with foil. Let rest for 30 minutes. Wearing heavy rubber gloves, pull the meat apart, discarding all the fat and bones. Sprinkle a little rub over the meat and spray with the apple juice mixture. Chop the meat with a chef's knife or a cleaver to your preferred texture. I like it pretty coarse, but many like it chopped fine.

Cozy Corner

Memphis

▼▼

I've only eaten at Cozy Corner a few times, but it's quickly become one of my favorite barbecue joints anywhere. Some may doubt the ambience, but this is a barbecue joint. When I am in line and the pitmaster is right in front of me with a pitchfork-type tool moving things around and I can see the real wood fire burning underneath, I am thinking "five-star ambience." Robert was that pitmaster's name and he was more than happy to talk with the customers while he worked and even posed for a picture. This is a famous barbecue joint. There are half a dozen books on the counter, all of which sing the praises of Cozy Corner. There are dozens of pictures of celebrities who have eaten there, many of them posing with the lovely owner, Desiree Robinson. She always has time to say hi to the customers. But none of that stuff is what makes Cozy Corner so good. The food is what makes it so good. They have good Memphis pork shoulder and ribs. I love the ribs here, real full-size spareribs cooked smoky and tender. They have good beans and the bologna sandwich is one of the best in town, but there's more. Cozy Corner is a perfect example of my feeling that the barbecue joints in Memphis all do their own thing. Cozy Corner is most famous for their smoked Cornish hens. I don't think I've ever even seen Cornish hens in another barbecue joint, and that's fine. They would have a hard time making them as good as this place does. The hen is a little smoky and a little salty. The skin is crusty and the meat is moist and tender. A Cornish hen at Cozy Corner is one of the best barbecue meals you're going to find anywhere. They're also pretty well known for their chicken wings. When I was there last, Robert had the top shelf of the cooker loaded with wings. They're smoky and tender and tossed in the wonderful Cozy Corner barbecue sauce. I'd suggest the hot, but make sure your sweet tea is full before you dig in. I'm sure looking forward to delivering a copy of this book to them to take its place on the counter. I think I'll have lunch while I'm there, too. A Cornish hen with a couple wings on the side, beans, and a sweet tea.

Robert, the pitmaster, shows off the ribs at Cozy Corner in Memphis, Tennessee.

Smoked Cornish Hens Cozy Corner Style

2 Cornish hens

Dr. BBQ's Tennessee Barbecue Rub (page 63)

These are really good and pretty simple. Cozy Corner seems to cook them kind of hot so I do, too.

• Yield: 2 to 4 servings

Prepare the cooker for indirect cooking at 400°F. Tuck the wings back on the hens and season them liberally all over inside and out with the rub. Put the hens on the cooker for 1 hour. Check for an internal temp of at least 160°F in the breast and 180°F in the thigh, but they should be higher than that. Remove to a platter, tent with foil, and rest for 10 minutes.

Here I am with Miss Desiree Robinson, the proprietor of Cozy Corner.

The Rendezvous

Memphis

www.hogsfly.com

▼▼

Without a doubt, the most famous barbecue joint in Memphis is the Rendezvous. It's been there since 1948; that's a good start. It's in the basement and you can only get in through the alley. They serve a very unique type of rib. There's lot's of funky stuff hanging on the walls and ceiling. The newest waiters have been working there for twenty years. What more could you ask for? I measure a barbecue joint by much more than the food. To me the character of the place is a big selling point, and this place is a gold mine. The Rendezvous is also home of the dry rib, but when mine came to the table the waiter simply pointed out the hot and mild barbecue sauce on the table and asked if I needed another beer (I did). So unless you want the tourist rap about dry ribs they don't seem to care much about it. The bigger story is how the ribs are cooked. The sign outside says charcoal ribs. I think that's a good description. I'd probably call them grilled ribs. Of course presidents, Elvis, Justin Timberlake, and even the Rolling Stones would tell you that the Rendezvous rules. They all still eat there regularly, except maybe Elvis. If you like your ribs falling off the bone tender you may want to go somewhere else. The ribs at the Rendezvous are a little chewy, but since they're baby back ribs they're good that way. They taste excellent and really don't need any sauce. I like the ribs at the Rendezvous. They have other things on the menu, but I don't think those things get ordered very much. It's a rib joint.

Rendezvous-Style Charcoal Ribs

2 slabs loin back ribs, each
21 pound or less

Dr. BBQ's Tennessee
Barbecue Rub (page 63),
as needed

1/2 cup Dr. BBQ's Tennessee
Barbecue Sauce (page 63)

1/4 cup apple cider vinegar

The trick to doing these at home is the setup. The Rendezvous cooks them direct, but way above the fire. They eventually move them down to finish, but this setup isn't practical with most home grills. If you can cook direct and at least 14 inches from the fire, you can cook them direct, over a medium fire built with lump charcoal, flipping often, for 2 to 3 hours, or until tender. If you can't get the meat far enough away from the fire to cook direct, you'll need to cook them indirect and hot, at 400°F. This will produce a similar result. These ribs are not intended to be falling-from-the-bone tender—they should have a little chew and some crunchy edges. • **Yield: 2 to 4 servings**

Prepare the cooker as suggested above. Peel the membrane from the back of the ribs and season lightly with the rub. Cook until done as suggested above. Remove to a platter. Combine the barbecue sauce and the vinegar. Brush the ribs lightly with the mixture. Sprinkle the meaty side of the ribs liberally with additional barbecue rub

Interstate Barbecue

Memphis

www.jimneelysinterstatebarbecue.com

▼▼

Jim Neely's Interstate Barbecue once served me one of the best slabs of ribs I've eaten. I didn't ask for them any particular way, I just wanted them the way they serve them. Well, what I got was a slab of whole spareribs with a good coating of sauce. This isn't usually my preference but I can eat them that way. Man, I'm glad I let them serve me their way. The ribs were cooked just right, tender, smoky, and juicy, and the sauce was the perfect complement. You know how you sometimes remember eating something years later and how good it was? That's what I'm reliving right now as I type this. Man, those things were good. I also tried my first barbecue spaghetti that day. This is a truly Memphis dish that involves the cooked pasta with a sauce that's pretty much just straight barbecue sauce. It seems they thin it with a little something but not much. Neely's serves it as a side dish and it has no meat in it. It's actually pretty good once you get over the fact that it looks like Italian spaghetti but tastes like barbecue sauce. Other places in Memphis add chopped pork and charge a little more for it. I'd guess that many eat this as the "poor man's special" at Interstate. As for me, I hope I always have enough cash in my pocket for the ribs.

Barbecue Spaghetti

2 cups Dr. BBQ's Tennessee
Barbecue Sauce (page 63)

½ cup tomato sauce

1 cup chopped smoked
pork (page 172)

1 pound spaghetti, cooked
al dente

This is the signature barbecue dish in Memphis as far as I'm concerned. • **Yield: 4 servings as a main course or 8 as a side dish**

In a saucepan, combine the barbecue sauce, tomato sauce, and the chopped pork. Bring to a boil, reduce the heat, and simmer for five minutes.

In a big bowl, toss the cooked spaghetti with the sauce.

Here I am indulging in some barbecue spaghetti; can't beat it!

Paradise Ridge Grille

Nashville

▼▼▼

The Paradise Ridge Grille is owned by some very good friends of mine. I first met Buddy and Charlie Babb at a cookoff in Tennessee. It seems they'd been cooking some barbecue at the local Moose Lodge, and when Buddy went to the cookoff in Cookeville, Tennessee, he saw many big beautiful barbecue pits, and he decided that they needed one. That was the fall of 1998 and by spring they had Black Betty, a big beauty made by David Klose. Having that nice pit gave them the inspiration to go to some cookoffs. They cooked around Tennessee that first year, getting the feel of things. I cooked next to them in Lebanon that year under the big oak tree and we became friends. When 2000 came around Charlie and Buddy were getting pretty good at this, and they won the big prestigious Blue Ridge Barbecue Festival in Tryon, North Carolina. Then they won the World Barbecue Association Championship that was held in Tennessee later that year. This was a good start! Charlie had seen the big lines for the barbecue vendors at Tryon and he wanted in on that. He had a store in Nashville, but barbecue was calling him. He bought a commercial cooker, enlisted a few friends as well as his mom, affectionately known as Granny on the barbecue circuit. Paradise Ridge Catering and Vending was born. They did very well that first year at Tryon and they were hooked. They traveled the country and did up to seventeen big barbecue events a year while also building a solid catering business at home. The Babbs are not just barbecue cooks. They'll fry you some catfish, serve you amazing desserts, and even cook up some fine dining. (See Buddy's lobster dish in my first book). The next step was surely a restaurant, and when Scully's, a place that they used to frequent, shut down it was a natural for the Paradise Ridge Grille to move in. So in July 2005 they did move in and were open for business on the twenty-second. It's a really nice place on the end of a big strip mall. You'll see Black Betty outside and when you go in you'll see the World Championship trophy along with dozens of other awards. There's a nice bar and plenty of TVs, but it's all about the food here. The big Nashville paper *The Tennessean* says they have the best catfish in town and I agree. My other favorite is the chicken and dumplings. Oh yeah, they serve barbecue here, too. World-class barbecue. Try the ribs or the pulled pork; you'll see why they won. Don't skip one of Granny's desserts, either. I'm proud to know the Babb family and I visit them every chance I get.

Steaks with Paradise Ridge Grille Seasoning

2 choice-grade rib-eye steaks, 12 ounces each

Paradise Ridge Grille Seasoning (recipe follows), as needed

2 tablespoons butter, softened

This isn't the famous rub that they sell at the restaurant, but it's a good one. Simple and tasty.

• Yield: 2 servings

Prepare the grill for hot and direct cooking. Season the steaks liberally on both sides with the Paradise Ridge Grille Seasoning. Put the steaks directly on the grill at an angle to the grate. Cook for 3 minutes. Rotate, don't flip the steaks, 90 degrees to encourage those cool crosshatch grill marks. Cook another 3 minutes, or until the bottom of the steak is nicely browned. Flip the steaks and cook until the internal temp reaches 130°F for medium-rare. Remove each steak to its own plate and top each with 1 tablespoon of the butter. Let rest a few minutes before cutting.

Paradise Ridge Grille Seasoning

1 cup Lawry's Seasoned Salt

½ cup finely ground black pepper

¼ cup granulated onion

¼ cup granulated garlic

• Yield: 2 cups

Mix together and store in an airtight container.

Amazin' Blazin' BBQ Cookoff

Wilson County Fair

Lebanon

www.wilsoncountyfair.net

▼▼

The third weekend in August you will always find me in Lebanon, Tennessee. It's about half an hour east of Nashville right off I-40. The Wilson County Fair is in Lebanon, and that's where the Amazin' Blazin' BBQ Cookoff is held. It's run by three ladies who will make you want to move to Lebanon. Wanda Bates, Kristina McKee, and Maryann Fosby put on the cookoff that is my favorite of the year. They have a nice parklike setting with electric and water for us to hook up to, they have a really nice pavilion for the common events of the weekend, and they treat each and every one of us like we are their absolute favorite. I think we all are their favorite. It's a great example of people who are passionate about what they are doing. The girls live in Lebanon and love the fair and support it with everything they have. It's the biggest and best county fair in Tennessee. I remember my first trip there from Chicago. I was amazed that there was actually a pickle-making contest and an apple pie contest and a knitting contest. They even have a nice air-conditioned building to hold all of the winners on display. They don't have a county fair in Cook County, where Chicago is, and if they did it wouldn't be anything like this one. It's great. Get yourself a foot-long corn dog and a fresh-squeezed lemonade and enjoy the fair. There's a big midway if rides are your thing and lots of entertainment. You'll see tractors and trucks and goats and hogs and cattle and ducks. The poultry pen is near the cookoff and there are always rumors that one of the Weddingtons has stolen a chicken to cook. It's possible.

So when the three Barbecue Babes decided to have a cookoff at the fair, it had to be just as good as the rest of the fair. They have done that and more. They have a low entry fee and high prize money. They give us gifts all throughout the weekend and even come around once in a while just to hug us. That's my favorite part. Kristina and Wanda work in the cattle business, so they added a steak cookoff on Friday night. So on top of all the other great stuff, everyone eats steak on Friday in Lebanon, so don't be late.

Fast Eddy's Championship Steak Recipe

2 prime-grade rib-eye steaks, well aged and 1½ inches thick (you'll have to go to a high-end butcher shop for these)

Montreal-type steak seasoning, as needed*

Garlic salt, as needed

4 tablespoons butter, divided in half

*Montreal steak seasoning is a common product originally marketed by McCormick but many other companies now make it.

In 2002 my buddy Fast Eddy won the steak cookoff at the Amazin' Blazin'. He cooked it at 275°F in his FEC100 pellet cooker. He cooked two steaks. I tasted the one he didn't turn in and it was great. Here's what he did. • **Yield: 2 to 4 servings**

Prepare the cooker for indirect cooking at 275°F, using hickory wood for flavor. Dust the steaks lightly on both sides with the steak seasoning and the garlic salt. Cook for 30 minutes. Flip and top each steak with 1 tablespoon of the butter. Cook until the internal temp in the center of the steak is 140°F. Remove to a plate with the buttered side down and top each steak with another tablespoon of the butter. Let rest for 5 minutes.

Jack Daniel's World Championship Barbecue Cookoff

Every October in Lynchburg

www.jackdaniels.com

▼▼

Lynchburg, Tennessee, is a big tourist attraction any time of year. It's a nice little Tennessee town and home to the Jack Daniel's distillery. But the single biggest day of the year in Lynchburg is the day of the barbecue cookoff. My friend David Roper tells me that when he applied for a job as a tour guide at Jack Daniel's, the first thing they told him was not to bother staying for the interview if he couldn't work the weekend of the barbecue, because everyone was required to work then. David got the job as a tour guide and he's become a colorful member of the team. Be sure to stop by the distillery for a tour while you're in Lynchburg, but the big party is in Wiseman Park right behind the old square. About fifty of the best barbecue teams in the world meet up there every October for the World Championship. It's strictly invite only, and they have teams that come from all corners of the world. I've seen teams from Japan, Australia, France, Switzerland, Germany, England, and Ireland. Canada and Mexico are regularly represented, as are Puerto Rico and Jamaica. Then you add a bunch of state champions from the U.S. and you've got quite a field. I'm proud to have competed a few times and won a few awards at "The Jack," as it's known around the barbecue circuit. The cooks get pretty serious on Saturday during the judging and don't have much time to visit with the visitors, so the folks at Jack Daniel's provide plenty of other things for the visitors to do. About 20,000 of them will line the paths of the park to see the Jack Daniel's Race Car, artisans building things out of discarded barrels, a lady making homemade soap, and a host of other fun country things. There's also some of the best barbecue vendors in the country lined up as you enter the park, so nobody goes away hungry. One of the highlights of the cookoff is the dessert competition. The cooks love to show off in this category and the displays are awesome. My friends Rod and Sheri Gray were the dessert winners at The Jack in 2002, and they've been nice enough to share their winning recipe here. I've also included a recipe for a grits pie from Marsha Russell. It's a great side dish with some Tennessee barbecue. Marsha is the receptionist at Jack Daniel's, a lifelong resident of Lynchburg, a great cook, and my good friend. When you go to Lynchburg be sure to say hi to her for me.

Sheri Gray's First-Place Caramel Apple Crunch

The Base

2 cups flour

2 cups uncooked oats (not instant)

1½ cup brown sugar

1½ cup melted butter

1 teaspoon baking soda

The Caramel Mixture

1½ cups caramel topping

½ cup flour

The Filling

2 cups apples, peeled, cored, and sliced

½ cup pecans, chopped

Sheri and her husband Rod are from Kansas and they cook under the name Pellet Envy because they use only pellet-fired cookers, and they do very well. At the Jack Daniel's World Championship in 2002 they entered this dessert and took first place. That's no small accomplishment—the cooks go all out in this category and the desserts are all fabulous. • **Yield: 20 servings**

Preheat the oven to 350°F.

To make the base: Combine all ingredients in a bowl and mix well. Press half of the mixture into a lightly greased 9×13-inch pan. Bake for 8 to 9 minutes. Save the other half for topping.

To make the caramel mixture: Mix the caramel topping and the flour together in a small saucepan and bring it to a boil, continuing to boil for 3 to 5 minutes, stirring constantly.

To make the filling: Combine the apples and pecans.

Top the baked base with the filling, add the caramel mixture, and top with the other half of the base. Bake for 20 to 25 minutes.

Let cool, then refrigerate to ease cutting. Serve the cut bars at room temperature, topped with ice cream.

Marsha's Grits Pie

½ cup uncooked quick-cooking grits

½ teaspoon salt

1 cup chopped fresh pineapple

4 ounces cream cheese

3 eggs

1 cup sugar

½ cup milk

¼ teaspoon vanilla extract

Two 9-inch graham cracker piecrusts

• Yield: 12 servings

Preheat the oven to 300°F.

In a medium saucepan, bring 2 cups water to a boil. Add the grits and salt, and return to a boil. Cover, reduce the heat to low, and cook 5 minutes, stirring occasionally. Remove from heat.

Combine the grits, pineapple, and cream cheese in the bowl of a mixer and beat until smooth. Add the eggs one at a time. Add the sugar, milk, and vanilla; process until smooth. Pour into the crusts.

Bake for 1 hour, or until mixture is set.

Texas

Dr. BBQ's Texas Barbecue Rub

Dr. BBQ's Texas Barbecue Sauce

Obie Obermark (Grand Prairie)

Obie-Cue's Ranch House Beans

Obie's Always Juicy Fajitas

International Barbecue Cookers Association/Lynn and Jeff Shivers (Arlington)

Dirty Rice from Lynn Shivers

David Klose, BBQ Pit Builder (Houston)

Margaritas à la Klose

Dave Klose's Grilled Shrimp

Bananas Foster, Klose Style

Bill and Barbara Milroy, Texas Rib Rangers (Denton)

Cerveza Beans

Railhead Smokehouse (Fort Worth)

Burn's Bar-B-Q (Houston)

Goode Company (Houston)

Meyer's Smokehouse (Elgin)

Black's BBQ (Lockhart)

Smitty's (Lockhart)

Southside Market & BBQ (Elgin)

House Park Bar-B-Que (Austin)

Kreuz Market (Lockhart)

Salt Lick BBQ (Driftwood)

Louie Mueller Barbecue (Taylor)

Clem Mikeska's (Temple)

Texas Brisket

Buttered Potatoes

Dr. BBQ's Texas Pinto Beans

Pumpkin Flan with Caramel Sauce

▼▼▼▼

When it comes to barbecue, Texas is as big as it gets. But barbecue isn't a big deal in Texas. Not because they don't love it, they do. It's not a big deal to them because it's just part of everyday life. They couldn't live without it and wouldn't consider it. Barbecue is everywhere in Texas. When you fly into Dallas, you can get some barbecue right in the airport. Granted it's Dickey's, part of a restaurant chain, but I had a pretty good brisket sandwich there.

I have heard and read all about Texas barbecue over the years, and I have been to Texas occasionally, even had some barbecue there, but in the past barbecue was not my primary reason for visiting the Lone Star State like it was this time. I've also met plenty of good Texas barbecue guys, even had one act as a mentor to me way back, but to write this properly I needed to make a special trip to Texas for a little research. I called a few old friends, surfed around the Net, and consulted Robb Walsh's wonderful book *Legends of Texas BBQ*. The end result was a whirlwind trip in the middle of Texas, a.k.a. the Barbecue Belt.

Texas is a huge state, and I couldn't possibly see it all. Besides, a complete book covering all of the barbecue in Texas would be bigger than *War and Peace*, and would be best written by a native Texan. They take that stuff real seriously. When I first got in Obie Obermark's truck to go to lunch, I told him I had noticed that most Texans are quite happy to be there, and they love Texas. He wholeheartedly agreed. It's an interesting vibe. Many places that I go, I meet people who think that all their problems would be solved if they could just move to the next county, or better yet, move to some glamorous place like Taos or Aspen or Mount Pilot. Not Texans, they're staying. The pride they have in their state is really invigorating to see. It seems every business you see is called Texas this and Lone Star that, North Texas that and Big Tex this. There are Texas flags proudly displayed everywhere and huge statues of famous Texans stand proudly right along the highway.

During my trip, I had the pleasure of acting as a judge at a cookoff in the town of Angleton, Texas. The cookoff was pure Texas. It was part of a small festival set up near the courthouse. The event included many locals serving food, some craft vendors, live music, and the arrival of Santa Claus along with Mrs. Claus via a fire truck. The cookoff was for nothing more than a good time and to raise a little money for charity. There was absolutely no prize money. Around the country, not many cooks will show up to cook for zero prize money, but in Angleton they had fifty cooks. Of course, there are many barbecue cooks and teams in the area, and there may have been a little side betting going on, but the main reason most of the folks were there was to have some fun. Many had their booths decorated in a Christmas theme, and goodwill was in the air. Bravo Angleton! I hope I can make it back someday.

My trip also included visits with some very active old barbecue friends. Dave Klose is the pit builder extraordinaire from Houston, Obie Obermark is a legendary barbecue rub purveyor, and Lynn and Jeff Shivers are the torchbearers for the International Barbecue Cookers Association, which oversees the majority of the barbecue cookoffs in Texas. These folks have had a huge influence in the world of barbecue, not only in Texas, but all around the country.

Last but certainly not least on my trip was a visit to each of the places on a long list of old barbecue joints. What a treat that was. I highly recommend a vacation to visit the legendary Texas barbecue joints. Some of them have become a little bit touristy, but it's still well worth the trip.

One important thing I need to discuss here is barbecue sauce. It's a subject that transcends all of Texas barbecue. The common belief is that Texas barbecue is served without sauce. The only possible exception is a splash of hot sauce. At the cookoff in Angleton, the chicken and ribs were mostly without sauce, with a few exceptions that were lightly glazed. It's against the rules to serve it on the side, so the cooks must decide whether to serve it on the meat or not, and most chose not to.

But then I realized that there is a barbecue sauce recipe included in Walter Jetton's *LBJ Barbecue Cook Book*. How could that be? At the barbecue joints I visited, all but a couple of old hard-core places did have barbecue sauce available. This will come as a big surprise to some, but a couple of places even served it on the food. (No, these were not yuppie northern transplants who did this. One was in the heart of Austin and has been there since 1943!) The sauce in these restaurants was not a sweet sticky sauce, nor was it a biting vinegar sauce, but it was clearly made for the barbecue, and people were using it. These sauces were very nondescript, and kind of a thin gravy, made to complement the meat but definitely not to take center stage. I'm told that some of them include meat drippings in the sauce and I believe that, although I never saw one that separated like I would expect in that case. Most of them were very good, and I enjoyed creating my version (see page 94). I will admit that I didn't see any sweet barbecue sauce in the restaurants, but I'm not a big fan of those anyway, so I was fine with it.

One side note to the sauce story. I've always been suspicious that some Texans were closet users of the sweet sticky sauces enjoyed on barbecue around the rest of the country, so while in between my two lunches one day in Lockhart, the official barbecue capital of Texas, I paid a visit to the local grocery store. There on the shelf front and center were KC Masterpiece, Bull's-Eye, Sweet Baby Ray's, Head Country, and a few house-brand barbecue sauces with names like Peach Habanero and Lime Cilantro. I'm pretty sure those last two were for tourists, but I suspect there were a few Texans buying the others, all of which are very sweet and very popular all around the country.

All in all I give Texas barbecue a perfect 10. Read on for some great individual experiences.

These nice ladies organized the judging at the Angleton, Texas, contest
I attended: Joy, Arlene, and Kathy, with Karin in the front.

Dr. BBQ's Texas Barbecue Rub

1/4 cup salt

3 tablespoons finely ground black pepper

2 teaspoons granulated garlic

2 teaspoons onion powder

1 teaspoon white sugar

This is my version of a typically good Texas barbecue joint rub. Note how simple it is. • **Yield: 1/2 cup**

Combine all ingredients in a bowl and mix well.

Dr. BBQ's Texas Barbecue Sauce

4 tablespoons butter

1/3 cup minced onion

1 clove garlic, crushed and minced

2 tablespoons flour

1 1/2 cups beef broth

1 cup tomato sauce

1 tablespoon Worcestershire sauce

1 tablespoon cider vinegar

1 tablespoon lemon juice

1 teaspoon finely ground black pepper

1/2 teaspoon brown sugar

This sauce is pretty typical of what I was served in the barbecue joints of Texas. • **Yield: About 3 cups**

In a medium saucepan over medium heat, melt the butter. Add the onion and garlic and cook 2 minutes. Add the flour and cook, stirring constantly, until the onion is soft. This will take about 4 minutes. Add all the other ingredients, stirring to blend. Bring to a boil, reduce to a simmer, and cook 15 minutes.

Obie Obermark

Obie-Cue's Texas Spice
Grand Prairie
www.obiecue.com

▼▼▼

By all accounts, Obie Obermark is a true barbecue man. He spends his days making, selling, shipping, creating, and promoting barbecue rubs for his company, aptly named Obie-Cue's Texas Spice. In his own words, "a rub would be any dry powder applied to a meat's surface prior to cooking." No argument from me. His labels boast a Texas flag–inspired logo and product names like Steakmaker, Texas Soul, BBQ Bomber, Big Bull's Texas Brisket Rub and Yankeeblaster. You can see them all and buy them at www.obiecue.com.

Obie is a tall Texan, claiming to be in his furry period when we had lunch, which I took to mean his hair and beard were grown long. When I asked him to take me to his favorite barbecue restaurant, he declined, saying that competition food had spoiled him. He suggested an upscale Mexican restaurant that was his favorite. I assure you he knows about more than barbecue, because La Margarita in Irving, Texas, was outstanding. It's a pretty safe bet that Obie is an old hippie, based on his free-thinking attitude and his stories about living a full-tilt yoga life in the past, which included a vegetarian diet. He's eating meat these days, and we're all better off for it. His rubs have won at least three World Championships, and a long list of other major awards. It's hard to put a hard number on these things because he sells a lot of these rubs, and not everyone admits to using them when they win. Selling barbecue products can be a very secretive business. If a cook is doing very well in competitions, he probably doesn't want anyone to know exactly what he's using. Obie understands that very well. He doesn't compete anymore, but he did, and is one of the founders of the IBCA (International Barbecue Cookers Association). He is still very active in competition barbecue, too. He is a host of the Annual Traders Village cookoff in Grand Prairie, Texas, and lends his name and effort to a chicken cookoff that raises a good amount of money for charity.

Traders Village is also his base of operations for the rub business. It's a huge Texas-sized flea market, where Obie has a permanent store. He's also had a long, strong mail-order business, and of course now enjoys a busy Internet business. If you ever get the chance to spend a little time with Obie, do it. He's an interesting guy who likes to talk about the downside of liquid-based barbecue and the great advantages to dry seasoning. He is also a passionate character outside of barbecue with a love for Texas music. He's even a DJ one day a week on KNON in Dallas, playing Texas Renegade music. Here's a couple of great recipes from Obie.

Obie-Cue's Ranch House Beans

1 pound dried pinto beans

3 pieces bacon, chopped

1 medium onion, chopped

One 15-ounce can tomato sauce

2 tablespoons BBQ Bomber (This is one of Obie's great products. You can substitute a sweet chile–flavored rub, but Obie's is the best.)

2 tablespoons chili powder

Sort and rinse the beans. Place in a large pot with 8 cups water and bring to a boil. Cook 2 minutes, then cover and let sit 1 hour.

Cook the bacon in a skillet until done, then remove to a paper towel to drain, retaining the grease. Cook the onion in the same skillet over medium heat until transparent and lightly browned.

Drain and rinse the beans. Return to the pot with the tomato sauce and enough water to cover the beans plus one-half inch. Add the BBQ Bomber, chili powder, and onions and simmer, covered, for 1 hour.

Obie's Always Juicy Fajitas

One 3-pound skirt steak, trimmed of excess fat and membrane

½ cup beer or 2 tablespoons lemon juice plus 6 tablespoons water

Obie-Cue's Original Fajita Seasoning, as needed

2 tablespoons cooking oil

2 large onions, sliced

2 small green bell peppers, sliced

3 or 4 jalapeño or serrano peppers, seeded and sliced (optional)

1 medium tomato, cut into chunks

12 flour tortillas

Salsa picante

Obie says, "Obie-Cue's Original Fajita Seasoning was the first blend that I ever made, and it won our second World Championship, winning 'Best Rub on the Planet' in 1998." • Yield: 12 fajitas

Lightly dampen the meat with the beer or diluted lemon juice and heavily coat it with Obie-Cue's Original Fajita Seasoning. Fold the skirt over 3 or 4 times and place in a gallon zip-lock bag with the beer or lemon juice. Refrigerate at least 6 hours or preferably overnight, to give the tenderizer time to work.

Remove the skirt steak from the bag and drain. Slow-grill over a low, very smoky fire just to warm the pink center. Remove from the fire and cut into 4 equal pieces. Cut each piece into ½-inch strips the long way, making sure to cut across the grain of the meat.

Over high heat, in a large heavy skillet, heat the cooking oil to near smoking. To keep from overloading the skillet, cook your fajitas in two batches. Add half the sliced onions and sauté, tossing or stirring vigorously, until the onions begin wilting, then add half of the green peppers and optional jalapeño or serrano peppers and continue stirring until the peppers start to wilt. Add half of the meat strips and stir well to combine. Turn the heat down to medium and cook for 3 minutes with occasional stirring. Add half of the tomatoes, stir well, and transfer to a serving platter. Repeat with remaining meat, onions, peppers, and tomatoes.

Serve with flour tortillas for rolling, and lots of salsa picante.

International Barbecue Cookers
Association/Lynn and Jeff Shivers

Arlington
www.ibcabbq.org

▼▼▼

No discussion of Texas barbecue would be complete without mention of Lynn and Jeff Shivers. I wanted to learn about the IBCA, so I paid them a visit. They are founding members of the IBCA, longtime cookoff participants, and sort of a walking encyclopedia of Texas cookoffs. They're also really nice folks. I've told this story many times, but I'm gonna tell it one more time here. In the days before the active Internet, many of the barbecue folks from around the country only heard about each other through the barbecue newsletters, until October at the American Royal. There we all bellied up to the barbecue bar for a few days so we could size each other up and have a party. It was always great fun, and we all made some lifelong friends there. So one day when I was still pretty green, I was talking to Lynn Shivers about cooking brisket. This was a big thrill for a guy from Chicago. Lynn told me that Jeff liked to hold his cooked brisket in an empty ice chest for six hours before slicing it. This was an epiphany for me. I was familiar with the cooler holding technique, but never realized it could be part of the cooking process, or that anyone would plan on resting a brisket for that long. I always add that it was so nice of Lynn to share one of Jeff's secrets

with me. These days, Jeff says he'd have shared it, too. Guess we'll never know.

Lynn and Jeff were part of the group that in 1989 began the IBCA. Along with Doug Beich, Terry Blount, Henry Cutaia, Jim Hudgins, Tom Kennedy, Obie Obermark, and Waldo Strein, they created it to regulate the scoring for the growing number of barbecue cookoffs around Texas. While in Texas, I was invited to an IBCA meeting with the Shivers. Unfortunately, there was a bit of an ice storm the day of the meeting, and nobody showed up except us and Hubert Green. The IBCA meetings are held at North Main Barbecue in Euless, Texas, where Hubert is the proprietor. There are many new upstart barbecue associations these days, and frankly, most of them just use a modified version of somebody else's rules, but in 1989, there was very little groundwork. These folks had to be creative and visionary. Their rules and procedures are largely unchanged almost twenty years later, so it seems they did a great job. In typical Texas fashion, the rules are pretty much clear-cut with a no-bull approach. No garnish is allowed, just a piece of aluminum foil in the bottom of the box so the hot meat doesn't sit directly on the Styrofoam. They tell you how many ribs or slices of brisket to include, and how to place them in the box so there is no attempt at marking the box for a friendly judge to identify. The chicken is presented as an uncut half chicken. In a contest with over sixty entries, they turn in two halves. A raffle ticket is split. You get half and the other half is taped to your box. At the awards ceremony, the tickets are peeled off, and the cook with the matching half wins. If you lose your half of the ticket, the award goes unclaimed. This is the way CASI (Chili Appreciation Society International) does it, and they were sanctioning chili cookoffs in Texas long before the IBCA came along, so it's fair to assume that's where the IBCA got the idea.

The judging is done in elimination rounds, so that presumably the best entries all end up at the final table. This way the same final judges get to try each contending box. It's a good system. It takes some time to judge a preliminary round or two, and the entries may be an hour old before the final judging. But it'll be the same for each and every box, so it's fair. I have judged one of their contests, in Angleton, Texas, and it was a great experience. The Angleton cookoff was actually officiated by Texas Gulf Coast BBQ

Cookers Association (TGCBCA), which is one of the "Pits" of the IBCA. The "Pits" are regional groups that make up the IBCA.

The head judges that day were Arlene Adams and Kathy Ritchie, and the system worked flawlessly. These ladies were all business, and the cooks were very confident in them. Because of the simplicity of the system, they can use some local folks to judge. Although many of the locals have done it many times before, there is no need for a formal training session apart from the five minutes before judging. On the day I judged, the food was wonderful, and I made some new friends. The Grand Champion was Kevin Jackson, a.k.a. Green Grass Cookers, from Richmond, Texas. Because of the system, I'm sure I tried some of his food, but there was no way to know which it was. I like it that way. Jeff Shivers is currently serving a second term as executive director of the IBCA, and Lynn Shivers is the secretary/treasurer. Lynn has held her position since 1997, and in 1999 it was written into the by-laws that it is a permanent position until she decides that she doesn't want it anymore. I don't see that happening any time soon.

Dirty Rice
from Lynn Shivers

1 pound Jimmy Dean sausage (I use hot)

½ cup chopped green bell pepper

½ cup chopped green onions

1½ cups rice

¼ teaspoon cayenne pepper

½ teaspoon minced garlic

3 cups water or chicken broth (I usually use the bouillon cubes)

2 tablespoons butter at room temperature

Salt and black pepper to taste

Here is Lynn's recipe for a nonbarbecue accompaniment that goes great not only with barbecue and grilled meats, but also with roasts and chops. • **Yield: About 8 servings**

Combine the sausage, bell pepper, and green onions in a nonmetallic bowl and microwave on high for 3 minutes. Drain off any fat, stir the mixture, and microwave it again for 3 minutes, or until the sausage isn't pink any longer.

While that is cooking, combine the rice, cayenne, garlic, and water or broth in a saucepan, bring it to a boil, reduce the heat to a simmer, cover, and cook for 20 minutes, or until the water is all absorbed.

When the rice is done, transfer it to a large bowl and add the sausage mixture, stirring well. Add the butter, salt, and pepper and stir.

David Klose, BBQ Pit Builder

Houston

www.bbqpits.com

▼▼

I've known Dave Klose for quite a while now, but when I decided to write this story, I figured I should go to Houston and see him. I gave him a call and told him I'd be paying a visit. In his typical attitude, he said, "Come on down, any time is good." The first thing you should know about Dave Klose is that he's a damn nice guy. He's used that virtue to build a successful business manufacturing barbecue pits. (A barbecue pit can be any kind of cooker; they are all descendants of the hand-dug pits of old.) It may seem weird to have a whole business building pits, but Dave's business is in Houston, Texas. Cooking barbecue is like religion in Texas, and barbecue pits are common home cooking equipment. Dave also builds the great big ones that you tow behind your truck. He's even had a hand in the building of the World's Largest Barbecue Pit as well as the World's Largest Grill.

Dave is a very interesting guy, claiming to be a connoisseur of both great coffee and great Champagne. I didn't have a chance on the trip to partake of his expertise in these two subjects, but he did give me a wonderful bottle of balsamic vinegar that leads me to believe anything he says about fine food and drink.

His tales of cooking in strange locations all over the world seem to go on and on. He told me a story about a pit he'd built being delivered to a private island via a Chinook helicopter. When I asked what he thought his biggest influence on barbecue has been, he said the promotion of American barbecue in Europe, and his creativity in the evolution of the barbecue pit. Admittedly he hasn't sold a huge number of cookers overseas, but he and his pits are very well known around the world.

As for the creativity, it is unmatched. This is a guy who could easily rest on his laurels and sell the same old style of cookers, but that's just not Dave. His innovations continue to change the way people cook barbecue. He uses NASA insulation on his fireboxes and has been known to fire his .44 into a pit to test the strength of the steel. I recently saw a pit he made with 24-karat gold wheels and a satellite dish mounted on it. His innovative attitude also extends to the style and flair he brings to the look of these masterpieces. Some people just see more details than the rest of us, and Dave Klose is one of those people. Another example is his early understanding of and support of the Internet. He was promoting barbecue on the Internet before most of us had a computer. His Web address is www.bbqpits.com, and it has a users' forum that has been there a long time.

The day I visited BBQ Pits by Klose, they had about a dozen new prototypes of a home-size steel and stainless steel grill. There were also some beautiful new high-dome cookers, and an old chuck wagon that Dave seemed very happy to have reclaimed from a previous owner, and of course a bunch of big shiny new trailer rigs. Dave says that his shop has been working full speed for seventeen years and every pit is sold before it's built. I also got to see some of Dave's favorite old cooker creations. There is the phone booth from Sarajevo, in former Yugoslavia, the antique baby buggy, and the fabricated giant beer bottle, all functional barbecue pits. When he saw my shiny red rental car, his first reaction was that it would make a nice barbecue pit if we gutted it. That's how Dave Klose thinks, speaks, lives, and breathes.

After the full tour and some great conversation, Dave took me to Burn's Bar-B-Q for lunch. I've seen Dave take people to Burn's on the Food Network, but hadn't been there myself. We were allowed in the back to see the pits, and it was an awesome sight. There was some barbecue moving in this little place. No fancy production line here, just a good old barbecue kitchen. Burn's is listed in my Texas restaurant reviews, but here's a tip. Go visit Dave and get him to take you there! He often wears a black cowboy hat, but make no mistake, Dave Klose is one of the good guys.

Here's David Klose having lunch at Burn's Bar-B-Q in Houston, Texas.

Margaritas à la Klose

One 12-ounce can of Minute Maid Limeade

1 empty Minute Maid can ³/₄ full of Herradura Silver Tequila

3 tablespoons Cointreau

1 lime

4 lime slices for garnish

When Dave was hitting the barbecue circuit hard, he always had a blender nearby to whip up some of these. He also usually had some Hooters Girls nearby, but that's a different subject. • **Yield: 4 servings**

Combine all ingredients except the limes in a blender and fill the rest of the blender with ice. Crush slowly at first, then speed up to achieve the proper slush consistency. You may have to pour a little out to add enough ice for proper consistency, depending on the size of your blender. Squeeze juice from half the lime into it, and blend for a few additional seconds. Using slices cut from the remaining half, rim 4 margarita glasses, then dip the glasses in margarita salt. Fill the glasses with the blended mixture and squeeze lime juice on top. Add lime slices to the rims.

Dave Klose's Grilled Shrimp

The Marinade

½ cup red wine

½ cup teriyaki sauce

½ cup Worcestershire sauce

¼ cup soy sauce

1 cup brown sugar

1 can Coca-Cola

¼ cup stone crab claw meat or regular crabmeat

The Shrimp

1 pound jumbo shrimp (preferably 10 to 16 count), tails on, peeled, butterflied deeply, deveined, and washed thoroughly

10 to 16 chicken tender strips, flattened with a mallet and sliced ¼ inch thick by 3 to 4 inches long (same as number of shrimp)

10 to 16 strips of lean bacon, cut in 4-inch-long pieces (same as number of shrimp)

Dr. BBQ's Texas Barbecue Rub (page 94)

Dave Klose says that this recipe is "an exceptional taste experience," and it's very quick and easy to make. Serve it with Dirty Rice from Lynn Shivers (page 100).

• Yield: 4 servings

In a saucepan, combine all the marinade ingredients and stir well. Heat and stir until the sugar has melted. Transfer to a glass or ceramic bowl.

Take the crabmeat and place it in each cut in the shrimp. Lay the chicken strips on top of the crabmeat. Wrap each shrimp with a bacon strip and secure with a toothpick. Place the shrimp in the marinade and let sit for 45 minutes.

While the shrimp are marinating, prepare a charcoal fire and let the coals burn down to white. Add soaked chunks of apple wood to the coals.

Sprinkle the shrimp with the barbecue seasoning.

Grill the shrimp over the coals for about 8 minutes, turning occasionally.

Bananas Foster, Klose Style

3 tablespoons butter

½ cup light brown sugar, firmly packed

Pinch ground nutmeg

Pinch ground cinnamon

3 firm bananas, peeled and cut into 2-inch slices

3 tablespoons Mexican vanilla extract

1 tablespoon maple syrup

¼ cup Jack Daniel's whiskey

Vanilla ice cream

Here is Dave Klose's take on that famous New Orleans dessert, bananas Foster. In the early 1900s, New Orleans was the number-one fruit port in the U.S., and Caribbean bananas were a primary import.

• Yield: 4 to 6 servings

Melt the butter in a large, heavy skillet. Add the sugar and spices and stir until melted.

Add the banana slices, vanilla, and syrup and cook until tender, about 2 minutes.

Remove the skillet from the heat, add the Jack Daniel's, don't stir, and carefully ignite.

Serve hot over ice cream.

Bill and Barbara Milroy,
Texas Rib Rangers

Denton
www.texasribrangers.com

▼▼

In 1977, Bill Milroy was a volunteer firefighter cooking up barbecue to raise money for the local fire department when he discovered the world of barbecue competition. Now, thirty years later, Bill and his wife Barbara devote themselves to barbecue full-time, traveling the country and entering competitions, selling their award-winning rubs and sauces, and teaching others the art of smoke and spice.

Over the years, the Milroys have won more than 500 awards at events like the Jack Daniel's World Championship Invitational Barbecue, the National BBQ Association Awards of Excellence and Fiery Foods & Barbecue's Scovies. They've been awarded the "Best on the Planet" title at the American Royal four times in five years.

As any true Texan would, Bill uses mesquite chunks in all of his cookers.

Bill believes that with so many variables involved in crafting true barbecue, consistency is a tough but necessary goal. For him, that consistency comes not from the cooker, the wood, the cut of meat, or even the cook himself, but from the spice rub and sauce. Texas Rib Rangers makes and sells a dozen products, including rubs, sauces, and a jalapeño pepper relish. Consistency in competition has always been important for this champion, who was one of the founding members of the North Texas Area BBQ Cookers Association. Bill helped NTABCA come up with a set of rules—after the first competitions pitted whole chickens against spareribs against brisket or pork butt or even steak. (The group eventually settled on seven slices of beef brisket, an intact chicken, and seven spareribs.)

But barbecue isn't just about the right wood or the right rubs, it's about a lifestyle. Since giving up his day job as a salesman for a bread company fourteen years ago, this husband-and-wife team have been attached at the hip. "If you see one of us, you're gonna see us both," says Bill. Twenty years ago, when they met, Barbara knew nothing about barbecue, but she soon became addicted to the results—and the life. It was she who persuaded Bill to quit the bread company, a move he now says he wishes he'd done sooner. Now that their kids are grown, the pair is free to roam as they please, and roam they do, entering competitions, going to trade shows, catering, and teaching, from one end of the country to the other. "It's the greatest thing in the world," Bill says.

I know Bill and Barbara are putting together a book of their own, so I didn't ask them for a recipe. Here's a Texas recipe I think they'd like. I know I like it.

Cerveza Beans

2 cups dried pinto beans, sorted and rinsed clean

¼ cup chopped jalapeño peppers

12 ounces dark Mexican beer, such as Negra Modelo

1 small onion, chopped

1 large tomato, peeled and chopped

1 tablespoon salt

1 tablespoon Worcestershire sauce

A great accompaniment to any barbecue.
• **Yield 6 to 8 servings**

Cover the beans with water and soak overnight. Drain the beans.

Cover the beans with fresh water, bring to a boil, reduce the heat, and simmer until the beans are done, 2 to 2½ hours. Drain the beans again, reserving 1 to 2 cups of the bean water.

Combine the remaining ingredients, the beans, and the reserved bean liquid. Simmer the beans for 30 minutes to blend the flavors, or until the liquid has been reduced to the desired amount. Add more salt if needed.

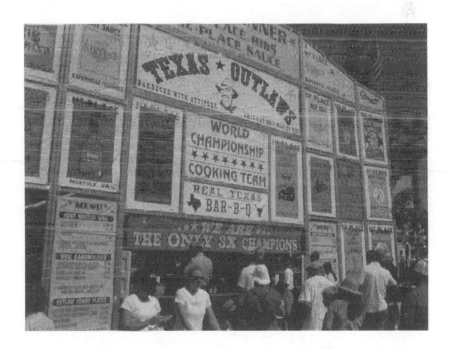

Texas Barbecue Joints

This is not a story about every barbecue joint in Texas. It's a story about the dozen I went to on a recent visit. I had heard about most of them for years. These places have become very famous. With the popularity of barbecue across the country, the places where true barbecue has been practiced and crafted for generations have become "museums" that people want to visit. Some are completely unchanged and unaffected, with the exception of a good bit of business from tourists. Others have opted to sell a few T-shirts and hats with their name on it, just because people ask. Some have huge mail-order businesses set up off-site to feed the Internet tourists. Others have built big new shrines to barbecue near the main road. The dining halls at the new Kreuz Market in Lockhart must seat 1,000 guests. They re-created the original pits when they moved, and they just made more of them. The story goes that they brought some hot coals from the original place to start the first fire at the new place. It's a well-known story among barbecue fanatics, but I guess I need to tell it here.

Back in 1900, Kreuz Market was a butcher shop that began selling smoked meats to customers. The typical reason for this among old butcher shops was for preservation of meat that was getting old. The Kreuz Market was later sold to the Schmitt family. When the patriarch of the Schmitt family passed on, he left the building to a daughter and the business to a son. Many years later they parted ways, with the Kreuz Market moving to a big beautiful new facility, and Smitty's opening in the old location. For me this is a good thing. It created two great places out of one. My advice is to definitely eat at both, but don't skip the third great barbecue joint in Lockhart, which is Black's, owned by the original family, and while they have broken tradition by offering barbecue sauce and forks, they are as authentic as you are going to find. There is another famous place in Lockhart called Chisolm Trail Barbecue, but I just couldn't eat any more on my two visits.

Another huge place and a relative newcomer to the Texas hill country is the Salt Lick in Driftwood, just south of Austin. You see, they didn't start serving barbecue at the Salt Lick until 1969, which may sound like a long run in most places, but around Austin they're a newcomer. Michael Rodriguez is the catering manager and a friend of mine, so I got the full tour and some history of the Salt Lick while I was there. They have built a place that seats 1,000 around the original open pit, which they still use every day. The Salt Lick is a beautiful place with two main buildings built out of stone that was quarried on the ranch where the restaurant is located. It's such a warm and comfortable place that they have to ask the guests to limit their dining to ninety minutes, so everyone can get some of their barbecue. Speaking of their barbecue, well, it's real good. They are meticulous about what they serve here. The sauce is made in small batches on-site, and the pies are all homemade.

I stayed in Austin for most of my adventure, and found many great places within an hour's drive. Here's the schedule I kept. Let's just say I skipped breakfast on these days.

December 1: lunch at Railhead in Fort Worth.

December 2: lunch at Burn's in Houston with Dave Klose. Dinner at Goode Co., also in Houston.

December 3: I judged chicken and ribs at the cookoff in Angleton, then had dinner at Meyer's Smokehouse in Elgin.

December 4: I had an early lunch at Black's, a second lunch at Smitty's, both in Lockhart, and a dinner at Southside Market in Elgin.

December 5: I had an early lunch at House Park in Austin and a late lunch at Kreuz Market in Lockhart.

December 6: I had an early lunch at the Salt Lick in Driftwood, then early dinner at Louie Mueller Barbecue in Taylor.

December 7: I had lunch at Clem Mikeska's in Temple, then the IBCA meeting at North Main Barbecue in Euless.

After eating at each of these places I filled out my own custom-made review form for my own reference. This was a lot of barbecue to eat, and I figured it would all be a blur if I didn't document it as I went. My plan was to sample the brisket, sausage, and beans at each place. Those seem to be the most popular menu items in Texas. I also planned to try the ribs whenever I felt like it, and any item that was exclusive to the place and sounded good. You'll see some ratings by number. This was spontaneous, and I didn't do it everywhere. I left it all in for your consideration anyway.

My plan worked pretty well except for the sausage. I found that I just didn't much care for Texas barbecue sausage. It's typically beef and kind of greasy. I'm okay with greasy food when it's appropriate, but when I found myself eating a sausage at Smitty's with my hands and wiping it on the butcher paper to degrease it. I tapped out on the sausage. I did try it one more time at the Salt Lick, mainly because I knew their sausage was good and definitely not greasy. When I got done I realized that my initial reactions were probably the best I was going to have, so I've just written them here as is, with just the slightest bit of editing. Hope you like them.

Railhead Smokehouse

Location: Fort Worth

My order: Two-way combo: sliced beef and sausage. Beans, CS (coleslaw) and PS (potato salad), white bread, pickle spear, and onion slices. Ice-cold schooner of Shiner Bock.

Brisket: Crusty, sliced thick by hand. Greasy and juicy. Pretty good. 7

Sausage: Pretty mediocre. Sliced thin. 5

Ribs: N/A

Smokiness and seasoning: Probably salt and pepper. Smoky enough, but not too much. Just right for me. Probably cooked over wood.

Sauce: Typical and uneventful. Served on the side, warm, in a cup. Not sweet, not spicy. 5

Beans: Dried pintos in a thin sauce. Good chili powder flavor. Not spicy. 8

Type of service: Cafeteria style. Very casual.

Ambience: Texas beer joint, with a half wall between the bar and the restaurant.

Special features: Texas flag over the bar. Really cold beer and T-shirts that say "Life's too short to live in Dallas." Cement floor.

Observations: Interesting that this is a famous barbecue joint known far and wide, yet to most of the clientele it's just a neighborhood beer joint. There were at least a dozen men sitting at tables just having a few beers, and more than a few family types stopping for some barbecue. It's almost like a step back in time, with barbecue.

Overall rating: I liked the comfortable feel and the nonchalant attitude towards the barbecue. This is what Famous Dave's is in its dreams. 7

Burn's Bar-B-Q

Location: Houston

My order: Three-way combo: ribs, brisket, and sausage. Double beans and a can of orange soda from a machine. White bread and pickles.

Brisket: Good, a little firm and maybe dry, but the sauce made it okay. 7

Sausage: Tasty and kind of red in color. Sliced on the major bias, so they were like strips. Great way to serve it. I think it helped the taste. 9

Ribs: Full spares, tender and juicy. Cooked just right. 9

Smokiness and seasoning: Probably salt and pepper. Smoky enough, but not too much. Just right for me. Cooked over wood in great old steel pits.

Sauce: Thin and tasty. Great balance. Might have some drippings added. Served warm, poured over all the meat. A very good complement. Not overwhelming or sticky.

Beans: Dried pintos with a thin sauce flavored with chili powder. Not spicy. Some chunks of very cooked onion and pepper and some cubed meat. Probably beef. 8

Type of service: Order, pay, get a number. They check your ticket before they give you your food. Picnic tables outside are the only seating.

Ambience: Funky old house–type setting in a questionable neighborhood. All the signs are homemade. Smoky walls. Beautiful.

Special features: Sign lying next to the porch says "Vacation." Sign inside says "Yes we have dog scraps, just ask."

Observations: Wonderful old African-American barbecue joint. Thanks to Dave Klose I got the full treatment. 9.5!

Goode Company (Kirby Road)

Location: Houston

My order: Three-way combo: brisket, jalapeño sausage, and ribs. Pinto beans, jambalaya, and jalapeño cheese bread. Pickles, onion, and jalapeño available.

Brisket: Soft, moist, and tender. Cut into small parts of a slice, kind of thin. 7

Sausage: Seemed very homemade. Not very spicy considering it was called jalapeño. Sliced on the bias, thinly. 7

Ribs: St. Louis–cut spares. Not peeled, with some cellophane character to the membrane. Generally good. Had sort of a reheated texture to them. 7

Smokiness and seasoning: Not much of either.

Sauce: Offered in the line, I opted for a little bowl on the side, served warm. It was good. I think it was a little spicy, but it might have been the food. Thin and not sweet.

Beans: Real pintos. Kind of bland. 5

Type of service: Cafeteria.

Ambience: Old wooden place. Wood floor. Small inside with a big seating area outside. A big buffalo head and a Brahma bull head are there. So is a rattlesnake skin and many old license plates. The staff was nice, but very businesslike. It's a high-volume place.

Special features: Jalapeño cheese bread was good but light on the jalapeños, and I never found the cheese. Still a nice touch.

Two kinds of beans, and jambalaya offered as a side, although the jambalaya wasn't much more than some sticky rice.

Observations: This is a very famous and popular place. They seem to own a couple blocks in the area with a Goode Mexican restaurant, a Goode honky-tonk, and a Goode seafood restaurant all right there. There was also a big mail-order business based right there pushing pecan pies, and a big commissary. That could explain the ribs that seemed reheated. The food was pretty sparse, except for the huge scoop of the lame jambalaya. There is a Ben and Jerry's store a few blocks south. 6 for Goode, and 9 for Ben and Jerry's.

Meyer's Smokehouse

Location: Elgin

My order: Two-way combo: brisket and sausage. Beans, creamed corn, white bread, pickles, and onion. Buttermilk pie for dessert.

Brisket: Pretty good, crusty. 8

Sausage: One long link cut in half. Kind of greasy. 7

Ribs: N/A

Smokiness and seasoning: Nothing stood out, decent balance.

Sauce: Typical, uneventful.

Beans: Basic pintos. Not much seasoning.

Type of service: Cafeteria.

Ambience: Nice big feel, butcher case near the line to see piles of sausage. Friendly servers. Desserts line the counter as you wait.

Special features: Creamed corn, was really just corn. A big crock of beans on the condiment table, I guess so you could have seconds. The little buttermilk pie was interesting, but tasted just okay. Seems to be made by a third party.

Observations: This is one of the main sausage places, and I just don't find the sausage to be very good. I think maybe sausage is best made of pork, not beef like all the Texas sausage seems to be. I did take this order to go, but it wasn't an issue. 7

Black's BBQ

Location: Lockhart

My order: Three slices of brisket, three slices of boneless pork loin, and one ring of sausage. A peach half, a bowl of beans, white bread, and sauce on the side. Diet Pepsi.

Brisket: Very good. 9

Sausage: This one was a little different. Seemed homemade without binders. It was

Robert, the pitmaster at Black's BBQ, and I in Lockhart, Texas.

a little mealy because of that, but at least it had some character.

Ribs: N/A

Misc. Boneless pork loin was a treat. Seems to be popular in Lockhart. It was the rib end, and was moist and smoky.

Smokiness and seasoning: Simple seasoning, but a good smoky taste. I asked and was told that they use post oak.

Sauce: Typical simple Texas sauce, served warm at its own station. Very good accompaniment to the smoky meat.

Beans: Tasty pintos, with a kind of beef broth juice.

Type of service: Cafeteria, with a little cold bar, then hot sides, and then to the carving station. Serve yourself white bread.

Ambience: This place is beautiful. It's old and funky, but just right. The carving is done on big beautiful butcher blocks. The place has been around since the 1930s, but moved to the current location in the '70s. I doubt that it's been touched since. This is the real deal and just might be the finest barbecue joint on the planet. Lots of deerheads and longhorns, and an antique stove used as a counter.

Special features: The ambience steals the show, but the food is great. I love the unique beans. This was my first experience with peaches as a side, and I liked them. Just canned peach halves.

Observations: Nothing here is a sellout to progress, unless absolutely necessary. No bull, great original barbecue joint. Gonna be hard to beat. 9.75

Smitty's

Location: Lockhart

My order: Three slices of brisket, one slice of pork chop, and a ring of sausage. Couple slices of white bread and a Diet Coke.

Brisket: It was good, sliced through both muscles. 9

Sausage: Greasy and terrible skin. 5

Ribs: N/A

Misc.: Bone-in pork loin. Delicious and perfectly done. 10

Smokiness and seasoning: Salt and pepper, I'm sure. Smoke just right. Tasty meat.

Sauce: They don't have any. Don't even ask. Hot sauce on the table.

Beans: It was a separate line, and I forgot to get them.

Type of service: You walk up to a small butcher counter near a pit. They get a hunk from the pit and slice off what you want on a big cool round butcher block. Then it's weighed on an old-fashioned butcher scale, and wrapped up in brown paper with white bread. You get a plastic knife. Then you enter the dining hall, and there's a different counter where you get beans, soda or beer, cheese, pickles, dessert or whatever.

Ambience: Interesting, but maybe a little too contrived. You walk in and feel the heat of a couple of burning logs at your feet. They burn outside the pit, but somehow the draft sucks the smoke and heat into the pit. (Could this be a trick?) The dining hall is a cool old room, with new tables built in the old style. Cheap folding chairs add to the feeling that the room is less than it seems.

Special features: Famous for what they don't have, barbecue sauce and forks. They have prime rib, too, which I didn't try.

Observations: I don't like the elitist crap about no sauce and no forks. I'm not a sauce guy, but it's ridiculous not to offer something. Same with the forks. You feel like an ass eating a pork chop with your hands, or cutting the sausage link with the knife, while holding it with your hand. This place has arguably the most famous pits in the world, but the dining experience suffers because of that crap. If you go, take a fork with you. 8

Southside Market & BBQ

Location: Elgin

My order: Two-way combo: beef ribs and brisket. Beans and white bread. Big Red soda.

Brisket: Two different kinds were on my plate, I'm not sure why. Might have been point and flat. The flat was way too smoky for me. Might have been use of mesquite. Done well. 6

Sausage: I skipped it. I'm tired of the same old greasy beef sausage I've had lately on this trip.

Ribs: N/A

Misc.: Beef ribs were really good, not too meaty but tasty. 9

Smokiness and seasoning: Probably salt and pepper. The beef ribs were great and so was the point, but the brisket flat was too smoky.

Sauce: Good stuff. Very typical to what I've been tasting. Complements the meat nicely, but nondescript.

Beans: Basic pintos in kind of a bean gravy.

Type of service: High-volume double-line cafeteria.

Ambience: Big wooden cool place. Lots of room and hunting trophies all over. I saw a bear rug on the wall and a cougar or bobcat or something.

Special features: They have a meat counter with fresh meat, and lots of sausage. The building also contains a big sausage plant. This is the original Elgin Hot Gut place. Elgin is the sausage capitol of Texas, by proclamation. They had sauce for sale by the jar, and even by the gallon.

Observations: Big, busy place. Probably not much different than years ago, except for the volume. This place could move some food. 9

House Park Bar-B-Que

Location: Austin

My order: I ordered a combo plate, but the sausage wasn't ready yet so I had a brisket sandwich plate with beans, and a tea.

Brisket: Very tender and good. A little crust. Served on a big bun with a little sauce. 8.5

Sausage: N/A

Ribs: N/A

Smokiness and seasoning: All nicely balanced. They cook with oak for heat and a little mesquite for flavor.

Sauce: They emphasized to me that it was homemade and they thought it was good, so they put some on the food. I agree. Not overpowering at all.

Beans: Tasty pintos. Seemed to be a little more seasoned than most.

Type of service: A simple walk up and order. Take your plate away. There is a station with real silverware and napkins.

Ambience: Beautiful old barbecue joint. The walls are thick with the patina of smoke. Tables and chairs inside, and picnic tables outside. Kind of dark and right out of a movie.

Special features: Open for lunch only, and they only serve brisket, sausage, and chicken halves. The sign outside says "Need no teef to eat my beef."

Observations: Near downtown, and a typical urban "lunch only" place, but this one is a barbecue joint that has been unchanged since 1943. 8.5

Kreuz Market

Location: Lockhart

My order: Two slices of beef, a slice of pork chop, and a slice of prime rib. There was no prime rib, so I added another slice of beef. White bread, pintos, and a bottle of Shiner Bock.

Brisket: There was beef shoulder clod instead of brisket. It was excellent, with a beef chuck taste, quite different than the brisket I've been eating on this trip. 10

Sausage: I'm not eating that any longer.

Ribs: N/A

Misc.: Pork chop was actually a thick slice of bone-in pork loin. It was the rib end, and very tasty with a huge smoke ring. My piece was a little dry on the end, but still very good. 9

Smokiness and seasoning: Seemed to have something more than salt and pepper, but not enough to distract. The smokiness was just right. Post oak was the wood of choice, with a legendary yard of woodpiles in different degrees of readiness.

Sauce: None, don't even ask.

Beans: Pretty basic pinto beans in pinto gravy.

Type of service: Butcher shop walk-up. Get your meat with bread and a plastic knife. Go into the dining hall for another service area with drinks, German potatoes, beans, cheese, pickles, etc.

Ambience: The business dates back to 1900. The building is obviously not old, but it has a great feel. Big and roomy with lots of interesting old stuff on the walls. There are a series of huge pits built exactly like the originals. The pits are right there in the big dining hall, and are really impressive. I'd heard the stories about the big new building and I didn't expect to like it as much as I did.

Special features: The granddaddy of Texas butcher shop barbecue. Huge seating areas, huge pits, and huge piles of wood outside.

Observations: It may be a new building built to feed thousands of tourists, but the food is still excellent and the ambience is great, albeit not old. I still don't like the concept of no forks and no barbecue sauce, but I can live with it to eat here. I'd still recommend bringing a fork, though. They did a good job of moving the old place to the big road. Don't skip Kreuz Market. 9.5

Salt Lick BBQ

Location: Driftwood

My order: Three-way combo: brisket, ribs, and sausage. Beans, pull-apart white bread, Diet Coke. It came nicely arranged on the plate.

Brisket: Very good. They serve you the flat, unless you ask for the point. I got some of both. 9

Sausage: This was good sausage, not greasy at all. Beef and pork together. 8

Ribs: A full sparerib with a light glaze. Done just right. 9

Misc.: Great-looking pies and cobblers, but I had to skip them.

Smokiness and seasoning: Just right. Everything is finished on the wood-burning open pit for a nice final hint of smoke.

Sauce: I only had a splash, but it's good. It's very popular, and has a little more character than most I've tried. It's served in a nice little thermos pitcher

Beans: A big bowl of tasty beans. These have a good amount of spice in them.

Type of service: Waitress, but the kitchen is wide open to see.

Ambience: Unreal! This place is beautiful, with a very casual ranch-type atmosphere. The buildings are all stone with a great warm feel and cool stuff everywhere. 11!

Special features: A great old stone open pit, which was there in the beginning in 1969. Neat little banquet rooms everywhere, and a huge 500-seat outdoor pavilion. A big off-site USDA kitchen services the big mail-order business.

Observations: This place is big volume, but really doesn't feel like it. There is plenty of room out in the country, so nothing seems cramped. The quality of the food is high priority, and it's well done. 9

Louie Mueller Barbecue

Location: Taylor

My order: Three slices of brisket, jalapeño sausage, beans, a slice of cheese, white bread, and a bottle of Shiner Bock.

Brisket: Really good. Moist and tender. How can all these places have such good brisket? 9

Sausage: Best I've had. I saw the grinder in back, so I asked and was told it's made on sight. It looked pretty overcooked, but still had plenty of life in it. I asked if they always cooked it so much, and was told that they didn't cook it all so much, but they always offered it that way because many like it. Put me on that list. Good jalapeño taste, but not very spicy. 9

Ribs: N/A

Misc.: I finally ordered a slice of cheese with my meal as it's a common item at the butcher shop–type places. It was just a slice of room-temp mild Cheddar with a dried end from not having been ordered lately. It was fine, but had no attachment to the barbecue for me.

Smokiness and seasoning: Just right. From another brick pit.

Sauce: Weak. Thin and no taste.

Beans: Typical. Good but just a side to the barbecue.

Type of service: Counter. Hard to call it cafeteria because there's no real line. You just walk up and tell them what you want. I said beef, sausage, and beans, and they gave me some. The beef was weighed and the sausage was a link.

Ambience: Like a museum piece. It couldn't be older or funkier and remain standing. There are patches of sheet metal where the wood floor is giving up. The walls haven't been painted or washed in decades and the old tables and chairs have lost all of their varnish a long time ago. It all matches in some bizarre way. There are some great old artifacts, like an ancient jukebox and the sign from the original Louie Mueller Food Store, which opened in 1946. Bobby Mueller runs the pits, with one waitress/cashier when I was there. The *Oprah* show was on and she was watching it. I had planned to also eat at Rudy Mikeska's, an old joint right across the street, but dining at Louie Mueller's is like getting laid. Afterwards all you want to do is relax and savor how good that just was. If I hadn't quit smoking years ago, a cig would have been the perfect finish.

Special features: You're not going to believe this, but they have wireless Internet access. You know this by reading the sign that's handwritten on butcher paper and taped to the refrigerator. They also offer a chipotle sausage that I wish I'd tried. This is an old place with a no-bull attitude. They have forks and barbecue sauce. They don't have to pretend to be an old authentic barbecue joint. It's quite obvious that it is one.

Observations: This place is great. Go here last. 9.75

Clem Mikeska's

Location: Temple

My order: Beef, ribs, and buttered potatoes, served with sauce and homemade bread. Diet Coke.

Brisket: No brisket here. They call it sirloin, but they told me it was tri-tip, which is part of the sirloin. It was delicious, with a roast beef kind of taste that brisket never has. 10

Sausage: N/A

Ribs: Great ribs, simple, nicely red, tender and moist. 10

Misc.: Buttered potatoes. Probably baked first, then peeled, chopped and served with butter. Simple and tasty. They also have great homemade sliced white bread. 10

Smokiness and seasoning: They sell a seasoning salt, so I assume that's what's on the meat. Not overpowering, really helped the meat. The smokiness was obvious, but good. Great red color on everything.

Sauce: The best sauce I've had in Texas. Probably includes drippings, but it's not greasy. You could probably call it a gravy. Great stuff.

Beans: N/A

Type of service: Cafeteria, with the carving station first and right there in front of you. Beautiful.

Ambience: It's a small woodsy room, with tons of deer heads, etc. There seems to be a huge catering operation right behind.

Special features: The sirloin, of course, and the unique sides, like the crushed potatoes and the pea salad.

Observations: This is a simple, updated place with great food. Hard to compare tri-tip and buttered potatoes with the typical brisket and pintos, but this is some of the best food you'll find anywhere. I'd never drive from Austin to Dallas without stopping at Clem Mikeska's. 9.5

Texas Brisket

One 10-pound choice-grade whole packer-trimmed brisket

Dr. BBQ's Texas Barbecue Rub, as needed (page 94)

Texas mop sauce (recipe follows)

I was amazed at how good the brisket was at almost all of the places I ate in Texas.

The prep was simple everywhere—season it and cook it. I think the key is to stay busy. They sell so much of it that it's always fresh. • **Yield 8 to 10 servings**

Prepare the cooker for indirect cooking at 235°F, using oak wood for flavor.

Season the brisket liberally with the rub.

Put the pan of mop sauce in the cooker. Put the brisket in the cooker and cook for 4 hours without peeking. Open the cooker and flip the brisket over. Apply a heavy dose of the mop sauce. Repeat the mopping once an hour until the brisket reaches an internal temp of 195°F in the center of the flat muscle. This will take 8 to 10 hours, depending on your cooker.

Mop the brisket one last time and then wrap in a double layer of heavy-duty aluminum foil. Let the brisket rest on the counter for 1 hour.

Unwrap the brisket and move it to a cutting board. Discard the fat cap. Slice the brisket through both muscles and across the grain.

Texas Mop Sauce

One 12-ounce beer

Juice of 1 lemon

1 cup coffee

1 medium onion, finely chopped

2 cloves garlic, crushed

1 tablespoon chili powder

Combine in a disposable foil pan. Place in the cooker while the brisket is cooking.

Buttered Potatoes

3 pounds russet potatoes, peeled and quartered

1 stick butter

½ cup minced onion

2 cloves garlic, crushed and minced

3 tablespoons flour

1 teaspoon finely ground black pepper

½ teaspoon chopped parsley

I'm not sure how Clem Mikeska's makes theirs, but they inspired me to come up with a similar recipe. Here's how I make mine. • **Yield: About 6 servings**

Place the potatoes in a kettle of salted water and cook until tender, about 10 minutes. In a small saucepan, melt the butter over medium heat. Add the onion and garlic and cook 2 minutes. Add the flour and pepper and cook until the onions are tender, about another 4 minutes. Remove from the heat and set aside. When the potatoes are done drain them well. Transfer to a large bowl. Crush the potatoes coarsely with a spoon, being careful not to mash them. Drizzle the butter-onion mixture over the potatoes, distributing it as evenly as possible. Toss the potatoes to coat. Top with the parsley.

Dr. BBQ's Texas Pinto Beans

1 pound dried pinto beans

3 tablespoons bacon fat or vegetable oil

1 medium onion, chopped fine

One 10-ounce can diced tomatoes with green chile

One 14-ounce can low-sodium beef broth

1 cup water

1 cup coffee

1 tablespoon chili powder

1 tablespoon brown sugar

1 tablespoon hot sauce

1 teaspoon black pepper

1 to 2 teaspoons salt

In Texas barbecue joints, the beans are generally very good, but not much more than simmered pinto beans. The result is a pretty uneventful product, basically just beans in bean gravy. I like them that way, but prefer a little more seasoning in mine. • **Yield: 10 servings**

The night before you plan to cook, place the beans in a large glass bowl and cover with water by a couple of inches. Let soak overnight. Discard any beans that float.

In a Dutch oven over medium heat, melt the bacon fat. Add the onion and sauté for a few minutes until soft. Add all of the remaining ingredients except the salt. Bring to a boil and reduce to a low simmer. Cook until the beans are tender, about 6 hours. Add 1 teaspoon of the salt and taste the beans. If they need additional salt, add it to taste.

Robert and some of their famous sausage hanging in the pit at Black's BBQ

Pumpkin Flan with Caramel Sauce

2 cups sugar

3½ cups milk

1 vanilla bean

6 eggs

1 teaspoon ground cinnamon

1 teaspoon ground nutmeg

1 teaspoon ground ginger

1 tablespoon dark rum

1 cup canned pumpkin

You might have to go to a yuppified Texas barbecue joint to get a dessert like this one, but it's mighty good. • Yield: 6 servings

Preheat the over to 350°F.

In a medium saucepan, combine 1 cup sugar and ⅔ cup water. Cook over medium heat, stirring until the sugar is dissolved. Increase the heat and boil until the mix is light brown. Reduce the heat and simmer until the syrup is an amber color, swirling the pan occasionally to push any crystals back in the syrup. Allow to cool slightly and pour evenly into six warmed custard cups so that this caramel sauce coats them.

Slit the vanilla bean and scrape out the seeds. Add them to the milk; scald the milk. Remove from heat and allow to cool. Remove the vanilla bean and reserve for another use.

Beat the eggs, spices, and rum together until foamy. Mix in remaining sugar and pumpkin. Gradually add the milk, stirring until the sugar is dissolved.

Pour the mixture into the custard cups. Place the cups in a pan with enough hot water to come halfway up the sides of the cups.

Bake for 60 to 70 minutes, or until a thin knife inserted halfway between the center and the edge of the custard comes out clean. Cool and refrigerate to chill.

To serve, run a thin knife around the outside of the cup and invert the custard onto a dish. Let the custard sit at room temperature for 10 minutes before serving.

The North

Dr. BBQ's Northern Barbecue Rub

Dr. BBQ's Northern Barbecue Sauce

Charlie Robinson of Robinson's #1 Ribs (Chicago, Illinois)

1982 Ribs

The Illinois State BBQ Championships (Shannon, Illinois)

Ray's Double Boar's Tooth Butt to Butt Recipe

The Pie Lady's Apple Praline Pie

Weber Grills

Smoky Sirloin Tip Roast

Bratwurst (Wisconsin)

Bratwash

Dr. BBQ's Favorite Bratwurst

Sprecher Brewery (Glendale, Wisconsin)

Sprecher Cream Soda Barbecue Sauce

The Great Pork BarbeQlossal (Des Moines, Iowa)

Mini World's Largest Porkburger

Raccoon Flats Achiote Marinade

Hawgeyes BBQ (Ankeny, Iowa)

Mrs. Tucker's "Trash"

Mr. Tucker's Favorite Home-Style Ranch Dressing

Ribfests

Ribfest Ribs

City BBQ (Columbus, Ohio)

City-Style Barbecue Burrito

The Canadian Barbecue Championship (Barrie, Ontario)

Steak and Potatoes on a Plank

Yes, there is barbecue up north. Once you leave the big four barbecue areas, the barbecue joints get pretty spread out, and the food gets more diverse, but there are some wonderful people, places, and food to be found. I spent the first forty-some years of my life in Chicago, and the first subject in this chapter, Charlie Robinson, is the guy who won the first cookoff I ever attended in 1982. By barbecue standards, that's not very long ago, but it's half of my life. The Chicago area is also the home of Weber-Stephens, and it would be hard to deny their influence on the world of barbecue. I decided to skip all the boiled rib faux barbecue joints of the North, and look a little deeper.

It may not be traditional southern barbecue, but the grilled bratwurst in Wisconsin surely has a kinship to it. Let's also remember that Iowa is the number-one hog-producing state in the U.S., and Minnesota is number three. They have been cooking some of those hogs over a fire up there for a long time—they just don't talk about it much. Even Ohio is in on the barbecue movement up north. Cleveland is the birthplace of the big ribfest-selling events that have become so popular all around the country, and Columbus boasts one of the best barbecue restaurants in the country.

When you talk about barbecue up north, you are usually talking about ribs, with chicken close behind. The long, slow cooking of pork shoulders and big beef briskets that folks down south are accustomed to seems pretty radical to northerners, unless of course they have migrated from the South. There's no question that as the country shrinks because of cheap airline tickets and the Internet, barbecue is spreading. Barbecue is a hot topic among foodies everywhere, and smokers are now selling like hotcakes all throughout the country.

Without a doubt, the sauce is an important part of the appeal of barbecue up north. While the barbecue belters consider sauce to be a condiment, up north it's often the main attraction. I'm not a big fan of any barbecue sauce, especially in large quantities, but it's a clear fact that many people love the stuff. It took a little creative license to form a chapter about barbecue in the North, so please don't be mad if I missed your favorite place or story. Hopefully I'll find it someday, too.

Dr. BBQ's Northern Barbecue Rub

½ cup brown sugar

¼ cup salt

¼ cup Lawry's Seasoned Salt

2 tablespoons granulated garlic

1 tablespoon onion powder

1 tablespoon lemon pepper

1 tablespoon chili powder

1 tablespoon paprika

2 teaspoons ground allspice

1 teaspoon cayenne pepper

1 teaspoon finely ground black pepper

• Yield: About 1½ cups

Mix together and store in an airtight container.

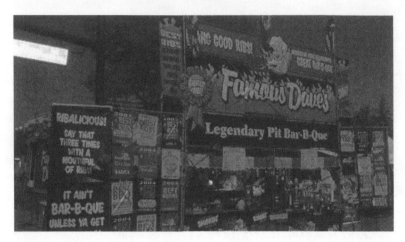

Dr. BBQ's Northern Barbecue Sauce

One 18-ounce bottle Kraft Original barbecue sauce

½ cup honey

1 teaspoon granulated garlic

1 teaspoon onion powder

1 teaspoon Dr. BBQ's Northern Barbecue Rub (recipe above)

1 teaspoon dry mustard

½ teaspoon finely ground black pepper

¼ teaspoon ground allspice

• Yield: About 2 cups

Whisk all the ingredients together in a bowl. Store in a closed container in the refrigerator.

Charlie Robinson of Robinson's #1 Ribs

Chicago, Illinois

www.rib1.com

▼▼

Charlie Robinson is a famous barbecue man in Chicago. He was the winner of the first ever Mike Royko Ribfest, which is still legendary in Chicago. It holds a special place in my heart as well since it was my first cookoff. Of course, since it was in 1982 it was just about everybody's first cookoff. I didn't place that day but it was a great learning experience that set the tone for my career. Charlie, on the other hand, did win, and has since parlayed that win into a successful chain of restaurants as well as a solid barbecue sauce business. I happen to think his food is very good and when I'm in Chicago I usually stop and get some.

Charlie grew up in Lambert, Mississippi, and his first job was picking cotton. His family were sharecroppers and life was tough. "Many times," he writes, "all we had to eat was milk and cornbread with sugar. But everyone in the neighborhood shared when someone killed a hog. So I rose from a three-room shotgun house in Mississippi to the top of the barbecue charts in the early 1980s when my original barbecue dominated the Mike Royko Rib Festival."

Charlie graduated from York College in Nebraska and is now the president and CEO of Robinson's #1 Ribs, with three locations. His sauce is sold in supermarkets all over Illinois and is even used aboard United Airlines planes. His ribs and chicken are covered with his special barbecue rub and sit in the refrigerator overnight to "let the flavors season every morsel." The next day, the meat is slow-cooked in a specially constructed hickory wood smoker at 250°F. Constant turning keeps the internal temp of the meat under 200 degrees and, as he puts it, "the slow cooking guarantees juicy tenderness." I think I'll fly up to Chicago soon and get some of those ribs!

1982 Ribs

1 quart white vinegar

1 red bell pepper, cut in strips

1 green bell pepper, cut in strips

1 jalapeño pepper, cut in strips

¼ cup soy sauce

2 slabs baby back ribs, about 2 pound each

Dr. BBQ's Northern Barbecue Rub, as needed (page 126)

Dr. BBQ's Northern Barbecue Sauce, as needed (page 126)

As I remember it, shortly after his big win Charlie Robinson was the subject of a big article in one of the Chicago papers. Here's the method I remember him describing at that time. He said the vinegar baste would help render the fat and the peppers just made it taste good. I may remember this wrong, but I know I did the vinegar basting as part of my cooking process for years. I added the jalapeño and the soy sauce. This recipe requires advance preparation. • **Yield: 2 to 4 servings**

Three days before you plan to cook, pour a cup of the vinegar out. Put the pepper and jalapeño strips in the vinegar bottle to soak. Add the soy sauce and mix well.

When you're ready to cook, prepare the cooker for indirect cooking at 250°F, using hickory wood for flavor.

Peel the membrane off the back of the ribs and season them lightly with the rub.

Put the ribs on the cooker and leave them for 1 hour. Strain the vinegar and place it in a clean spray bottle. Discard the peppers or use them for something else. After 1 hour open the cooker and spray heavily with the vinegar. After another 30 minutes, spray the ribs, flip them, and spray again. Repeat this every half hour until the ribs are tender to the touch. This should take a total of 4 to 5 hours.

Brush the ribs with barbecue sauce, then flip and sauce the other side, finishing with the meaty side up. Cook for 15 minutes. Remove to a platter and serve.

The Illinois State BBQ Championships

Shannon, Illinois

www.ilstatebbqchampionship.com

▼▼

There is great history at the Illinois State BBQ Championships. It began in 1991 and was the brainchild of Jim Burns. Jim was the owner of King James BBQ in West Chicago, Illinois, where it all began. Jim had been competing in some barbecue cookoffs around the country, and wanted to bring one to Illinois. The old Mike Royko Ribfest had been held in Chicago for the past eight years, but this new event was sanctioned by the Kansas City Barbeque Society and required cooking briskets and pork all night. The concept was pretty radical to most of the locals. The first year was small and we were all pretty naïve. I think there were about a dozen teams. Truth be told, most of us didn't know much about real barbecue, but we gave it a shot. I met John and Sue Beadle that weekend, who are very good barbecue cooks, and they became my mentors. Jim hosted the event for five years, but then sold his restaurant. Luckily for us, Mike Lake was part of the Illinois barbecue family, and he decided to help by moving the event to Shannon, Illinois, where he and his lovely wife, Theresa, live. Since 1996 they have immersed themselves in this great event, and it is known as one of the best cookoffs in the country. The event is held in a nice park in a small rural town, surrounded by cornfields. It has become known as the Barbecue Field of Dreams. Mike and Theresa have worked tirelessly on this cookoff. In 1999 Mike created the Butt to Butt cookoff to get some additional big-name teams to attend his cookoff. He invited six teams that had won the pork category at a major cookoff to participate in a separate winner-takes-all pork butt cookoff for $1,000 cash, a plaque, and the coveted boar's tooth necklace. This turned out to be a very smart move. Almost all the legends of barbecue have participated in the Butt to Butt over the years. It's now a sought-after invitation and a big deal to win. The greatest thing is that the teams come once for the Butt to Butt, but then become regulars because they have such a good time. I am a longtime supporter of this cookoff and have participated in and won the Butt to Butt twice. I wear the boar's tooth necklace proudly. Shannon is also the home of a very competitive pie contest. The burly barbecue guys compete against the local church ladies and all other comers. One of Mike's neighbors, Donna Lessman, is affectionately known as the Pie Lady, because she has dominated the contest. Last I heard she was retiring, but you never know. Shannon is also the place where the tradition of passing a bottle of ice-cold Dr. McGillicuddy's Vanilla Schnapps began. Toss the cap and pass it until it's gone. Shannon is the second weekend in July. I'll see you there.

Ray's Double Boar's Tooth Butt to Butt Recipe

2 pork butts, 7 to 8 pounds each

Dr. BBQ's Northern Barbecue Rub, as needed (page 126)

2 tablespoons turbinado sugar (Sugar in the Raw)

Dr. BBQ's Kansas City Barbecue Sauce, as needed (page 5)

2 tablespoons apple juice

Since I've won the Butt to Butt twice, I guess I'll use my own recipe here. When you win you get the coveted boar's tooth necklace and so far I'm the only cook with two. For this recipe I actually cooked two butts to two different degrees of doneness. The reason was to be able to pull the meat from one and slice the other one. It makes for a nice presentation and shows the judges two methods of cooking a pork butt. • **Yield: About 25 servings**

Prepare the cooker for indirect cooking at 235°F, using cherry wood for flavor.

Season one of the butts heavily with the rub and put it in the cooker fat side up. Trim the fat cap off the second butt and butterfly it by cutting along the flat part of the blade bone. You may need to have a butcher do this for you. Season this butt heavily with the rub and the sugar. Cover and return it to the refrigerator. After the first butt has cooked for 5 hours, add the butterflied butt to the cooker, opening it up to cook. Now just let them cook.

The first one will be done when the internal temp reaches 195°F, and the butterflied one will be done when it reaches an internal temp of 175°F. If one finishes ahead of the other, just wrap it tightly in heavy-duty foil and let it rest on the counter. When ready, slide the fat cap off the first butt. With your hands, pull the meat, discarding any bone, fat, or other stuff that you don't want to eat. Sprinkle a light dusting of rub on the meat. Add the apple juice and about the same amount of sauce. Toss lightly to coat.

The second butt will be sliced. Remove the bone and slice against the grain, about ½ inch thick. For my winning presentation I put a pile of pulled meat in the box, spreading it evenly. Then I laid six slices that had sauce brushed on half of each slice nicely on top in a cascade fashion. For serving guests, I'd put the pulled meat on a big platter and lay all the slices on top. Then I'd drizzle it all with sauce.

The Pie Lady's Apple Praline Pie

Pastry for a double-crust pie

The Filling

6 cups peeled and thinly sliced apples

³⁄₄ cup sugar

¼ cup flour

1 teaspoon ground cinnamon

¼ teaspoon salt

2 tablespoons butter or margarine

The Topping

¼ cup butter or margarine

½ cup firmly packed brown sugar

2 tablespoons half-and-half

½ cup chopped pecans

Thanks to Donna Lessman from Shannon, Illinois.
• Yield: 8 servings

Preheat the oven to 350°F.

Roll out half the pastry and fit it into a pie plate.

Make the filling: In a large bowl, combine the apples, sugar, flour, cinnamon, and salt; toss lightly. Spoon the apple mixture into the pastry-lined pan. Dot with butter or margarine. Top with second crust and flute the edge. Cut slits in several places. Bake at 350°F for 50 to 55 minutes, or until apples are tender.

Make the topping: In a small saucepan, melt the butter or margarine, then stir in the brown sugar and half-and-half. Heat slowly to boiling; stir in pecans. Spread over top of pie. Return to oven for 5 minutes, or until bubbly.

Weber Grills

www.weber.com

▼▼▼

While on the subject of Chicago and barbecue I should mention Weber Grills. In 1952, George Stephen, a welder at the Weber Brothers Metal Works in Chicago, was totally frustrated. He owned a flat, open, brazier-type grill, similar to a hibachi, and not only did it not have a lid, the food that he grilled was so close to the coals that a thin layer of ash covered it. George's job was welding together large metal spheres to make buoys for the Coast Guard to use on Lake Michigan. In one of the defining moments in grilling history, George had a brainstorm: Maybe a half a buoy with a lid would make a good grill. He added legs to the bottom of the buoy and a handle to the lid, and the Weber kettle grill was invented. The only problem was that it wouldn't stay lit. A neighbor advised him to punch holes in the lid for more oxygen, and the kettle-type grill was perfected.

He hired Mike Kempster to be his primary salesman for the grill at Weber Brothers and the rest is grilling history. Mike went on to become executive vice president of Weber-Stephen Products Company. Inexpensive Weber charcoal grills captured the imagination of the entire country during the late '50s and early '60s, and soon nearly every suburban family owned a kettle-style grill, also called a barbecue, and most of them were made by Weber.

After decades of new models and innovations, Weber remains the premier company producing not only charcoal grills, but also the Summit and Genesis gas grills, plus specialty units like the Smokey Mountain Cooker Smoker and portable grills for tailgaters. Many of the true barbecuers today got their start grilling on a Weber-Stephen kettle grill, and most of us still have one. Some people even collect them, like John and Teresa Espinoza of Clovis, California, who have ten, including a forty-four-year-old Weber that they purchased in 1962. However, their favorite is a 36-inch Ranch Kettle that cooks 18 tri-tips at the same time! I've used Weber kettles for many years and still have three of them. I even used one at my first cookoff back in 1982. The following recipe is all over the Internet nowadays, but I think a version of it originated in a Weber Kettle cookbook a long time ago.

Smoky Sirloin Tip Roast

1 choice-grade sirloin tip roast, 3 to 4 pounds

2 to 3 tablespoons olive oil

Dr. BBQ's Northern Barbecue Rub (page 126)

This is a perfect thing to cook on the Weber kettle. Prepare the grill for indirect cooking per Weber's instructions, with coals banked on both sides and a drip pan in the middle. • **Yield: 6–8 servings**

Prepare the cooker for indirect cooking at 300°F, using cherry wood for flavor.

Rub the roast with the olive oil to coat. Season liberally with the rub, then put it in the cooker. Cook until an internal temp of 135°F is reached for medium-rare. This should take about 1 hour. Remove to a platter and tent with foil. Let rest for 15 minutes. Slice thinly and serve.

Barbecue in Wisconsin

Barbecue is alive and well in Wisconsin, and has been for many years. Admittedly it's mostly grilling, but I'm not a snob about that. I remember as a kid in the '60s going with my family to the VFW on the Rock River in Fort Atkinson for a chicken barbecue. They had a big block pit set up and were grilling chicken halves, just like you'd see in the South, but this was in Wisconsin! They also served great breakfast on Sunday mornings at that VFW, and still do, but that's another story. Wisconsin is also the home of

Mad Dog and Merrill, a couple of fun-loving grilling experts. These guys do grilling/ entertainment demos all around the country, but their roots and daily radio show come from Appleton. It's estimated that these guys have cooked 10,000 bratwursts at Lambeau Field, home of the Green Bay Packers. As a lifelong Chicago Bears fan, the Packers are my sworn enemy for life, but I like Mad Dog and Merrill anyway. You might even hear me as a guest on their show from time to time.

Bratwurst

▼▼

If 10,000 brats seems like a lot to you, you've never been to Wisconsin. They just plain love the things. Don't get me wrong, I like them, too, but not as much as the folks in Wisconsin do. They celebrate "Take Your Brat to Work Day" each spring, where you stop and buy a brat or two on your way to work. I'd bet most of those brats never see the lunch hour. It's a great fundraising event, and they sell huge amounts of brats, but it just wouldn't work outside Wisconsin.

There is a funny but informational

Wisconsin-based Web page about brats at www.bratwurstpages.com. It's hosted by Jim Schroeder from Jefferson, Wisconsin. I've been to Jefferson many times, and when I'm there I buy my brats at Schroedl's, a great old-time butcher shop that I wish was near my home. In one excerpt on the Bratwurst Pages, they mention that sometimes people even eat brats without any beer. That was news to me. Speaking of beer, here's my favorite recipe from the Bratwurst Pages. It's the perfect accompaniment to a bratwurst.

Bratwash

1 case of beer

1 cooler

3 bags of ice (cubes)

Remove cans from recyclable cardboard holder. Place cans in cooler, intermingling with ice cubes. Chill 45 minutes and serve. • **Yield: Serves 8 guests (or 2 Wisconsinites)**

The brat is a descendant of a German sausage made with veal and pork. Most of the brats that you'll find today are made exclusively from pork. They generally come in two different styles, a cooked white sausage kind of like a big white hot dog, or a fresh sausage in casing that looks like a typical Italian sausage. You can mail order the authentic item from www.usinger.com. in Milwaukee. I like them both, but prefer the texture of the fresh. I cook them using the same treatment, but the white ones get done a little quicker.

Dr. BBQ's Favorite Bratwurst

10 links of bratwurst

1 stick butter

1 large onion, sliced thin

1 can beer

1 aluminum foil pan

Rolls for serving

Mustard (optional)

Cooking the brats properly is a big deal. The typical accompaniments are beer, onions, butter, and sometimes mustard and sauerkraut. Many cooks like to boil or simmer the brats in the beer, butter, and onions and then grill them. The thinking is that the brat will be cooked and all the fat will be gone. Yeah, so will all the flavor. My favorite method incorporates all the required brat ingredients and conserves the great flavors of them all. • **Yield: 6 to 8 servings**

Prepare the grill for direct cooking and medium heat.

Place the pan on one side of the grill and add the stick of butter. Put the brats on the other side of the grill directly on the grate. When the butter melts, add the sliced onion to the pan. Toss the onion occasionally. Flip the brats as needed. When the onions get soft, add the can of beer. As the brats get nicely browned add them to the pan. Don't worry about them being done all the way because they are going to continue to cook in the pan. You can add more beer if it's needed, but we want to reduce it down by the end so don't add too much.

When everything is in the pan, cover it with foil and cook for 15 minutes. Remove the foil and let the mixture reduce until it's just soft onions and brats. Remove from the heat. Serve the brats on sausage rolls with the onions and some mustard, if desired.

Sprecher Brewery

Glendale, Wisconsin

www.sprecherbrewery.com

▼▼

In Wisconsin they really like beer. And since beer goes so well with barbecue, it seems fair to offer up a great little old-world brewery to visit on your barbecue road trip. The beer here will only be served in big 16-ounce bottles, so it's a bit of an upgrade from the bratwash recipe. Matter of fact, the beer at Sprecher is an upgrade from just about any other beer. There is a long tradition of brewing in Milwaukee, and these guys are doing a fine job of keeping it strong. They also make a line of fantastic premium sodas that I like better than the beer! There's a world class root beer, an equally great cream soda, and a few other interesting flavors such as Orange Dream and Ravin' Red.

I first became familiar with these products when I met Scott McGlinchey at a cookoff in Wisconsin. Scott has a great relationship with the folks at Sprecher and usually has some of the hometown product around at a cookoff for sampling. He also sells a barbecue sauce that he makes using Sprecher root beer, and it's great stuff. I've been meaning to make a cream soda barbecue sauce for a long time now, so all these things collided to finally make that happen. It's great on grilled pork chops and ribs.

Sprecher Cream Soda Barbecue Sauce

2 tablespoons butter

2 tablespoons vegetable oil

1 cup finely chopped red onion

1 jalapeño pepper, seeded, deveined and minced

2 tablespoons flour

16 ounces Sprecher cream soda, or another premium brand

1/4 cup brown sugar

3 tablespoons Worcestershire sauce

2 tablespoons freshly squeezed lemon juice

1 tablespoon white vinegar

1 tablespoon soy sauce

1/2 teaspoon finely ground black pepper

1 tablespoon paprika

3 tablespoons tomato paste

• Yield: About 2½ cups

In a medium saucepan over medium heat, melt the butter with the oil. Add the onion and jalapeño and cook until tender. Add the flour and blend well. Add all the ingredients except the paprika and tomato paste and mix well. Bring to a boil and reduce to simmer. Cover and cook for about 15 minutes, stirring occasionally. Pour the sauce in a blender or use an immersion blender and puree until smooth, about 30 seconds in a blender or a minute with the immersion blender. Return to the heat and whisk in the paprika and tomato paste. Cook for an additional 5 minutes.

The Great Pork BarbeQlossal

Des Moines, Iowa
www.pork.org

▼▼

Any event with the word "pork" in the name has got to be good. If that's not good enough, BarbeQlossal is actually a part of World Pork Expo. How's that for a name? World Pork Expo is the trade show for everyone in the world who is involved in the pork industry. The barbecue cooks are there for a few days, so we get to walk through the show, and I must admit that I don't know what half the products are even for. But I don't really need to as long as the producers keep bringing those delicious hogs to market. It is an excellent place to get yourself a pair of shoelaces with pigs on them or a pig hat, jacket, wind chime, earrings, or just about anything else you can think of. These folks like to eat pork, too, so they host The Great Pork BarbeQlossal, and we cook a lot of it. The rules here are a little different than at most of the cookoffs I attend. Predictably we don't cook any chicken or beef at this one. The categories are pork ribs, pork loin, pork shoulder, and whole hog. There are usually about eighty teams, and it's quite a sight when the eighty whole hogs are ready to be carved. The pork producers in attendance know when this will happen and they come out strong to eat. It really is a fun contest, put together by my good friend Anne Rehnstrom, who works for the Pork Board. You'll see many other creative uses of pork while at BarbeQlossal, too. There are usually a couple of sponsors cooking lots of their product to give away, and there's always Speed Herrig with his big trailer from his barbecue sauce company, Cookies. Speed spends the week visiting with people and cooking pork to give away. In 2006 my friend Mike Tucker decided to cook the World's Largest Porkburger during the BarbeQlossal, just for fun. I was honored to be asked to garnish the porkburger. I used Maytag blue cheese, a wonderful Iowa product, some bacon, and a few regular old burger items. At the official weigh in the burger weighed 43.3 pounds and was declared the World's Largest Porkburger by all in attendance. The Pork Queen was there as well as the President of the Pork Board and many other pork enthusiasts. Mike even brought his mascot, a stuffed beaver, out for the event. A grand time was had by all. World Pork Expo is held each June at the beautiful Iowa State Fairgrounds in Des Moines.

Mini World's Largest Porkburger

2 pounds bulk Italian sausage, hot or mild

1 loaf of round bread, uncut and 8 to 10 inches wide

4 leaves lettuce

Dr. BBQ's Northern Barbecue Sauce, as needed (page 126)

Hot sauce, as needed (I used Dirty Dick's Hot Sauce)

1 cup crumbled blue cheese, Maytag preferred

1 cup cooked, crumbled bacon

½ cup sliced yellow peppers from a jar

1 medium onion, sliced and grilled

1 tomato, thinly sliced

Here's a manageable size with all the same great ingredients as the big one. The original was made of Italian sausage, which is always 100 percent pork.

• **Yield: 8 servings**

Prepare the cooker for indirect cooking at 300°F.

Form the sausage into a big patty. You'll need to make it bigger than the bread to account for a little shrinkage. It's okay if it's thick. Form the burger as tightly as you can.

Transfer it to the cooker. You'll need to flip it one time and might need to rotate it so it cooks evenly. Cook the burger to an internal temp of 160°F. This should take about 2 hours.

Split the loaf of bread, and if it's too high just cut a slab out of the middle. Place the bottom bun on a plate. Top with the lettuce leaves. Now move the burger on top of the lettuce. Brush lightly with barbecue sauce. Add a shake or two of hot sauce and brush again. Top with cheese, bacon, peppers, onion, and tomato. Add the top bun and cut into 8 wedges to serve.

The World's Largest Pork Burger is officially weighed in and overseen by Danita Rodibaugh, president of the National Pork Board; Roger Davidson, from Horizon Smokers; Mike Tucker from Hawgeyes BBQ; Bob Dykhuis, NPPC Board Member; Dr. BBQ; and Wayne Peugh, vice president of the National Pork Board.

Raccoon Flats
Achiote Marinade

5 tablespoons achiote seeds (about 2 ounces)

1½ tablespoons dried Mexican oregano

1½ tablespoons black peppercorns

1¼ teaspoons cumin seeds

½ teaspoon whole cloves

6 inches of ½-inch-diameter canela (Mexican cinnamon), or 1½ teaspoons regular cinnamon

1 teaspoon salt, plus more if needed

14 large cloves garlic, roughly chopped

1½ cups sour orange juice, or 1 cup fresh lime juice plus ½ cup fresh orange juice

This recipe comes from the 2002 BarbeQlossal Grand Champions. Raccoon Flats is a team made up of two brothers, Paul and John Lengeling from Iowa. They're real nice guys and real good cooks. You'll always see them coming because they drive a 1977 Dodge motor home lovingly known as the Shagmobile. According to Paul it really is worth a trip to a Mexican or Latin grocery store to get the achiote seeds, Mexican oregano, canela, and the sour orange juice. Sounds good to me. This is the marinade Raccoon Flats uses on their whole hog, but it's equally good on pork butts, whole boneless loins, or even pork chops. This is enough marinade for one pork butt, a whole pork loin, or a dozen chops. Marinate the butt overnight and the loin or chops for just several hours. • **Yield: About 2 cups**

Blend the first six ingredients in a grinder and grind until it becomes a very fine mixture. Transfer the ground spices to a blender and add the salt, garlic, and sour orange juice. Blend until the mixture is smooth. Let the marinade steep for several hours to let the flavors develop.

Hawgeyes BBQ

Ankeny, Iowa

www.hawgeyesbbq.com

▼▼

Mike Tucker is the brains behind Hawgeyes BBQ. Mike is in the landscaping business in Ankeny, Iowa, and he was looking for something to expand his business, so in 1995 he brought in some big smokers. It seemed like a fun product and the bonus was he could cook on them. They were having so much fun that Mike and his cooking partner and faithful Hawgeyes employee Bret Wram decided to cook in some contests. They're near Des Moines and the Great Pork BarbeQlossal, so they began competing, and in 1999 they were the Grand Champions. Like so many of us, they had the barbecue bug, but competing regularly wasn't really their thing. So in 2000 Hawgeyes opened a barbecue stand at the landscaping yard. They had been selling some sauces, rubs, and accessories at their store, but things were starting to come around on the Internet and Mike had hired Dan Thorton, who was already a good computer guy, so www.hawgeyesbbq.com was born. These days they have a very busy Internet store because they mix the new with the old. They have all the automation you could want, but if you want to talk to someone they are always friendly and available. Dan also takes great pride in packing the glass bottles very well and shipping orders in a timely fashion. They also bring in all kinds of small-batch interesting products. All the designer products that have been born from the cookoff circuit can be found at Hawgeyes. It's a fun place to shop because no place else has as many great products. I'd be remiss if I didn't mention that Mike Tucker likes to help people. He started by giving away surplus Christmas trees to the needy, but now he buys trees just for that reason and he gathers together a bunch of food to give away along with the trees. The Iowa Barbeque Society has joined in, and now it's a big event in Des Moines. They even feed the folks some barbecue pork sandwiches. Mike also spearheaded the Ribs for Kids program, where they take a group of inner city kids up to the Cookies Barbecue Sauce plant and give them a little seminar about cooking. Each kid gets a small grill and they have a cookoff. These kids aren't used to being treated so well, and they really appreciate it. Mike gets help from Cookies and the Iowa Barbeque Society, but when you do as much as Mike does people are happy to help out. His newest project is Senior Q. Folks around the country are encouraged to cook some barbecue and bring it to some seniors. It's all about doing your own thing. If you feed one lonely lady and spend a little time with her, you are a winner. If you can, feed a whole nursing home: The KCBS *Bullsheet* and the *National Barbecue News* have both agreed to print pictures and stories to thank the folks that are getting involved in Senior Q. I predict this will be another big success initiated by Mike Tucker. He's a good man.

I asked Mike Tucker for a recipe to include here and he sent me a favorite from his mom and a favorite from his dad. That's the kind of guy Mike Tucker is.

Mrs. Tucker's "Trash"

1 box extra-thick pretzels

Half a regular-size box of Rice Chex

Half a regular-size box of Cheerios

Half a regular-size box of Corn Chex

1 pound peanuts (not Spanish)

1 pound cashews

1½ cups vegetable oil

2 teaspoons celery salt

2 teaspoons chili powder

3 teaspoons Tabasco sauce

4 tablespoons Worcestershire sauce

½ stick melted butter

She cooks it in the oven, but I'd cook it in the barbecue pit. • Yield: Makes a bunch

Preheat the oven or cooker at 350°F.

In a large pan, combine the first six ingredients. Toss to blend. In a medium bowl, mix together the oil, spices, Tabasco, and Worcestershire. Mix in the melted butter. Pour over the dry ingredients. Mix well, place in a roasting pan, and bake, stirring every 15 to 20 minutes.

Cook for 1 to 1½ hours, or until golden brown. Stir it again when done.

Cool and store in an airtight container or zip-lock bags.

Mr. Tucker's Favorite Home-Style Ranch Dressing

2 cups mayonnaise

2 cups buttermilk

2 tablespoons lemon juice

1 teaspoon garlic powder

3 teaspoons minced green onion

2 tablespoons chopped fresh parsley

1 teaspoon finely ground black pepper

1 teaspoon salt

Great for dipping raw vegetables.

• Yield: 1 quart

Combine all the ingredients in the order given. Whisk until smooth.

Ribfests

A ribfest is a very special kind of barbecue festival. They are often hyped as a barbecue contest, but that's really not what they are all about. They are primarily about selling ribs. I mean tons of ribs. I mean truckloads of ribs. I mean thousands and thousands of dollars worth of ribs. Yes, they sell some pork, brisket, sausage, and chicken along with side dishes, but it's really all about the ribs. And it's really all about the selling of the ribs. A ribfest is a traveling food show. The rib vendors are mostly independent businesses that travel the country doing a ribfest in a different town each week. Some have restaurants and catering operations at home and most of them have a good sauce business, but they are mostly in the business of selling ribs at ribfests. They all have massive commercial cookers and a great big façade of signs. Some ribfests have limited the height of the signs because they were getting dangerous, but they still allow them to be 20 to 30 feet high. These guys are great showmen. They all have big grills in the fronts of their booths with ribs piled high and getting the full sauce treatment. The sights and smells are wonderful. I've even seen them with fans blowing the smoke out into the crowd, and the fans love it. I like these events because they do so much to get people talking about and eating barbecue. I used to live near the big ribfest in Naperville, Illinois, and I usually attended. The people wait in long lines in the summer sun to buy a sampler or a slab, and many of them meet their friends who've been in other lines so they can compare and find their favorite of the day. I almost forgot, but the ribfests all have winners, too. The ribs and sauce will be judged, and somebody wins. There are good cash prizes at most ribfests and that is part of the reason the contestants come, but the winner will also get the bragging rights and will probably sell more ribs than everybody else. Ribfests are held all over the country these days and are very popular. When I Googled "ribfest" there were over 100,000 results listed. Find a ribfest near you, get in line, and enjoy some ribs.

Ribfest Ribs

2 slabs St. Louis–cut ribs, about 2 ½ pounds each

Barbecue rub of your choice, as needed

Barbecue sauce of your choice, as needed

Most of the big ribfest guys use St. Louis–cut ribs weighing about 2 1/2 pounds per slab. Most of them cook in big commercial gas-fired barbecue pits as hot as is reasonable and they don't use very much or very strong wood for flavor. Most of them finish the ribs on a big open grill near the front of their booth while brushing them with barbecue sauce. It's a fun thing to see big piles of ribs on these big grills with fire and smoke everywhere. The result is a pretty good rib with caramelized sweet barbecue sauce on it. The volume doesn't allow the big sellers to remove the membrane, so I don't call for it here. The ribfest guys just put the grill heat to it and kind of crisp it up. (If I were you I'd peel the membrane.) They all have a signature rub and sauce that they sell, so I've left the choice of rub and sauce open here. There are plenty of rub and sauce recipes in this book, or you can use the rub and sauce that you buy from your favorite ribfest team. There is no central location to find these guys. Do that rifbest search again and you'll find them. • **Yield: About 4 servings**

Prepare the cooker for indirect cooking at 275°F, using a small amount of apple wood for flavor.

Season the ribs lightly and put them in the cooker. Cook until tender; this should take about 4 hours.

Prepare a grill for direct cooking at medium heat. Transfer the ribs to the grill and brush with barbecue sauce. Turn and brush the other side. Continue this process until the ribs are as caramelized as you like.

City BBQ

Columbus, Ohio

www.citybbq.com

▼▼

My first visit to Columbus, Ohio, was in 1996, and all I did was pass through on my way to the new cookoff in Nelsonville, Ohio. That weekend the cookoff was won by a nice group of guys from Columbus using the name the BBQ Boys. I got to know them as Jim Budros, John Kean, and Mike Taylor, and in 1997 they won the brisket category at the American Royal. This was a big accomplishment for three guys from Ohio, because there just wasn't much barbecue there. The BBQ Boys didn't like it that way, so they decided they needed to open a restaurant in Columbus so the people there could enjoy some real barbecue. The original BBQ Boys have other successful careers and none of them could run the day-to-day operations, so they brought in Rick Malir. Rick has done a great job, and City BBQ will have nine locations by the end of 2007. The food is still prepared fresh at each location and the recipes are the same ones the team used to win the awards. City BBQ is a newer barbecue joint, but very much in the tradition of the great old ones. They treat every item on the menu as if they were cooking for their friends and family.

City-Style Barbecue Burrito

1 pound leftover brisket, preferably from City BBQ

Two 4-ounce cans mild green chiles

2 to 3 tablespoons taco seasoning, or to taste

½ cup salsa

8 flour tortillas

Rice and cheese, if desired

• Yield: 8 burritos

Heat the brisket, covered, in the microwave on high for 2 minutes. Shred it with your hands.

Add the remaining ingredients except the tortillas and mix thoroughly. Return to the microwave and cook on high until heated through, probably another 1 to 2 minutes.

Put the tortillas in the microwave and cook for 30 seconds.

Spoon the filling onto the tortillas and roll up burrito style. Feel free to add rice and cheese if you like.

The Canadian Barbecue Championship

Barrie, Ontario

www.canadianbbqassociation.com

▼▼▼

Barbecue is alive and well in Canada. That should be no surprise—Canadians have enjoyed smoking meat, fish, and game for centuries, so it wasn't much of a stretch for them to take up American barbecue. A group of enthusiasts have been having smaller but fun cookoffs for a while now, but in 2004 the Canadian Barbecue Association was formed with big plans. It was spearheaded by David Coulson, an exec with Napoleon Grills, and Kirk Sharpley, who works with Chef Ted Reader, well-known in Canada as "King of the Q." They wanted to bring a big barbecue event to Canada for everyone to enjoy, so they worked with the folks who run Kempenfest in Barrie. It's a huge festival held over the three-day Civic Holiday weekend on the shore of Kempenfelt Bay that includes many arts and crafts booths, beer tents, food booths, and a carnival. The turnout of people is in the 250,000 range. Adding a barbecue cookoff was a great fit, and I'm proud to be a part of it. They import me annually to act as the head judge. We've put our heads together to create an event that is a great cross between the traditional American barbecue cookoff and a culinary event that would be more familiar to the chefs of the world. One-third of the judging is done on-site, which inspires wonderful booths and great hospitality for everyone to enjoy. I'm very proud to have played a part in the creation of this event. The interest has been strong since the beginning and continues to grow every year. All the grill and smoker companies in Canada have joined in, and the future is very bright. On top of all that, the Canadian Barbecue Championship is held in August, which is a very nice time of year to be in Canada.

Steak and Potatoes on a Plank

2 beef tenderloin steaks, 10 to 12 ounces each

Montreal steak spice, as needed (this is a common grocery store item)

1 cedar plank, soaked in water for at least 1 hour

2 cups leftover mashed potatoes, cold from the refrigerator (note: mashed potatoes are best 1 day old, since freshly mashed potatoes will run off the plank while cooking)

2 tablespoons freshly grated Parmesan cheese

1 tablespoon minced fresh chives

This recipe comes from David Coulson of Barrie, Ontario. David works for Napoleon Grills and has been instrumental in setting up the Canadian Barbecue Championship. He's also a pretty good guy and can even cook a little. David says, "The nice part of this meal is the juices from the steak run up and into the potatoes, making them creamy on the inside but golden on the outside with a wonderful smoke flavor from the board." Sounds good to me. • **Yield: 2 servings**

Preheat the grill to high (500°–550°F).

Season the beef steaks liberally with the spice, pressing it into the meat to adhere. Sear the beef tenderloin steaks on one side for 2 to 3 minutes.

Place the steaks, seared side up, onto a pre-soaked cedar plank, evenly spaced, and surround each steak with cold mashed potatoes, leaving the top of the seared steak exposed.

Turn the grill down to medium.

Place the plank back on the grill and bake for 15 to 20 minutes, for medium-rare, with the grill lid closed.

When finished, the potatoes should be golden brown. Turn the grill off, or close all the vents if using charcoal. Sprinkle the grated cheese and fresh chives on the potatoes and let sit for a minute with the heat off and the lid closed.

Bring the plank to the table for serving. Use a new plank as a trivet to set it on.

The South

Dr. BBQ's Southern Barbecue Rub

Dr. BBQ's Southern Barbecue Sauce

Big Bob Gibson Bar-B-Q (Decatur, Alabama)

Chicken with White Barbecue Sauce

Dr. BBQ's Alabama White Barbecue Sauce

Lemon Pie with Meringue

Dreamland Bar-B-Que Ribs (Tuscaloosa, Alabama)

Dreamer Ribs

The National BBQ News and The National Barbecue Festival (Douglas, Georgia)

Grilled Chocolate Bananas

Jack's Old South (Vienna, Georgia)

Jack's Old South Peach Baked Beans

Barbecue in Florida

Home BBQ Grilled Cheese Steak

Sonny's Real Pit Bar-B-Q

Sliced Smoked Pork Shoulder

Moonlite Bar-B-Q (Owensboro, Kentucky)

Old Hickory Pit Bar-B-Q (Owensboro, Kentucky)

Precious Blood Parish Barbecue Picnic (Owensboro, Kentucky)

Barbecued Mutton, Owensboro Style

Kentucky Barbecue Mopping Dip

Dr. BBQ's Kentucky Burgoo

▼▼▼▼▼

It's a daunting task to write about barbecue in the southern United States in one short chapter. First thing I have to do is to define the South. For this book it'll be everything south and east of St. Louis, but not including Tennessee, Texas, and North Carolina, which all have their own chapters. Even a rabid barbecue enthusiast such as myself can't get to every great little place and meet every legendary pitmaster in the South, so let me apologize to the ones I haven't gotten to yet. My love of barbecue will probably get me there sometime, and I look forward to those visits. For now we're gonna talk about the people, places, and things that I have experienced in the South, and that have helped make true American barbecue what it is today.

I firmly believe that barbecue as we know it in America was created by people who were poor and only had access to the lesser cuts of meat. I'm sure it was slave food, but it also came from poor white folks. They had to make the best with what they had, and barbecue is all about that. Up north it's often perceived that barbecue is an African-American tradition, but in the South it isn't. Blacks and whites have the same passion for real barbecue. In my experience around Chicago, the majority of the white people migrated through Ellis Island from Europe, while the black people came from the American South. No barbecue in Europe, lots of barbecue in the South. Therefore I say barbecue is a Southern thing, not a black or white thing.

I think the pace of life in the South has a lot to do with the love of barbecue as well. Sitting next to your cooker for the whole day just to have a good dinner isn't something most people up north will do, although that is changing. But to hang around all day cooking barbecue is a well-respected tradition in the South. It's just a different way of looking at things. Don't get me wrong, it's not like an island thing where you put everything off because you want to sit under the palm tree today. It's more of an appreciation of watching the wind blow through the trees and seeing squirrels playing in the grass while the smoke is rising. Southerners enjoy those things and they are good things to do while the barbecue takes its time.

Even throughout the South there are different incarnations of barbecue. In Kentucky they love to cook mutton. Sounds good to me. In northern Alabama you'll find my friends at Big Bob Gibson dunking their freshly smoked chickens in their legendary white sauce, and in Georgia and South Carolina you can find a bunch of folks who love a mustard-based sauce on their barbecue. Of course, these are the well-known traditions.

There are lots of areas where the sauce gets real unique, too. My friend Mikey Johnson tells me about a region in Alabama that likes barbecue sauce with Worcestershire sauce as a main ingredient. But Tommy Houston in Virginia also uses a sauce like that. I think these regional sauces are exactly that: regional. I know the white sauce originated in Bob Gibson's backyard, and I'd bet many of the others have a similar origin. Some seem to have spread to a wider acceptance than others, but all are originals that just sprang up where they were.

Now, the meat is a little different story. They seem to cook a lot of pork in the South, because hogs are plentiful. So are chickens, and they do get cooked regularly on the barbecue pit, but a whole bunch of them are getting fried in the cast-iron skillet, too. I love barbecue, but I fully endorse the frying of some of the chickens. (I'm okay with a few becoming chicken and dumplings also.) The barbecue cooking method is similar no matter where you go. The meat is near a wood fire, either above it or on the side of it. If it's above it's either far enough away that it can cook a long time or there is a barrier between the fire and the food. I think the results are similar; however, there are purists who claim to taste a big difference when the drippings go directly on the fire. I really don't. Nowadays many barbecue restaurants use gas-fueled cookers, even some of the old legendary joints. The truth is that the new-fangled gas cookers do pretty good if they are used properly. Of course, I'd rather see a cool old wood-burning pit, but I do understand the need for progress. I support all methods of barbecue and there's no better place to experience them than the southern United States.

Dr. BBQ's Southern Barbecue Rub

3 tablespoons salt

3 tablespoons celery salt

1 tablespoon finely ground black pepper

1 tablespoon onion powder

1 tablespoon garlic powder

1 tablespoon paprika

$\frac{1}{2}$ tablespoon cayenne pepper

$\frac{1}{2}$ tablespoon dried thyme leaves

• Yield: About $\frac{3}{4}$ cup

Mix together and store in an airtight container.

Dr. BBQ's Southern Barbecue Sauce

2 to 3 tablespoons bacon grease

$\frac{1}{2}$ cup minced onion

2 cloves garlic, minced

$1\frac{1}{3}$ cups ketchup

$\frac{2}{3}$ cup yellow mustard

$\frac{1}{2}$ cup brown sugar

$\frac{1}{4}$ cup Worcestershire sauce

2 tablespoons hot sauce (I used Frank's)

1 teaspoon finely ground black pepper

1 teaspoon salt

• Yield: About $2\frac{1}{2}$ cups

In a medium saucepan, heat the bacon grease over medium heat. Add the onion and garlic and cook until soft, stirring often. This should take 4 to 5 minutes. Add all of the other ingredients, stirring well, and simmer for 15 minutes.

Big Bob Gibson Bar-B-Q

Decatur, Alabama

www.bigbobgibsonbbq.com

▼▼▼

The folks at Big Bob Gibson seem to get a lot of space in my books, and rightfully so. They are good friends, but they also run one of the finest barbecue businesses in the country. In recent years, Chris Lilly has been the high-profile member of the team, but Big Bob's was selling barbecue in Decatur for sixty-five years before Chris ever came to work for them. I recently spent a couple hours talking about the history with Don McLemore in his office at the flagship restaurant. Don is the friendly white-haired gentleman you'll always find near the door of the restaurant. He's also the grandson of Big Bob Gibson. Big Bob was a railroad worker who chose another path in 1925 when he began selling barbecue in his yard. By all accounts he was cooking chicken and using the now-legendary white sauce from the beginning, and it's a safe bet he also cooked some whole hogs or maybe pork shoulders. The restaurant had a few locations in the early years, all in the Decatur area, but in 1952 Big Bob's daughter Catherine came aboard and they settled in at a location on Sixth Avenue, which is still a main thoroughfare through the area. That turned out to be a very wise business move. Their success allowed them to build a new building at that site that still stands in the shadow of the current restaurant. Look across the parking lot as you enter and you'll see the telltale smokestacks on the unassuming copy center next door. In 1977, Catherine's son Don joined the business, and the popularity continued to grow. With Don's guidance they added all the right menu items and promoted their catering business, all the while continuing to use the same recipes and goodwill that Big Bob started with so many years ago. In 1987, they built the restaurant that you see now on the adjacent property along Sixth Avenue. It's a fine example of a barbecue joint. When you enter you'll be greeted warmly as you stand among the towering Memphis in May trophies. Two are for the overall World Championship and six for first-place pork shoulder. You'll also see countless other awards and press clippings, all from the biggest and best contests and events.

In 1991, two important things happened at Big Bob's. Don's daughter Amy and her husband, Chris Lilly, joined the team, and they opened a second restaurant near the flourishing new Beltline area in Decatur. That's where you'll find Chris these days when he's not taping a TV show or cooking at some fancy chef event. Chris is a really likable guy who has helped take barbecue to a new level. Our friend John Markus says that walking into a barbecue event with Chris is like walking in with Bruce Springsteen. It's true, but I'm not sure he even knows it. So the addition of Chris brought a push to the barbecue sauce business where they added a great new red sauce to the legendary white sauce. They've since added a few additional sauces and a dry rub, but the championship red and the white sauce are the most popular. Chris also became the head cook of the newly formed barbecue cookoff team. They figured if they could win a few cookoffs, it might help the business. That was a pretty good idea! They've won a bunch and that has parlayed into Big Bob Gibson becoming one of the biggest names in barbecue today. Now they cook annually at the Big Apple Barbecue Block Party in New York City as well as the South Beach Food and Wine festival in Miami. Yes, the restaurants and catering business have flourished, too. They've even been invited to cook at the James Beard House, where I was proud to assist. It seems these guys have done it all in the barbecue business, leading the way with most of it. But I doubt if they are done. I think you'll see more from them real soon.

I guess I should tell you a little about the food, too. Aside from all the history and lore, they also serve some great barbecue at Big Bob Gibson. Of course the World Championship pork shoulder is a good choice, and so are the ribs. They serve whole spareribs because that's what the folks in Decatur like. They also must like slaw on their sandwiches, too, because that's how they are served. Who said that was only a Carolina thing? The chicken is legendary, split down the back and cooked over wood in the old-style brick pits. As soon as the chicken comes out of

the pit it gets dunked in a vat of Big Bob Gibson white barbecue sauce, just like it's been done for more than eighty years. No need to mess with perfection.

And last but not least, my favorite, the turkey. It's succulent white meat sliced and served as juicy as any turkey I've had anywhere. I rarely eat anything else. Well, okay, I usually have some Brunswick stew and sometimes a baked potato. They have these gigantic potatoes that you can get stuffed with the barbecue meat of your choice. That's hard to finish, they're so big. They also do a similar treatment to a simple salad and it's very popular. And I can't forget about the pies. It's hard to leave Big Bob Gibson Bar-B-Q without having a slice of pie. The pies are very simple—chocolate, lemon, or coconut topped with an outrageously high meringue—but they are the perfect ending to a great barbecue meal. Wherever you're driving to, take the side trip to Decatur and say hi to Don for me. You'll be glad you did.

Chicken with
White Barbecue Sauce

I frying chicken, about 4 pounds, quartered

Dr. BBQ's Southern Barbecue Rub (page 155)

1 double recipe Dr. BBQ's Alabama White Barbecue Sauce, divided (recipe follows)

Here's my version of this wonderful Alabama favorite. • **Yield: 4 servings**

Prepare the cooker for indirect cooking at 300°F, using a small amount of hickory wood for flavor. Season the chicken liberally with the rub and put it in the cooker. Arrange the breasts skin side up and start the thighs skin side down. Turn all the parts—breasts, thighs, legs, and wings—every twenty minutes until the chicken is done. The dark meat will be done when the internal temp reaches 180°F and the white meat will be done when it reaches 160°F. This should take $1\frac{1}{2}$ to 2 hours, depending on your cooker and the size of your chicken.

As the pieces get to the desired temp, take them off and immediately dunk them in one batch of the white sauce. Then transfer them to a platter and cover with foil. Repeat this process until all the chicken is done and on the platter. Discard the sauce that was used for dunking and serve with the second batch of white sauce at the table.

Dr. BBQ's Alabama White Barbecue Sauce

1 cup mayonnaise

¾ cup white vinegar

1 tablespoon lemon juice

1 tablespoon freshly ground black pepper

1 teaspoon sugar

1 teaspoon prepared horseradish

1 teaspoon salt

This is way different from most barbecue sauces!
• Yield: About 2 cups

Combine all ingredients in a bowl, mix well, and refrigerate.

Lemon Pie with Meringue

1 cup sugar

2 tablespoons flour

3 tablespoons cornstarch

1/4 teaspoon salt

2 lemons, juiced and zested

2 tablespoons butter

4 egg yolks, beaten

One 9-inch piecrust, baked

4 egg whites

6 tablespoons sugar

Mine's pretty good, but not as good as the one at Big Bob's. • **Yield: 6 to 8 servings**

Preheat the oven to 350°F.

In a medium saucepan, whisk together the sugar, flour, cornstarch, and salt. Stir in 1½ cups water, lemon juice, and lemon zest. Cook over medium-high heat, stirring frequently, until the mixture comes to a boil. Stir in the butter. Place the egg yolks in a small bowl and gradually whisk in ½ cup of the hot sugar mixture. Whisk the egg yolk mixture back into the remaining sugar mixture. Bring to a boil and continue to cook, stirring constantly, until thick. Remove from the heat. Pour the filling into the baked pastry shell.

In a large bowl, beat the egg whites until they are foamy. Add the sugar gradually, and continue to beat until stiff peaks form. Spread the meringue over the pie, making sure to anchor it to the crust.

Bake for 10 minutes, or until meringue is golden brown.

Serve chilled.

Dreamland Bar-B-Que Ribs

Tuscaloosa, Alabama

www.dreamlandbbq.com

▼▼

Ain't nothing like 'em nowhere" is what the advertising says, and I'm in full agreement. One of the best slabs of ribs I've ever eaten was at Dreamland in Tuscaloosa. There are some other locations now, but I always like to go to the original. Dreamland is near the University of Alabama and is said to have been a favorite of their legendary football coach, Bear Bryant. It's famous among barbecue lovers and has been for many years. Even before the current newfound popularity of the old barbecue joints, Dreamland had a cultlike following. It's really just a bar that serves ribs, plus bread, sauce, and beer. That's it. But frankly I don't think anyone would order anything else anyway. The ribs are that good. They are cooked direct over a real wood fire and served with one of my all-time favorite barbecue sauces. I won't even try to imitate this one. I suggest ordering it from them at www.dreamlandbbq.com. It was all created by John "Big Daddy" Bishop, who started selling ribs at this location in 1958. Big Daddy is not around anymore, but his recipes are. There is one important rule that is written on a sign at Dreamland. "No Farting!" Please obey this rule and you'll have a great time and a great meal at Dreamland.

Dreamer Ribs

Three racks of whole spareribs

Dr. BBQ's Southern Barbecue Rub (page 155), as needed

Dreamland BBQ Sauce, ordered from www.dreamlandbbq.com, or Dr. BBQ's Southern Barbecue Sauce (page 155) as a substitute

Like so many of the old barbecue joints, Dreamland uses a cooking method that just isn't practical with the equipment that most folks have at their disposal. I think my Friday Night Spareribs from my first book are pretty similar in texture, so I've borrowed that cooking technique. I'll use my Southern Rub on them but you'll have to order some Dreamland sauce for them to be authentic. If you must, substitute my Southern Barbecue Sauce and you'll be eating pretty well. • **Yield: 6 servings**

Prepare the cooker for indirect cooking at 250°F, using hickory and cherry wood for flavor.

Peel the membrane off the back of the ribs and trim the flap off. Trim any loose or thin meat off the meaty edge. Season lightly with the rub.

Put the ribs in the cooker and cook until tender. Use a rib rack if needed for space. This should take 5 to 6 hours. Check the ribs by sticking them with a toothpick. It should slide in easily. When the ribs are done, remove them to a platter and brush them liberally with the barbecue sauce. Tent with foil and let rest for 10 minutes.

When serving whole spareribs, you must always cut them apart individually for your guests. They just won't pull apart like back ribs will.

The National BBQ News

www.barbecuenews.com

▼▼▼

The story of the beginning of the *National Barbecue News* (NBBQN) is very similar to the stories of the Kansas City Barbeque Society (KCBS) and the International Barbecue Cookers Association (IBCA). A group of friends had discovered barbecue cookoffs, saw a need for a communication tool, and created one. In the case of the NBBQN the people were Dr. Don "Doc" Gillis and Joe Phelps. It seems that Doc and Joe were fishing buddies, but Doc had found a new hobby: cooking in barbecue contests. So in 1986, Doc talked Joe into being on his team. They began cooking and really enjoyed themselves, but like others involved in barbecue they saw a need to get the word out to the cooks. This was 1986, and there was no Internet or books or newspapers devoted to barbecue, so it was all word of mouth. Don and Joe also found cookoffs to be an expensive hobby, so they were looking for a way to support it. They didn't really have to look too far, since Joe and his wife, Carlene, were running the local paper, *The Coffee County News,* anyway, so a barbecue newspaper was the obvious idea. That was in 1990, and in 2007 they will celebrate seventeen successful years. The *National Barbecue News* is now read in all fifty states and at least six foreign countries. The wonderful thing they've done is to become a resource for everyone. They treat all the different sanctioning groups equally, they promote any and all barbecue business groups, and they go out of their way to support the backyarders out there who cook only for their families. In 2002, a smooth transition took place when Joe and Carlene's son Kell took over the paper. Kell says it wasn't much of a stretch since he had run the printing machine for every issue that had previously been printed. Kell is a great guy and always has a nice word to say, but I know his mom is keeping an eye on him just in case. The Phelpses, along with the late Doc Gillis, have done more than their share to promote barbecue. They've even started the National Barbecue Festival in their home-town of Douglas, Georgia. It's held every fall and consists of a big invitational cookoff known as "The Best of the Best," a bigger open cookoff, a backyard cookoff, and even a Kids-Q. About one hundred teams cook in Douglas, and all the town folk come out for it. Check their Web site for the info, and be there if you can.

Grilled Chocolate Bananas

6 bananas

1 big milk chocolate bar, broken into small pieces

Vanilla ice cream

Whipped cream

Chopped pecan pieces

Maraschino cherries

I asked Kell for his favorite recipe on the grill and this is what he gave me. I guess he's got a sweet tooth. • **Yield: 6 servings**

Prepare a grill for direct cooking over medium heat. Take a sharp knife and slit the bananas, leaving the skin intact, from end to end so the flat part is on the bottom. Go deep into the banana but do not cut the bottom part of the skin. Force the slits wide and stuff with pieces of the chocolate. Wrap the bananas in aluminum foil. Place them on the grill for about 10 minutes, or until the chocolate is melted and the bananas are partially cooked. Peel away the foil, then the banana peel, and scoop out the filling with a spoon. Put the filling from each banana in its own bowl. Top with vanilla ice cream, whipped cream, pecans, and a cherry on top.

Jack's Old South

Vienna, Georgia

www.jacksoldsouth.com

▼▼

Jack's Old South is many things these days, but they all revolve around Myron Mixon. Jack Mixon, the namesake of the restaurant, was Myron's father, and he passed away in 1996, a few months before Myron ever cooked in a barbecue contest. As of this writing the Jack's Old South cooking team has won an estimated 130 barbecue cookoffs. That's an amazing number. No one else is even close. Myron has won the Memphis in May World Championship twice and the hog division there four times. He lives in Vienna, Georgia, where the Big Pig Jig is held every October. You can see the grounds right off I-75 as you pass by Exit 109. It's the second biggest cookoff on the Memphis in May circuit, and he's won that one three times, too. He's usually wearing black, so he's become known as the Man in Black to the cookoff world, but he's certainly no bad guy. Myron is one of those cooks who loves to help other people learn about barbecue. He learned from his dad during family reunions and parties as he grew up, where barbecue was always served. This was south Georgia, after all.

They needed a sauce to serve with all this barbecue, so Myron's mom, Gaye Mixon, took an old family recipe for a mopping sauce and thickened it up, and Jack's Old South Barbecue Sauce was born. They've been selling it around Vienna since 1982 and you can order it on the JOS Web site. The family has had a few barbecue restaurants around Vienna, but these days Myron is living the barbecue dream. He's a well-known barbecue man with many promotional opportunities. There's the Jack's Old South line of cookers, the sauce that has been joined by a rub, and he does a lot of catering. There's also the Ultimate Cooking School, where you learn to cook barbecue from Myron Mixon over a two-day class. What an experience that is! There's still plenty of time for cookoffs, too. Myron cooks at twenty-five to thirty of those each year all across the country. He's been a competitor every year on *The All-Star BBQ Showdown* and he's even cooked on TV with Martha Stewart and Sara Moulton. All in all, I'd say Myron Mixon is a world-class barbecue man, and I'm sure Jack would be pleased at how his name is being carried on.

Jack's Old South Peach Baked Beans

6 strips bacon

1 red bell pepper, chopped

1 small onion, chopped

One #10 can Bush's Baked Beans (the big commercial size, 117 ounces)

4 cups prepared peach pie filling

• Yield: • Serves 20

Prepare the cooker for indirect cooking at 350°F, or preheat the oven at 350°F.

Fry the bacon in a skillet until crispy, then remove to drain. Add the bell pepper and onion and sauté until soft. Mix the beans and pie filling with the peppers, onions, and crumbled bacon. Put the mixture in a baking dish or aluminum pan (if cooking on smoker). Cook for 1 hour.

Barbecue in Florida

The whole state of Florida is very much overlooked as a place for barbecue. Tourists come to Florida and visit the beautiful beach towns and eat all the great seafood. They see the pretty manicured palm trees and resorts and they miss seeing what most of Florida really is. Just yesterday I saw a couple driving a convertible with the top down in Orlando. It's July here right now and in the mid-nineties. Add in the brutal humidity and the intense tropical sun and it would be pretty miserable in a convertible. But they were going to enjoy Florida like it is on the postcards. The truth is, most of Florida isn't like that at all. In my neighborhood the locals all drive big pickup trucks and had their air-conditioning on yesterday. Sound like the South? That's because it is. The middle of Florida is just south of the middle of Georgia and really not very different. So there are many old barbecue joints all over Florida and they are good. In general they aren't very flashy and none get written about very much, but there are plenty of them.

Just here in Lakeland there are three old ones and one fairly new one that is surely in the old tradition. I live near Granger & Son's, a funky old barbecue joint that was known as Garl's for most of its life. Mrs. Garl sold to Granger a while back, and he recently changed the name, but the barbecue there is still good and really popular with the locals. Friday night is steak night and the place is packed. Brother's Bar-B-Q is another good old barbecue joint in Lakeland on Martin Luther King Avenue. They serve a distinctly mustard-based sauce that many would say belongs only in South Carolina. I don't think so. Brother's has a big following in the African-American community of Lakeland. Then there's Jimbo's on Memorial, where everyone in Lakeland eats. They've been there since 1964 and I don't think they've changed a thing. I hope they never do. You'll get complimentary hush puppies, good barbecue with homemade sauce, and if you save room, apple pie with cider sauce. As you head to south Lakeland you'll find Happy Jack's Barbecue. Happy Jack's may not be the oldest barbecue joint in town, but you'd never know it. They've settled into an old gas station and the wood-burning pit sits near the road where everyone can see it. They even have carhops to bring your food right out to your truck. Yes, the lot is mostly full of pickup trucks. This is definitely not a tourist destination, but it's always one of my favorites.

That's just in Lakeland, but there are many more a short drive from my house. There's Peeble's, a legendary place in Auburndale that closes for a few months every summer because they don't have air-conditioning and no sensible Floridian would go there in the heat of summer. It's a great place with indoor block pits and outdoor bathrooms. Another favorite of mine is First Choice in Brandon. It's in a shopping mall but has a brick pit built into the wall in a very old and traditional fashion. This place always has a line out the door and with good reason. They slice the food to order and it's all good. Pay attention to the man slicing the meat. He'll probably ask you what you're having long before the cashier does. Then there's Black Water Barbecue in Orlando. These guys are friends and active cookoff champions. They know how to cook real barbecue and that's how they serve it. I like the turkey at Black Water.

There are many, many more great barbecue joints throughout Florida and they're often overlooked. When you come to Florida, look around for a barbecue joint. Even if you're at the beach there's probably one pretty close by. An interesting note about Florida barbecue is that while Florida is one of the biggest beef-producing states in the country these days, the meat of choice for barbecue in Florida is typically pork. That's probably a long tradition that began with all the wild hogs here. I haven't eaten a wild hog but hope to soon. I hear they're pretty good. You won't find those in the restaurants, though. They serve good old farm-raised pork.

There are some great cookoffs in Florida, too. I'm telling you, people in Florida love barbecue. The reason I moved to Lakeland in 2000 was because I'd been here for the big cookoff in February a few times and liked it here. I also knew it was a barbecue-friendly town. There's another big cookoff a couple towns over in Plant City every November. If you've ever been to Plant City you'll know that it's the place where most of Florida's strawberries are grown. You have to like them for that.

My third favorite cookoff in Florida is in Key Largo. What a great place for a cookoff. It's held in the park right on the beach. The people there have that great laid-back Keys attitude and you can go see the boat from the movie *The African Queen* while you're there. Come to Florida for the beaches, but don't skip the barbecue.

Home BBQ Grilled Cheese Steak

1 teaspoon salt

1 teaspoon freshly cracked black pepper

1/2 teaspoon granulated garlic

1 flank steak, butterflied

Extra virgin olive oil, as needed

1 cup finely chopped baby portobello mushrooms

1 cup finely chopped sweet onion (such as Vidalia)

1/2 cup finely chopped green bell pepper (optional)

1 cup shredded mozzarella cheese

3 toothpicks, soaked in water for 30 minutes

This great recipe comes from Kevin and Clara Bevington. They are simply the winningest barbecue team in Florida. Using the team name Homebbq.com, they've won eleven Grand Championships in Florida and have been second a whopping twenty times in the few short years they've been cooking. Kevin hosts www.homebbq.com, where you'll find lots of great barbecue information as well as his championship barbecue products.

In Kevin's words: "This recipe is one of our favorites, and it is fairly simple to make. Hopefully you had the butcher butterfly the flank steak for you. I know at my local grocery store, they do this without a problem. Also, make sure your ingredients are finely chopped, this is important so they cook thoroughly." • **Yield: 4 servings**

Prepare the grill for hot and direct cooking. You will need to have an indirect cooker available, too, or be able to switch over for the second cooking step. The indirect temp will need to be 375°F.

Mix the salt, pepper, and granulated garlic together in a bowl and set aside.

Open the flank steak completely, and tenderize it with a Jaccard tenderizer or tenderizing mallet. Lightly coat the top with extra virgin olive oil and rub in well. Lightly sprinkle one-quarter of the seasoning mixture on the oiled flank steak, evenly spread. Place the chopped mushrooms, onion, and bell pepper, if using, on the flank steak. Drizzle olive oil on top of the mushrooms, onions, and peppers. Spread the mozzarella cheese evenly on top. Sprinkle evenly with one-quarter of the seasoning. Roll up the flank steak to form a roll. Make sure the roll is even, and the filling ingredients aren't bunched in the middle. Secure the roll with the water-soaked toothpicks—make sure they don't break! Lightly coat the outside with olive oil and the remaining seasoning. Let the flank roll rest for 30 minutes.

Place the rolled flank steak on the direct grill. Cook the roll, turning occasionally, until it is nicely browned all over. This should take about 4 minutes. Wrap the rolled flank steak in heavy-duty aluminum foil and place in the indirect cooker for approximately 20 to 25 minutes, or until the meat reaches an internal temp of 135°F for medium-rare. Remove from the grill, unwrap the foil, and let stand for approximately 10 minutes (save the juice in the foil!). Cut into ¾-inch slices, and place on a platter. Drizzle reserved juice over the slices and serve.

Sonny's Real Pit Bar-B-Q

150 Locations Throughout the Southeast

www.sonnysbbq.com

▼▼

In 1968, Floyd "Sonny" Tillman and his wife, Lucille, opened the first Sonny's Real Pit Bar-B-Q in Gainesville, Florida. They served good wood-cooked food and treated people real nice. What a concept! Well, it worked and they built a very successful restaurant. In 1977, they began to franchise their concept and that worked, too. Sonny's is now the largest chain of barbecue restaurants in the country, with more than 150 locations in nine southern states. Good food and treating people nicely has paid off. In Florida you can't hardly swing a dead cat without hitting a Sonny's, but they all seem to be very successful. I'm usually suspect of chains, but I have to admit that every time I eat at Sonny's

I'm served a good meal. They have baby back and St. Louis ribs, chicken, beef, pulled pork, and my favorite, the sliced pork. It's sweet and smoky and served with the sauce on the side. Their Web site says the sliced pork is where it all began, and that would explain the success. This stuff is really good. They like to serve it on garlic bread, but I pass on that and have mine on a toasted bun. They have a few different sauces that people love and some great sides. I know some barbecuers who cook their own meat and go get Sonny's beans because they are so good. Sonny's advertises relentlessly and promotes themselves as "Feel Good Bar-B-Q." I know I feel good when I eat there.

Sliced Smoked Pork Shoulder

1 pork shoulder roast, 4 to 5 pounds, boned, trimmed, rolled, and tied (you might need a butcher for this cut)

Dr. BBQ's Southern Barbecue Rub, as needed (page 155)

With the popularity of pulled and chopped pork, sliced pork from the barbecue pit has almost been forgotten. If you trim the fat and cook it a little less it's mighty good stuff. • **Yield: About 8 servings**

Prepare the cooker for indirect cooking at 250°F, using oak wood for flavor.

Season the pork liberally with the rub. Put the pork in the cooker and smoke it until it reaches an internal temperature of 170°F. This should take 6 to 8 hours. Remove it from the cooker, tent loosely with foil, and let rest for 15 minutes. Slice it thin to serve.

Barbecue in Kentucky

Owensboro, Kentucky
"Barbecue Capital of the World"

Owensboro is well known as the home of barbecued mutton. These days it's really just lamb, but no matter. It's real popular there. I happen to like lamb, so I'm a big fan and go to Owensboro every chance I get. I recently asked a local why the folks around Owensboro had taken to mutton so well, and his answer was that in the early days it was the cheapest thing they could get for their big barbecues. Fair enough. Truth is, that fits the old theory that barbecue was a method for making the lesser cuts of meat taste good. I suspect there were some local sheep farmers back then, too, and there were cheap mutton cuts available, but these days most of the folks are eating it just because they like it

The cooking method is pretty typical: A fire is directly below the meat but far enough away that it's an indirect cooking method. They use very little dry rub but do mop their food along the way with a liquid that they call a "dip." It's an interesting combination of Worcestershire sauce, vinegar, lemon juice, salt, pepper, a little brown sugar, water, and sometimes a little tomato paste. I don't believe I've had anything quite like it anywhere else. They also use it on their barbecued chickens and pork shoulders and it works just fine with everything.

Another important part of the barbecue here is burgoo. It's really a stew and has nothing to do with any of the barbecue, but you won't find barbecue in Owensboro without burgoo alongside. In my opinion it's pretty similar to Brunswick stew, and they both seem to have come from the long list of soups/stews that were originally created to use up whatever was lying around.

Moonlite Bar-B-Q

Owensboro, Kentucky

www.moonlite.com

▼▼▼

There are many barbecue restaurants in Owensboro, but by far the most famous is Moonlite. It's also by far the biggest, boasting seating for 350, but it doesn't stop there. Moonlite Bar-B-Q has a large number of faithful carry-out customers, a big catering business, and they ship their menu items all over the world. On top of that they are a big meat purveyor that supplies mutton to at least one of the local parish picnics, and probably to all of them. This is a large business, but it's all run by the Bosley family, which has owned it since 1963. When you go, I'd suggest the buffet. The only catch is that the buffet is closed from 2:00 P.M. until 4:00 P.M., but that's just because it's slow then and the food

wouldn't be fresh. So go early or late and have the buffet. You'll find mutton two ways, chopped real fine like the locals seem to like it, but also pulled into big pieces the way I like it. There's also barbecued pork shoulder, and sometimes there are ribs and usually fried fish. There are greens and potatoes and the best little tender corn I've had anywhere. They have a big crock of burgoo, so be sure to try that. Last but not least, there are some beautiful homemade desserts. I think there was a salad bar, too, but I'm not sure. My behavior at Moonlite brings to mind the episode when Homer Simpson gets kicked out of the Chinese buffet restaurant by a guy yelling "Eat some vegetables!"

Old Hickory Pit Bar-B-Q

Owensboro, Kentucky

▼▼▼

If Moonlite is the big tourist attraction in town, Old Hickory is the local favorite. It's a very nice place with friendly waitresses and a busy carry-out counter right up front. It's a pretty safe bet that I was the only tourist in the place, and one young waitress sat with a lady who looked like her grandma in between

her duties. The menu is just what you'd expect to see in Owensboro, with barbecued mutton and burgoo as the featured items and barbecued pork close behind. As I looked at the menu I saw that I could order my mutton chopped or "from the pit." When I asked, the waitress told me that "from the pit" was pulled right from the big pieces of meat that were in the pit. You see, the chopped mutton is tossed with some of the dip and is held that way in batches waiting to be served. Don't mistake this for a sacrifice to convenience, as they like it to soak up some of the dip before serving. I ordered mine from the pit and it was good. The only thing is that the way they cook the mutton, it's meant to be served with the dip and can be a little dry without it. The good news is there is some dip right on the table, and since I like the bigger chunks I just added a little pour of dip and I was eating well. Of course, I had a cup of burgoo with my meal and it was excellent. I found the food at Old Hickory to be a little more tangy than at the other places I ate. My thought is that this is directly related to local preference as opposed to the taste preference of visitors. My suggestion would be to try them both.

Precious Blood Parish Barbecue Picnic

Owensboro, Kentucky

▼▼

I got a tip that the real barbecue in Owensboro was at the Catholic Church barbecues held each weekend throughout Davies County. Man, was that some good advice. I was sent a schedule of the barbecues, and later found it in multiple places on the Internet. This is a big deal! So I checked my schedule against theirs and found that I could attend the barbecue at the Precious Blood Church. I called the church and spoke with Penny Blandford, who passed me on to Bruce Tucker. She said Bruce would be cooking and could help me. Bruce was very nice on the phone and said they'd be glad to have me visit. I got there a few hours before serving time and the cooking was in full swing. What seemed like an army of workers were cooking 1,800 pounds of mutton hind quarters, 600 whole butterflied chickens, 600 pounds of pork butts, and an amazing 750 gallons of burgoo. They estimate that they fed 1,100 people at the event, but the bulk of the food was takeout, so I'll make a guess that more than 5,000 folks got fed on that day's cooking. The main barbecue pit brought a tear to my eye. It's eighty-five feet long and has a permanent metal roof over the whole thing. Seems the old wooden one burned down. The pit is dug about four feet down and there are steel side walls that are about three feet high, so the cooking is done approximately seven feet above the fire. The food all sits on these massive steel grates that have handles on the ends. When it comes time to move a grate or flip the chickens, it's easily done. For the chicken-flipping, two guys take a spare grate and place it on top of the chickens. Then with one graceful swoop they flip the whole thing, probably doing thirty birds at a time. It's way cool and very functional. Then they just take the new top grid off and move to the next grate of chickens. Down in the pit they burn big slabs of wood, mostly lumberyard waste of hickory and oak. The fire is constantly tended by a man with a garden hose. It seems he knows just by looking if the temp is right. These guys do a great job and it's all based on experience. This picnic has been going on since the 1950s. I spent some time with the pastor, the Reverend Brad Whistle, and it was obvious that this is one happy family church. They all wear red shirts for the occasion, printed for the day. After everyone is fed and the work is done they have a mass. Father Brad gleams when he tells me that the church is a sea of red. He's a very nice man leading a very nice parish.

But back to the food. There are two giant kettles of dip that season all the meat. One is for mopping during the cooking and the other is for wetting the food down after it's sliced. The lamb and pork are cooked for many hours and then the slicing takes place. Three industrial band saws are the tools for this job, each manned by two men. One man puts the whole piece of meat through the blade, bones and all, cutting it into slabs about an inch thick. The second guy moves the slabs into an empty ice chest. The meat is very tender at this point and breaks up as it's handled, resulting in nice serving-size chunks. Every now and then the second guy pours a little of the serving dip on the meat. When the ice chest is mostly full, it's closed up and left to marinate until needed. It's a very smooth process and it results in some great food.

Equally important is the burgoo. It's handled by another team of cooks and it's a big project. At Precious Blood they have a garage-type building with ten built-in kettles that can cook seventy-five gallons each. Five have an automatic stirring system and five must be stirred constantly by hand. They have these custom-made wooden paddles and have been doing it that way for many years. It's fun to see a man teaching his children how to stir the burgoo. For that reason alone I don't think they'll ever automate all of the kettles. The automation is simply for convenience. Each kettle requires at least three people to stir in shifts for six to eight hours, so you can see why a little automation was welcome. They tell me they only use all ten kettles one day a year, and that they use four of them a few times throughout the year. They also have a trailer so they can bring four kettles to the barbecue festival, but that's a story for another day. The burgoo is a popular item here. Much like the meat cutters, they have a very smooth system that transfers the burgoo from the kettles to wide-mouth gallon jugs. I think most of it is sold that way and taken home. So is much of the meat, taken away by the pound or by the whole chicken, but there is another option. You could go inside the auditorium and have an all-you-can-eat feast for $9 the day I was there. I couldn't pass that up. There's a line as you come in where you get some of everything and then you sit down in a family-style setting. I sat with some wonderful folks who attend many of the barbecues in the area. There are waitresses that bring more of everything to you so you certainly won't leave hungry. I think I had three cups of the burgoo and at least two helpings of mutton. The folks at Precious Blood were generous enough to share many tips and even a list of ingredients to help me with my dip and my burgoo recipes, but I must tell you that the good vibrations they have at their event will be impossible to match. The friendly people and the food were both outstanding, and I can't wait to go back.

Barbecued Mutton, Owensboro Style

1 whole leg of lamb, 3 to 4 pounds, butterflied

Salt and pepper

1 batch Kentucky Barbecue Mopping Dip (recipe follows)

¼ cup tomato paste

Mutton is simply an older lamb, and not many of them grow very old these days. You'll find it hard to actually find any old lamb in most places, so I just use lamb. In Owensboro they use hindquarters, but you're probably not going to find that cut either, so let's just use a butterflied leg of lamb. If you can't find that, get a new butcher!

• Yield: 6 to 8 servings

Prepare the grill for direct cooking at medium heat.

Lay the butterflied lamb open and sprinkle it lightly with salt and pepper. Put it on the grill and cook for 20 minutes.

Meanwhile, separate the dip into two equal portions. Add the tomato paste to one half and reserve that for serving. Use the plain half for mopping while the lamb is on the grill.

After the first 20 minutes, flip the lamb and baste with the dip. Do this every 20 minutes until the lamb reaches an internal temp of 160°F. This should take 1 to 2 hours.

Remove the lamb to a pan. Discard the mopping dip that you have been basting with. Now baste the lamb well with the reserved serving dip. Cover with foil and rest for 15 minutes. Slice or chop and serve with the remaining serving dip on the side.

Kentucky Barbecue
Mopping Dip

1 cup Worcestershire sauce

1 cup water

¼ cup cider vinegar

2 tablespoons brown sugar

1 tablespoon lemon juice

½ teaspoon ground black pepper

¼ teaspoon cayenne pepper

I was able to make this with a little help from my friends at Precious Blood Parish in Owensboro.

• Yield: 2⅓ cups

In a medium saucepan, whisk the ingredients together. Bring to a simmer, stirring to dissolve the sugar. Remove from the heat.

To make this into a serving dip, add ½ cup tomato paste.

Dr. BBQ takes a turn stirring the burgoo.

Dr. BBQ's Kentucky Burgoo

2 tablespoons pickling spices, wraped in a cheesecloth bundle

1 tablespoon salt

1 large chicken

3 pounds brisket trimmings or other lean beef

1 pound lean trimmed lamb, preferably from the leg

Vegetable oil

2 large onions, finely chopped

½ head cabbage, chopped fine

Two 28-ounce cans tomato puree

¾ cup vinegar

¾ cup Worcestershire sauce

Juice of 2 lemons

2 tablespoons ground black pepper

5 pounds potatoes, peeled and diced

2 cups frozen or fresh corn

Two 15-ounce cans lima beans, drained

Salt and hot sauce to taste

My friends at Precious Blood in Owensboro were generous enough to give me their list of ingredients, but the measurements were a parish secret. Using that list and going by what I tasted and saw that day, I've come up with my own recipe. They do their burgoo in 75-gallon batches using some serious industrial equipment, so I've changed a few things to fit the home kitchen. You'll need to grind the cooked meat if you want to get the texture right. You'll also need to stir the pot frequently for the last two hours. This is a big project but well worth the effort.

• Yield: Makes 3 to 4 gallons

In a big, heavy stockpot bring 6 quarts water, the pickling spice bundle, and salt to a boil. Add the chicken, beef, and lamb. Return to a boil, reduce to a simmer, and cook for 1 hour.

Meanwhile, in a separate sauté pan, heat the oil over medium heat and sauté the onion and cabbage for 10 to 15 minutes, until soft. Set aside.

When the meat is cooked remove it all to a platter to cool, keeping the liquid in the pot. Add the onion/cabbage mixture to the stockpot and continue simmering. Add the tomato puree, vinegar, Worcestershire, lemon juice, and black pepper to the pot and mix well.

When the meat has cooled, run it through a grinder, using the coarse plate. You can chop it by hand or use a food processor if you must, but the texture won't be the same as the original. Add the ground meat to the pot and continue cooking, stirring and scraping the bottom often. Return to a simmer. Add the potatoes and return to a simmer. Cook for 1 hour, stirring and scraping the bottom often. Puree the whole pot of burgoo with an immersion blender if you have one. If not, try to break up the potatoes as best you can. It'll just be a little chunkier, but it will be fine. Add the corn and lima beans and stir. Cook for another hour, stirring and scraping the bottom often. Check for salt and add some hot sauce if you like.

The East

Dr. BBQ's Eastern Barbecue Rub

Dr. BBQ's Eastern Barbecue Sauce

Daisy May's BBQ USA (New York City)

Adam's Pork Glaze

Blue Smoke (New York City)

Deviled Eggs

Dinosaur Bar-B-Que (New York City)

Smoked Lamb Shanks and Garlic Mashed Potatoes

Grill Kings BBQ Cookoff (Belmont Park, Long Island, New York)

Wing Ding Chicken Wings

Wing Ding Dry Rub

Peppers (Rehoboth Beach, Delaware)

Homemade Caribbean Hot Pepper Sauce

The New England Barbecue Society (Forestdale, Massachusetts)

Franken-Chicken

Chap's Pit Beef (Baltimore, Maryland)

Big Al's Pit Beef (Rosedale, Maryland)

Dr. BBQ's Recipe for Pit Beef

Creamy Horseradish Sauce

Waldorf Eggfest (Waldorf, Maryland)

Wess and Sally's Potato Skins

▼▼▼▼▼

Barbecue in the eastern United States is very interesting. Like so many things along the East Coast, there is a big difference between the way things are done in the big cities and the way they are done in the rest of the state. Drive a couple hours west out of New York City and you'll find a different world. There aren't a couple of barbecue joints in every town, though. The people there didn't grow up with it. Barbecue in the East has come a long way in recent years, but the truth is it gets lost among all the other food traditions along the East Coast. There are many ethnic and cultural food traditions that stand strong, but most of them come from places other than the American South. The weather has been a deterrent, too. As much as I'd like to see people "Barbecue All Year Long," the reality is it's cold and snowy in Vermont and New Hampshire a good part of the year and cooking outside is strictly for the hard-core enthusiasts. There's also an abundance of seafood along the East Coast, and the people have traditionally eaten a lot of that. The recent popularity of real southern barbecue has surely gotten their attention, but barbecue joints aren't going to be replacing the steak houses and Italian restaurants any time soon. Like all good cuisine, barbecue will find its place, and the invasion has begun.

In New York City chefs like Adam Perry Lang and Kenny Callaghan are cooking some very good barbecue, and a longtime Syracuse tradition has come to Harlem in the form of Dinosaur Bar-B-Que. There's even a big-time cookoff on Long Island now. Speaking of cookoffs, the New England Barbecue Society has been meeting and promoting barbecue events since 1995. They're based in Boston, but the word has spread far and wide. They now boast members from a dozen states and Puerto Rico. Baltimore has an old barbecue tradition known as pit beef, and there's a Big Green Egglest in Waldorf, Maryland. In Rehoboth Beach, Delaware, there's a collection of barbecue and hot sauces that you won't believe.

I think it's just getting started. Barbecue is good food and a fun tradition and the word is spreading fast in the Northeast. If you head south of Washington, D.C., you'll find that you are getting into barbecue country. Virginia may be part of the big city D.C. area, but drive out into the country and you'll find that you've entered the South. Barbecue is very popular here, and I'd suggest going to Danville for the big cookoff in the spring. It's a little different than the other regions, but barbecue is alive and well in the East.

Dr. BBQ's Eastern Barbecue Rub

½ cup salt

3 tablespoons coarsely ground black pepper

2 tablespoons garlic powder

2 tablespoons onion powder

2 tablespoons paprika

1 tablespoon dried basil leaves

1 tablespoon dried marjoram leaves

1 tablespoon white sugar

1 teaspoon ground allspice

• Yield: About 1¼ cups

Mix well and store in an airtight container.

Dr. BBQ's Eastern Barbecue Sauce

2 cups ketchup

½ cup molasses

¼ cup cider vinegar

¼ cup yellow mustard

2 tablespoons Worcestershire sauce

½ tablespoon granulated garlic

½ tablespoon onion powder

½ tablespoon finely ground black pepper

½ tablespoon hot sauce (I use Frank's)

• Yield: About 3 cups

In a medium saucepan, mix all the ingredients together over medium heat. Cook 5 minutes, stirring until well blended.

Daisy May's BBQ USA/Adam Perry Lang

New York City

www.daisymaysbbq.com

▼▼

This is not your typical barbecue joint or pitmaster story. Matter of fact, it's the only one of its kind. Adam Perry Lang grew up on Long Island and graduated from the Culinary Institute of America. He took a job at Le Cirque in Manhattan. Working for one of the best-known chefs in New York, Daniel Boulud, Adam honed his skills in the kitchen. He left with Daniel to help open a new restaurant named Daniel. From there he went to work at Chanterelle for a year as sous chef. These are not barbecue joints. These are among the finest restaurants in New York, manned by the finest chefs. Then Adam headed to France for a stint at Restaurant Guy Savoy and another stint at L'Espérance working for Marc Meneau. You can see that this is getting to be a world-class résumé, folks. He went back to New York for a year at Monzu, another fine restaurant. From there it was a gig as a private chef for someone he will never reveal, but obviously someone with unlimited money. He spent his time at the employer's New Mexico ranch, where he encountered some "displaced Texans" working as cowboys. In their spare time the cowboys built a barbecue pit and Adam began cooking on it. You see what's coming? This chef who knows more about meat than anyone I've ever

met is hanging out with some Texans who know about authentic barbecue. This was great inspiration for Adam Perry Lang. You don't get to the level he was at without a great passion for food and the quest to learn more about it. The magic that happens in a barbecue pit is something that just doesn't happen in a kitchen, even in the finest kitchens in the world. But the typical pitmaster doesn't have the skills to really perfect the technique to a consistent level of perfection like the great chefs do. The mix of classic French cooking technique and the unique elements that come from meat cooked in a barbecue pit was a great challenge to Adam. I can tell you that I've spent hours talking with him about this and I learn more every time. I hope I send a little back his way, too.

So Adam headed back to New York with a whole new cuisine in his pocket, ready to open a barbecue joint. He wanted it to be more than Adam Perry Lang's barbecue joint, so he named it Daisy May's. Who's Daisy May, you ask? Well, Daisy May was a cocker spaniel that lived on the ranch in New Mexico. Adam was also getting the cookoff bug, so he attended the American Royal in 2002 and became a Certified Barbecue Judge. He met Ed Roith and a bunch of other legendary pitmasters of the cookoff circuit and says he ate some amazing food. In 2003 Daisy May's BBQ USA opened. It was just a carryout/delivery place, but they also ran a fleet of New York food carts. Move over hot dogs, there's a barbecue man in town. This has all been wildly successful, and in 2006 Daisy May's added a dining room and extended the hours. The people of New York have clearly embraced the real barbecue that they serve. The food is the best barbecue in New York. I highly recommend the beef ribs. They're as good as Mr. Powdrell's (page 210), and his are about as good as they come. In the new dining room they will cook a whole suckling pig for you and a dozen or so of your friends. You have to order it forty-eight hours in advance, but that's just part of the adventure. The pig will be served on a custom cutting board and your guests will be given plastic aprons and gloves so that they aren't afraid to dig right in. Only in New York do you have a very civilized pig pickin'. Nice.

This story wouldn't be complete without telling you about Adam's rookie year on the cookoff circuit. He flew to Huntsville to help me at the Rocket City cookoff in 2005. He made some great ribs for the team that day and learned the ropes. Obviously this guy didn't need cooking lessons, he just needed to get a feel for the culture. His next stop was The Great Pork BarbeQlossal in Des Moines. Among all his other accomplishments, Adam was one of the Pork Board's Celebrated Chefs in 2005. But no Celebrated Chef had ever entered the cookoff before. He kicked that door down, getting a perfect score in ribs and winning the whole contest against one of the toughest fields of the year. This guy is a fast learner. For that victory he was invited to cook in the American Royal Invitational. No, he didn't win the toughest cookoff of the year, but he did win the pork shoulder category. Another amazing accomplishment by an amazing guy. When you're in New York, don't miss Daisy May's BBQ USA.

Adam's Pork Glaze

2 green apples, peeled and diced

2 tablespoons dark brown sugar

1 tablespoon butter

4 tablespoons Jack Daniel's whiskey

1 tablespoon yellow mustard

1 tablespoon ketchup

1 tablespoon crushed garlic

1 teaspoon coriander seed

1 teaspoon ground black pepper

1 teaspoon kosher salt

½ cup dark brown sugar

¼ cup honey

¼ cup apple cider vinegar

½ cup apricot preserves

This glaze is excellent on pork—both quick- and long-cooking cuts. It's meant to be used at the end of the cooking. **Yield: About 2½ cups**

Toss the diced apples in the brown sugar. Melt the butter in a frying pan over high heat. When the butter's slightly brown, add the diced apples. Cook until nicely caramelized, and then deglaze with the Jack Daniel's, being careful of possible flames. Cook off the alcohol and add 4 tablespoons water.

Place in a blender and puree. Add the remaining ingredients.

Puree further and reserve to glaze during the last half hour of indirect grilling or the last 5 minutes of direct grilling.

Blue Smoke

New York City

www.bluesmoke.com

▼▼▼

It was big news in the world of barbecue when Blue Smoke was opened in March of 2002. A real barbecue joint in Manhattan? Seemed kind of farfetched to most folks, but everybody was watching. They had Mike Mills of Memphis in May fame on board, and the folks at the Union Square Hospitality Group led by Danny Meyer surely know how to run a restaurant in New York, so maybe it would work. My first visit to Blue Smoke was a quick one, just picking up supplies to help Chris Lilly cook at the Beard House, but I did get to meet the Blue Smoke executive chef, Kenny Callaghan, that day. His interest and passion for barbecue were obvious, and he even came for the dinner that night. Since then I've been to Blue Smoke enough times to understand that they are serious about the barbecue, but they are running a restaurant in Manhattan. They completely get it and it seems the locals do, too. They serve very good barbecue. I like all three rib choices. The brisket and pork are both very good as well. But they also have an excellent jazz club downstairs and an amazing collection of top-shelf liquor. They have their own beer, Blue Smoke Original Ale, on tap and an eighteen-year-old bourbon bottled especially for them. It's really a unique place that can offer real barbecue with the service and amenities that are required to survive in New York. This is the kind of stuff that makes a great barbecue joint to me. Good barbecue, a friendly atmosphere, a good story, and a unique way of doing things. All things considered, I'd call Blue Smoke one great barbecue joint! Blue Smoke is also instrumental in the organizing of the Big Apple Block Party every June on the streets of Manhattan. It's a big party with food served by a dozen or so of the biggest and best barbecue joints from around the country. There's Southside Market from Elgin, Texas, Salt Lick from Austin, Ed Mitchell's from Wilson, North Carolina, Big Bob Gibson from Decatur, Alabama, the 17th Street Bar and Grill from Murphysboro, Illinois, and Blue Smoke all lined up and feeding the city dwellers. It's truly a sight to see and a huge success. I grew up in Chicago and never had an interest in going to New York. Now my life is much different and I love to go there, and when I'm there I always stop at Blue Smoke.

Deviled Eggs

6 hard-boiled eggs, peeled, cut in half

¼ to ⅓ cup mayonnaise

2 teaspoons hot sauce

1 teaspoon dry mustard

½ teaspoon dried thyme leaves

Salt and pepper to taste

Paprika for garnish

One of the staples at Blue Smoke is the deviled eggs. Who doesn't like a couple of these with their barbecue? • **Yield: 6 servings as an appetizer**

Put the yolks in a small bowl. Add the rest of the ingredients and mash it all thoroughly with a fork. Add more mayonnaise if needed to create a thick but creamy consistency. Fill the whites with this mixture. Top each egg with a shake of paprika.

Dinosaur Bar-B-Que

New York City

www.dinosaurbarbque.com

▼▼

I've always loved the "Dinosaur
Good Eatin' Prayer":
Get down on your knees
And put up your paws
Thank the good Lord
For the use of your jaws

There's a sense of humor in everything that Dinosaur Bar-B-Que does, including the graffiti that they encourage their customers to inscribe upon the bathroom walls of their three locations in Syracuse, Rochester, and New York City. One of their favorite graffiti is "Love at first sight is just lust with potential!"

They got their start by catering biker bashes like the Harley Rendezvous because they didn't like the food served at them. Because they didn't have any investment capital back in 1983, they sawed a 55-gallon drum in half, borrowed some used restaurant equipment, and launched their catering business with three sandwiches: Italian sausage with onions and peppers, a burger, and rib-eye steak. In addition to the biker events, they worked swap meets, tattoo shows, state fairs, and regional festivals.

Life on the road can wear you down, as I know so well, and in 1987 the partners decided that their own restaurant was the answer. They found the old N&H Tavern in downtown Syracuse, New York. But although they called themselves "Bar-B-Que," they weren't actually fixing it. So one of the partners, John Stage, decided to study 'cue by traveling the South to eat at as many barbecue places as he could. It was, in John's words, "like penetrating a secret society."

They opened the first Dinosaur Bar-B-Que in the fall of 1988, but times were rough before they established a regular customer base. So they added a bar and live bands playing mostly the blues, and soon their restaurant was a happening kinda place. They also launched a line of Dinosaur products, including Dinosaur Bar-B-Que Sensuous Slathering Sauce, which they nicknamed "The Mutha Sauce," and Wango Tango Habanero Hot BBQ Sauce.

"The restaurant biz is a lot like a Broadway show," says John. "When the curtain goes up, you'd better be ready." He adds: "We've been gambling for years, and as long as we continue to enjoy the business and have a couple of crazy ideas in our heads, the evolution of Dinosaur Bar-B-Que is bound to continue."

Smoked Lamb Shanks and Garlic Mashed Potatoes

4 large lamb shanks

2 to 3 tablespoons olive oil

Dr. BBQ's Eastern Barbecue Rub, as needed (page 184)

1 cup red wine

Garlic mashed potatoes (recipe follows)

Dr. BBQ's Eastern Barbecue Sauce, as needed (page 184)

Lamb shanks are my all-time favorite meal. They serve them at Dinosaur with garlic mashed potatoes. Here's my version of that great dish. • Yield: • Serves 4

Prepare the cooker for indirect cooking at 250°F, using cherry wood for flavor.

Rub the shanks with the oil, and then season them liberally with the rub. Place them in the cooker for 2 hours.

Transfer the shanks to an aluminum foil pan. Add the wine and ½ cup water, and cover tightly with foil. Return to the cooker. Cook until the shanks are tender, about 3 to 4 more hours.

Remove the pan from the cooker. Transfer the shanks to a platter and tent with foil. Serve on top of a big pile of the garlic mashed potatoes and drizzled with the barbecue sauce.

Garlic Mashed Potatoes

1 whole head of garlic

Olive oil

6 medium russet potatoes

¼ cup butter

⅓ to ⅔ cup milk

¼ cup sour cream

2 tablespoons snipped chives

Salt and pepper to taste

• Yield: 4 servings

Preheat the oven to 350°F.

Trim the head of garlic about ¼ inch. Drizzle olive oil over the head of garlic and wrap it in foil. Bake for 45 minutes. Squeeze the cloves out of the skins and mash them thoroughly; set aside.

Peel and quarter the potatoes and place them in a saucepan of boiling salted water. Boil for 15 to 25 minutes until they are easily pierced with a knife. Drain the potatoes, return them to the saucepan, and add the butter and ⅓ cup of the milk. Mash until the potatoes are a smooth consistency, adding more milk if necessary. The amount of milk will vary, depending on the potatoes.

Stir in the remaining ingredients and serve.

Grill Kings BBQ Cookoff

Belmont Park
Long Island, New York
www.grillkings.com

▼▼▼

There wasn't much interest in barbecue on Long Island a few years ago, and there definitely wasn't a cookoff. That was until the Grill Kings came along. Grill Kings is headed by Dean Camastro, and they're bringing barbecue to New York in a big way. As in so many places, the people of Long Island are hearing about the barbecue craze and they want in on it. So in 2003 Dean and his friends put together a backyard cookoff. A backyard cookoff is a little more laid back, with shorter cook times, than a typical sanctioned cookoff. The next year they held a Kansas City Barbeque Society (KCBS) judging class. They lined up sponsors and promoted their idea everywhere they could and eventually they had everything in place to hold a 2004 New York State Championship cookoff on Long Island. They even got a proclamation from the governor proclaiming it as such. They lined up cooks, judges, and contest reps (hey, this is New York, they weren't just hanging around) and had a cookoff. By 2006 there were over fifty teams, with some of them selling to the public. There's a beer tent, bands, and even gambling.

Well, you have to walk over to the betting parlor, but the cookoff is at Belmont Park. They have a bunch of great prizes along with some solid prize money, but the coolest thing of all is the Grand Champions belt. It's like a World Championship wrestling belt, or the belt for one of the thousand or so boxing championships. (Which is more legit these days? Boxing or wrestling?) The Grill Kings are real go-getters and their event has a bright future. They have been written up in all the New York newspapers, and the week before finds many of the cooks appearing on local TV cooking some barbecue to help promote the event. In 2005 I was lucky enough to get up there and cook in the Grill Kings event. It was a good day for me, since I won the championship belt. I don't usually carry trophies with me, but that one was so cool that I did. I have many great pictures of hot girls wearing it and posing with me. It's good to be the (Grill) King. The bad news is it's a traveling trophy. You keep it for a year and then the next guy gets it. I'll be back to get it someday.

Wing Ding Chicken Wings

Wing Ding Dry Rub, as needed (recipe follows)

12 whole chicken wings

I made this rub for chicken wings and cooked some one day at a contest at which Dirty Dick was helping me. He liked them so much he asked for the rub recipe and used it at the Grill Kings wing cookoff in 2006. He used his own sauce on them, and took first place. I prefer them dry. • **Yield: 12 to 24 pieces**

Prepare the grill for direct cooking at medium heat.

Trim the tips off the wings and slash them on the inside of the joint. Apply a liberal coating of the rub to all sides of the wings. Put the wings in a zip-lock bag and refrigerate them for 1 to 2 hours.

Put the wings on the grill and cook, turning frequently, until crispy and brown. You should see the juices bubbling on top of the wings. This should take 30 to 40 minutes.

Remove them to a platter and let rest for 5 minutes. You can serve them whole or cut them to make 24 pieces.

Wing Ding Dry Rub

1 tablespoon granulated garlic

1 tablespoon onion powder

1 tablespoon chili powder

1 tablespoon lemon pepper

1 tablespoon salt

1 tablespoon turbinado sugar (Sugar in the Raw)

1 teaspoon ground cumin

1 teaspoon ground paprika

1 teaspoon cayenne pepper

• **Yield: About ½ cup**

Mix together and store in an airtight container.

Peppers

Tanger Factory Outlet at Rehoboth Beach

Rehoboth Beach, Delaware

www.peppers.com

▼▼

Not many people can say their business all started with a Bloody Mary smorgasbord, but Peppers can. The Hearn family—dad Luther, son Chip, and sister Randi—along with Kris Charles run Peppers, a mega hot sauce and barbecue sauce business. That's where it all began. They owned the Starboard Restaurant in Rehoboth Beach, Delaware, and had the idea to offer forty-eight ingredients to make your own Bloody Mary. The people loved it, and the selections quickly grew, ultimately topping out at 650 options for your drink. What a concept! Rehoboth Beach is a big summer party hangout for East Coasters, and the Sunday morning Bloody Mary was a welcome hangover cure. Luther tells me they had a line out in the parking lot just to get in the Bloody Mary line, which got you into the line for a table. Needless to say, many of the items on the smorgasbord were hot sauces. The family would bring back exotic samples from vacations around the world and Luther would order them in for the restaurants. Of course, everybody wanted to buy a bottle of their favorite, so they opened a wooden shack in the parking lot to sell the hot sauces. This was wildly successful. These guys invented the hot sauce shop. The shack was replaced by a bigger one, and they started a mailing list, sending out catalogs so the customers could get the products in the off-season, too. I remember getting one of those catalogs many years ago. It was simply a few pages with exotic hot sauces, barbecue sauces, dry rubs, and chile powders listed with prices. They were making this up as they went along. They made many trips to the Caribbean to find new products to sell. Exotic sauces are commonplace now, but this stuff just wasn't being brought to the States before Peppers went and got it. At the same time they were building their own collection of hot sauces. They've since sold the restaurant, but the sauce collection is alive and well and over 2,000 bottles these days. The shack is gone, too, but only because they've moved to a big location at the local outlet mall. They always carried some barbecue sauces, but nowadays that's a big part of the business along with dry rubs, books, aprons, and all the other stuff that we use in the fiery kitchen. The Internet has been a great fit for them as well, and www.peppers.com keeps them quite busy.

These folks are true entrepreneurs and I like them very much. They're fun, too. Chip's business card lists him as an Ice Cream Artist because they also run The Ice Cream Store right on the boardwalk where you can cool down if you do too much hot sauce. Of course, you can buy a little hot sauce there, too. Rehoboth Beach is a hot summer place and Peppers makes it even hotter.

Homemade Caribbean Hot Pepper Sauce

½ **pound habanero chiles, seeds and stems removed (try to find the red habs; be careful when handling the habaneros, they're extremely hot—I use rubber gloves)**

1 **medium white onion, chopped**

2 **cloves garlic, minced**

1 **medium papaya, boiled until tender, peeled, seeded, and finely chopped**

1 **medium tomato, seeded and finely chopped**

½ **cup cider vinegar**

½ **cup lime juice**

2 **tablespoons dry mustard**

1 **teaspoon dried thyme leaves**

1 **teaspoon dried basil leaves**

½ **teaspoon ground nutmeg**

½ **teaspoon ground turmeric**

In case you can't find one of the 2,000 sauces at Peppers to fit your taste, here's a hot sauce recipe you can make at home. • **Yield: 3 to 4 cups**

Combine the chiles, onion, garlic, papaya, and tomato in a food processor and puree (you may have to do this in batches). Remove to a bowl. Combine the vinegar, lime juice, and 2 tablespoons water in a saucepan and heat until it reaches a slight boil, then sprinkle the mustard, thyme, basil, nutmeg, and turmeric into the liquid. Pour this hot, spiced mixture over the puree and mix thoroughly.

Let cool and store in an airtight container in the refrigerator for up to 8 weeks.

Barbecue in New England

The New England Barbecue Society

Forestdale, Massachusetts

www.nebs.org

▼▼

In 1991 a New Englander named Jerry Soucy went to the American Royal. He saw wonderful things and went home to start a cookoff in Massachusetts. In 1991 the Pig'n Pepper cookoff was born. That's where it began in New England, and it's a common story. The American Royal was started after a member saw the cookoff at Memphis in May and the story repeats itself everywhere. So after a few years the people who were cooking at the Pig'n Pepper wanted to organize. The original group was The New England Society for Wood Cookery, but a year later in 1995 the New England Barbecue Society (NEBS) was born. Their first event was the Snowshoe Grilling Contest, which is still held each February near Boston. It takes a hearty cook to attend a grilling contest in February. I guess these guys were onto "Barbecue All Year Long" before I was! It's really interesting to think about how a few dozen people in New England who were interested in learning about real barbecue found each other. Without Food TV, e-mail, and the Internet I don't know how popular barbecue would be there even today, let alone then. But they did find each other and many lifelong friends have been made over the years. These days the NEBS people work with the Kansas City Barbeque Society on most of their big cookoffs. They help promote and organize the cookoffs but let KCBS handle the scoring. This works well because it lends a credibility that attracts traveling teams from around the country. I've cooked in New Hampshire at one of their events and had a great time. In 2006 they were involved with thirteen barbecue cookoffs and seven grilling contests. They also hold social meetings on a regular basis at barbecue restaurants. The NEBS people do a lot to promote barbecue. They regularly hold cooking classes just to help spread the word, and you can often find a member cooking somewhere as a demonstration. There are over three hundred members and at least one hundred active cooking teams. Many of the members now cater and sell products and do other barbecue business–related things. Like many of us they travel to cookoffs in other places to cook and make new friends. Teams from the NEBS have won major awards at cookoffs in Arizona, California, Maryland, Pennsylvania, Georgia, Kansas City, and Tennessee. Barbecue has come a long way in New England thanks to the New England Barbecue Society.

Franken-Chicken

1 whole chicken, 3 to 4
pounds

Franken-Chicken 5-Spice
Brine (recipe follows)

Franken-Chicken Spice
Rub, as needed (recipe
follows)

8 cinnamon sticks

Franken-Chicken Maple
Glaze (recipe follows)

This recipe comes from Steve Farrin and Doug Pini, also known as I Smell Smoke. They won the NEBS Team of the Year award in 2005 and 2006.

From Steve: "There's a little story behind the recipe. We cooked two different chicken recipes for a contest. One of them included the brine and the other included the glaze. When the cooking was done the brined chicken was moist and flavorful but the sauce and rub on the skin were not very good. The glazed birds were not brined and came out a bit dry. We actually removed the skin from a glazed bird and put in on the breast of the brined bird and got first-place chicken. After that contest we combined the two recipes and won many awards, including third-place chicken in the American Royal Invitational." • Yield: 2 to 4 servings

A day before you plan to cook, clean and trim excess fat from the chicken. Place it into a large resealable plastic bag. Pour the brine over the chicken. Refrigerate for at least 12 hours or up to 24 hours.

Prepare the cooker for indirect cooking at 350°F, using maple or apple wood for flavor.

Remove the chicken from the brine and rinse lightly under cold water. Dry the chicken. Generously rub chicken inside and out with the spice rub. Truss the legs to ensure even cooking.

Put the cinnamon sticks on top of the coals just before putting the chicken on to cook. Put the chicken in the cooker and cook for 45 minutes. Then begin glazing the chicken with the glaze every 10 minutes, and cook until the internal temp of the chicken is 165°F and the juices run clear. This should take another 20 to 30 minutes.

Franken-Chicken 5-Spice Brine

½ cup kosher salt

½ cup light brown sugar

2 tablespoons 5-spice powder

1 whole lemon, sliced

1 cinnamon stick (3 inches long) broken in thirds

10 whole black peppercorns

Combine ingredients and 8 cups (2 quarts) water in a large bowl. Whisk to dissolve the salt and sugar.

Franken-Chicken Spice Rub

¼ cup kosher salt

¼ cup light brown sugar

¼ cup pure ancho chile powder (ground ancho chiles, not blended)

2 tablespoons ground black pepper

1 tablespoon lemon pepper

1 tablespoon garlic powder

1 tablespoon onion powder

½ teaspoon cayenne pepper

½ teaspoon celery seeds

Combine ingredients in a large bowl. Store in an airtight container.

Franken-Chicken Maple Glaze

2 cups pure maple syrup

2 cups light brown sugar

¼ cup balsamic vinegar

2 teaspoons ground chipotle pepper

1 stick unsalted butter, cut in tablespoon-size pieces and slightly softened

Heat the syrup, sugar, and vinegar in a medium saucepan. Simmer for 10 minutes until slightly thickened. Add the ground chipotle pepper and whisk in the butter 1 tablespoon at a time, continuously simmering and stirring to incorporate the butter.

Barbecue in Maryland

Chap's Pit Beef
Baltimore, Maryland

Big Al's Pit Beef
Rosedale, Maryland

▼▼

I had heard about pit beef for many years and was really happy when I had a free afternoon in Baltimore recently to check it out. The legend goes that the best pit beef stands are lined up on Pulaski Highway. Well, this sounded like a great way to spend a few hours. I'd eat half a sandwich at 3 or 4 of them, save the leftovers for a later meal, and then find a place to take a nap. Good news and bad news. I drove up and down Pulaski Highway and could only find two pit beef stands. The good news is there really doesn't need to be more than two. The two I tried were both great, even better than I had hoped for. What I knew about pit beef beforehand was that it's seasoned well on the outside, charred a bit, cooked to medium-rare, and sliced thin on a slicing machine. Well, that's exactly what I got and it was outstanding.

The first place I went to was **Chap's Pit Beef**. It seems to be an upscale pit beef stand. Chap's is in the parking lot of a seedy-looking strip joint, so upscale might not be the right word, but it's a pretty nice place with a few tables inside. You wait in line, pay your tab, and get your food from the man at the next window. There is a sign telling you that you won't be waited on if you're on your cell phone. They should have those in every restaurant. When you get to the next window you'll see a huge gas grill with beef roasts, hams, turkey breasts, pork roasts, and ribs on it. This grill looks like it's been there for a long time. It's very cool looking and the cooks move fast. I had beef on a kaiser roll, medium-rare with no horseradish sauce, and it was excellent. I can't wait to go back. They also offered a plate with an open-face beef sandwich with fries, all covered in gravy. I was pretty sure I couldn't eat two of those, so I passed.

The next stop was **Big Al's Pit Beef**. It's not very far from Chap's and the pit beef was just as good. I'd give them both a perfect score. Big Al's is a little funkier, although it's not in the parking lot of a seedy strip joint. You stand outside to order and again get your food at the next window. The server was wearing a do-rag with skulls on it the day I was there. I don't think this was a required uniform for the workers at Big Al's because the cook wasn't wearing one. He just had a shaved head. They obviously don't have a rule against tattoos for their help, either. Don't misunderstand this to mean bad service, it was very good service and equally good food. I don't think these guys get robbed much, either. This time I ordered some beach fries to go with my sandwich. These are seasoned fries, an idea borrowed from the nearby boardwalks of the eastern seaboard. I also saw a sign for burnt ends, so I ordered them, too. The fries were good. The burnt ends seemed to be just that. The pieces that got too cooked were reserved for this. I had chunks of turkey, pork, and beef in my order, all pretty crunchy.

They were only a couple bucks and a small portion so they made a nice side item. I had a long drive ahead of me that day, so I saved them for snacking on the trip.

It's my understanding that pit beef is sold in other parts of Baltimore, even at the ballpark by former Oriole star Boog Powell, but I'll go back to Chap's and Big Al's next time I'm there. Yes, both of them. I don't see how it could get any better.

Dr. BBQ's Recipe for Pit Beef

1 choice-grade bottom round roast, 3 to 4 pounds

2 to 3 tablespoons olive oil

Dr. BBQ's Eastern Barbecue Rub, as needed (page 184)

8 to 12 kaiser rolls, depending how thick you stack the beef

Creamy Horseradish Sauce (recipe follows)

The trick to this recipe is slicing the meat as thin as possible. A slicing machine is best, but with a sharp knife and a lot of patience you can do it.
• Yield: 8 to 12 servings

Prepare the grill for direct cooking at medium-high heat.

Rub the roast with the oil to coat. Season the roast liberally with the rub.

Put the roast on the grill and cook, turning occasionally, until the roast is nicely browned on all sides. Reduce the heat to low and continue cooking and turning until the roast reaches an internal temp of 125°F.

Remove from the heat, wrap tightly in aluminum foil, and rest for 20 minutes. Slice across the grain as thinly as possible and serve on kaiser rolls. Serve the horseradish sauce on the side.

Creamy Horseradish Sauce

⅔ cup sour cream

¼ cup prepared horseradish

2 green onions, finely chopped

1 teaspoon distilled white vinegar

1 teaspoon sugar

¾ teaspoon chopped fresh dill weed

Horseradish sauce is a classic condiment that's served with smoked or roasted meats, beef in particular, and cooked or raw vegetables. Since horseradish is very volatile and loses its flavor and aroma quickly, this simple sauce should be made close to serving time. For an added hit of heat, I sometimes add ground habanero chile. • Yield: ⅔ cup

Combine all the ingredients in a bowl and blend until well mixed. Allow the mixture to sit for 15 to 20 minutes to develop the flavors.

Waldorf Eggfest

Waldorf, Maryland

www.seasonaldistributors.com

▼▼

Every May in Waldorf, Maryland, the original Eggfest is held at Seasonal Distributors. Dale and Rona Kelley are the owners and they are really nice people. They love having all the Eggers come to their place for a party. It all starts Friday evening with a bus ride to Captain Billy's, an authentic Chesapeake Bay crab shack. The crabs, shrimp, and beer flow for hours. It's quite a feast and quite a party. Then we go back to the hotel for some rest before the big day on Saturday. Now, if you can't sleep, you'll probably find some Eggers in the parking lot cooking something and tipping a few. Saturday is the big day. Seasonal Lisa (Lisa Shumaker) has everything ready when we show up early in the morning. There are Eggs of all sizes in the parking lot just waiting to have their virginity taken, and the Eggers roll in with coolers of meat and beer. They bring canopies, tables, chairs, and all the comforts of a home kitchen to the party. When it's all set up it looks like a little city. The common thread is a Big Green Egg in every booth, smoking away. Big Green Egg enthusiasts bring many different talents to the party. There are plenty of photographers, a couple of championship cooking teams offering tips, and even a blues band made up of Eggers. Most days Dale even sings a song with them. There are Eggcessories for sale; they even sell a few of my books there. Then there's a door-prize raffle with the coveted Mini Egg as the grand prize. A good time is had by all. But it's not over yet. Back to the hotel for a quick shower and the "After Party" begins in the parking lot. A few Eggs will be fired up to cook the leftovers, but it's gotten so popular that some of the Eggers bring special food reserved just for the After Party. Some will tell you that this is the highlight of the event. Nobody has to drive home and we're all among friends, so you can really let loose if you want. I know I talk a lot about the Big Green Egg and the culture in my books, but it's just that much fun.

Wess and Sally's Potato Skins

4 medium white potatoes

Olive oil

Dizzy Pig Red Eye Express, as needed (this is a spicy barbecue rub available at www.dizzypig.com)

1 cup shredded Cheddar cheese

2 tablespoons minced chives, plus more for garnish

8 slices bacon, cooked and crumbled

½ cup sour cream

Wess and Sally Breeden are longtime members of the Big Green Egg family. They've been to every Eggfest in Waldorf and always cook some wonderful things when they're there. • **Yield: 8 skins**

Boil the potatoes in salted water until just tender, about 15 to 20 minutes. Remove from the water and let cool.

Prepare the grill for direct cooking at medium heat.

Cut the potatoes in half and scoop out the flesh, leaving a ¼ to ½-inch shell. Rub the skins inside and out with olive oil and sprinkle liberally with the Red Eye Express or another spicy rub.

Put the potatoes on heavy-duty foil or a grill topper for about an hour, or until brown and slightly crispy. Check after 30 minutes, and more frequently after that.

Top with the cheese, chives, and bacon. Cook for a few more minutes, until the cheese is melted.

Top with sour cream and additional chives to serve.

The West

Dr. BBQ's Western Barbecue Rub

Dr. BBQ's Western Barbecue Sauce

Mr. Powdrell's Barbeque House (Albuquerque, New Mexico)

Beef Ribs in the Style of Powdrell's Barbeque House

Robb's Ribs (Albuquerque, New Mexico)

Green Chile–Cheddar Cornbread

Habanero Barbecue Sauce

Rudy's Country Store and BBQ (Albuquerque, New Mexico)

Smoked Prime Rib

The National Fiery Foods & Barbecue Show
(Albuquerque, New Mexico)

Southwestern Chile-Marinated Grilled Quail

Grilled Ostrich Steaks with Fiery Bourbon-Teriyaki Marinade

Best of the West Nugget Rib Cookoff (Sparks, Nevada)

Dr. BBQ's Navy Grog

Big Jim's Hog Breath Ribs

BBQ at the Summit (Dillon, Colorado)

1-2-BBQ Jalapeño Poppers

Ranch House BBQ (Olympia, Washington)

Ranch House Beef Barley

The Western BBQ Association (Bellevue, Washington)

Two Loose Screws Barbecued Salmon

Tex Wasabi's—Guy Fieri (Santa Rosa, California)

Tex Wasabi's Short Ribs

Santa Maria–Style Tri-Tip Barbecue

Dr. BBQ's Tri-Tip

Dr. BBQ's Tri-Tip Rub

Barbecue out west is many different things, and some of them are pretty unique. My first thought is of cowboy barbecue, but there is no distinct style of cowboy barbecue. Most of what I can find about that is directly related to some advertising promotion, because cowboy barbecue is a pretty good catch phrase. Barbecue is very popular in Denver, even spawning the Rocky Mountain BBQ Association, but the food I've found is typical American barbecue. There's some excellent barbecue in Albuquerque and that's no surprise. Albuquerque is an all-around great food town with all the terrific New Mexican restaurants, a strong link to the West Texas barbecue tradition, and a big fiery foods and barbecue show. Sparks, Nevada, adjacent to Reno, has probably the best rib-tasting party you'll ever go to. Head up to Seattle and you'll find the wonderful salmon that they've been cooking over wood for many years, but you'll also find some serious barbecue enthusiasts. And last but not least, there is even barbecue in California. Not everyone in California eats sprouts. They love real barbecue and even created their own specialty, the tri-tip.

Californians love to grill fresh fish, too, when they're not eating it raw. One of my friends in California even combines barbecue and sushi at his restaurant, Tex Wasabi's! But all of the barbecue out west seems to be imported from somewhere else, with the obvious exception of the salmon. That makes sense to me because while the location of the actual first people who cooked American barbecue may be debatable, it's a safe bet that it was not west of the Mississippi River. But like everything else that's good, people take it with them when they move. Then they often blend the old with what they find in the new land. I happen to like that. We didn't invent pizza, tacos, or gyros either, but we sure do like to eat a lot of them. We make them the way we like them, so why shouldn't folks add New Mexican chiles to their barbecue sauce or sprouts to their sandwich? Tofu grills up nicely, or so I've heard. Let the folks out west join in the fun of barbecue. There's plenty to go around. I hope you enjoy this chapter, but remember that it's a long ride to explore western barbecue, so you'll probably need to make a couple trips out west, which is not a bad thing at all.

Dr. BBQ's Western Barbecue Rub

1/2 cup chili powder

1/2 cup brown sugar

2 tablespoons salt

2 tablespoons granulated garlic

2 tablespoons onion powder

1 tablespoon ground cumin

• Yield: 1¼ cups

Mix all the ingredients together and store in an airtight container.

Dr. BBQ's Western Barbecue Sauce

2 ancho chiles

2 to 3 tablespoons olive oil

1 medium onion, chopped

2 cloves garlic, crushed

1/2 cup reserved chile water

1/2 cup tomato sauce

1/4 cup soy sauce

2 tablespoons turbinado sugar (Sugar in the Raw)

1 tablespoon balsamic vinegar

1 tablespoon smoked paprika

1 teaspoon salt

1/2 teaspoon finely ground black pepper

• Yield: About 1½ cups

A few hours before making the sauce, soak the ancho chiles in a cup of water. When the chiles are soft, remove the seeds and stems and chop the chiles. Be sure to reserve the water for the sauce.

Put the oil in a medium saucepan over medium heat. Add the onion, garlic, and chiles, and cook for about 5 minutes. Add all the other ingredients, stirring as you go. Bring to a simmer and cook 5 minutes. Transfer the sauce to a blender and blend on high for 3 to 4 minutes, or until smooth. Transfer the sauce back to the saucepan and check for thickness. If you'd like it thicker, just cook it for a few minutes. If you'd like it thinner, mix in some more of the reserved chile water.

Mr. Powdrell's Barbeque House

Albuquerque, New Mexico
www.mrpowdrellsbbq.com

▼▼

Pete Powdrell is the living legend of Albuquerque barbecue. I spoke with him and his son Mike in their location way out on east Central Avenue in Albuquerque and picked Pete's brain for an hour or so. He grew up in the Panhandle of West Texas and his grandfather taught him how to 'cue the old-fashioned way. They dug a pit in the ground and threw in dry hickory wood for the fire and some green hickory for the smoke. Their cooking grate was chicken wire suspended three feet over the fire. They kept the fire going twenty-four hours a day until all the meat was smoked.

In 1969, Pete moved to Albuquerque and opened his first restaurant at Gibson and Carlisle. He served his customers barbecue but also offered "country cookin'" that used herbs from the restaurant's garden. He's still doing that, although Mike has taken over the day-to-day operation of the restaurant. The restaurant gets its hickory wood from Texas, sweet potatoes from Turkey, Texas, and its beans from the Estancia Valley in New Mexico as they have for decades. Change is not a good thing at Powdrell's!

Pete says that the secret of good barbecue is where you're from, and the seasonings and sauces vary regionally. He vows he'll never give up "old-style" barbecue, which means taking the time to do things right. He refuses to use gas cookers or wrap barbecue in aluminum foil. And he makes his own sauce right there in the restaurant.

Because he's from Texas, he loves brisket—he told me that brisket "allows you to cook it a long time." In this case it's fourteen to sixteen hours. He doesn't trim any of the fat off the brisket before cooking it.

"How do you know when it's done?" I asked him.

"When you can smell more meat than smoke," Pete replied.

And then Mike brought us lunch—not brisket but juicy prime beef ribs, smoked to perfection.

Beef Ribs in the Style of Powdrell's Barbeque House

One large meaty slab of beef ribs, preferably cut from the rib eye

Dr. BBQ's Western Barbecue Rub, as needed (page 208)

Dr. BBQ's Western Barbecue Sauce, as needed (page 208)

Very few restaurants will give up their prized recipes, so I usually don't even ask. Here is my best reincarnation of those wonderful ribs from Powdrell's. Be sure to use hickory wood to flavor the ribs and if possible get it from Texas like Mr. Powdrell does. • **Yield: 2 servings**

Fire up your barbecue unit for indirect cooking at 225°F, using hickory wood for flavor.

Season the ribs liberally with the rub. Place in the ribs in the smoker and cook for 4 to 5 hours, or until the meat is tender.

Remove from the cooker and lightly brush with the barbecue sauce. Tent loosely with foil. Let the ribs rest for 15 minutes before serving.

The legendary Mr. Powdrell and I at Mr. Powdrell's restaurant in Albuquerque, New Mexico.

Robb's Ribbs

Albuquerque, New Mexico

www.robbsribbs.com

▼▼

This is another fine Albuquerque barbecue joint. Its high ceilings and painted murals don't have the funkiness of many barbecue places, but the food is really good. Robb Richmond is a friendly bearded guy who's always there, and he makes a smokin' hot habanero barbecue sauce. I usually dip very lightly in that one and a little heavier in the mild. Robb is famous for his ribs, but I always get the pork loin sandwich.

It's nicely smoked and lightly seasoned, cooked just right. It comes on a great roll. I wish I was there right now. The beans are good and the green chile cornbread is better. I usually have both, chased by an El Modelo. What I really like about Robb's is the way he's mixed the local flavor with authentic barbecue. Many times this can become some kind of confusion cuisine that I don't like, but not here. Robb's is good.

Green Chile–Cheddar Cornbread

1 cup coarse cornmeal

1 cup all-purpose flour

2 teaspoons sugar

1 teaspoon baking soda

1 teaspoon baking powder

1 teaspoon salt

¼ teaspoon garlic powder

1½ cups buttermilk

¼ cup finely chopped roasted and peeled green chile

2 eggs, beaten

1 cup grated Cheddar cheese

Here's my spin on Robb's cornbread. I've made one addition, cheddar cheese, and this cranked-up cornbread goes well with all types of barbecue. You can also make it with blue cornmeal. That'll get your guests' attention! • **Yield: 6 servings**

Preheat the oven to 350°F.

Combine all the dry ingredients in a bowl.

Heat the buttermilk with the green chile for 3 minutes and then allow it to cool. Combine the eggs and cheese in a bowl. Add the milk mixture and the egg mixture to the dry ingredients and blend until smooth.

Pour this mixture into a greased 9-inch-square pan and bake for 40 to 50 minutes, or until the cornbread is browned and firm.

Habanero Barbecue Sauce

1 onion, chopped

2 tablespoons butter, margarine, or vegetable oil

3 cloves garlic, minced

2 cups ketchup

½ cup cider vinegar

¾ cup brown sugar

2 tablespoons lemon juice

2 tablespoons Worcestershire sauce

1 habanero chile, seeds and stem removed, minced and then crushed in a mortar

2 teaspoons dry mustard

¼ teaspoon freshly ground black pepper

Salt to taste

The habanero is the hottest chile in the world, so you don't need much of it. This is my version of a sauce made at Robb's Ribbs in Albuquerque. It is a finishing sauce for grilled or smoked beef, chicken, or pork, to be applied before serving or served on the side. • **Yield: 2 cups**

In a small skillet, sauté the onion in the butter until soft. Add the garlic and sauté for 2 minutes.

Combine the onion and garlic with all the remaining ingredients in a saucepan and whisk to blend. Bring to a boil over high heat. Reduce the heat and simmer, uncovered, for 30 minutes, stirring occasionally.

Rudy's Country Store and BBQ

Albuquerque, New Mexico

www.rudys.com

▼▼

When I'm in Albuquerque I usually stay on the north end near Rio Rancho, and I always eat at Rudy's at least once. Rudy's Country Store and BBQ is like a modernized version of the great butcher shop barbecue joints of Texas. That's no surprise, because that's exactly what it is. It started in Leon Springs, Texas, in 1989 and has opened additional locations, spreading throughout Texas and the Southwest. You stand in line and when it's your turn, the cashier tells your order to one of the men cutting the meat right behind her in plain view. He pulls a piece of pork or brisket or turkey or whatever you have ordered from the real wood-burning pits that are right behind him, also in plain view, and he cuts your meat to order, by hand. Then the cashier places it on the scale right in front of you and rings it up. Simplicity at its best, and the barbecue is excellent. They have great side dishes at Rudy's, too. I highly recommend the creamed corn, cold beer, and hot cobbler for dessert. One very interesting thing is that they offer brisket and lean brisket. If you just order brisket you'll probably get the very well-marbled point muscle and that's a good thing. Many barbecue cooks serve the flat muscle to the guests and save the point for themselves. So please don't order the lean. They also have prime rib on the weekends until it runs out. I'd recommend going early to get in on some of that. They promote themselves as the "Worst Barbecue in Texas," but don't believe it. Rudy's may be a chain, but it's first rate in my book.

Smoked Prime Rib

One prime-grade 4-pound rib-eye roast

½ cup Dr. BBQ's Texas Barbecue Rub (page 94)

Dr. BBQ's Western Barbecue Sauce, as needed (page 208)

Here is my take on this very popular smoked roast at Rudy's BBQ. • **Yield: About 8 servings**

Prepare your cooker for indirect cooking at 225°F, using oak wood for flavor.

Allow the roast to reach room temperature. Rub the roast thoroughly with the Texas rub. Place it in the smoker and cook it for 3 to 4 hours, or until the internal temperature reaches 150°F.

Remove the roast from the smoker and tent it loosely with foil. Let it rest for 20 minutes. Slice about ½ inch thick, and serve with the barbecue sauce on the side.

The National Fiery Foods
& Barbecue Show

Albuquerque, New Mexico

www.fiery-foods.com

▼▼▼

My friend Dave DeWitt and his wife, Mary Jane Wilan, produce the largest trade and consumer show featuring chile-based and barbecue products, the National Fiery Foods & Barbecue Show. At this writing the show is in its nineteenth year and in 2006 it attracted 14,000 people to Sandia Resort and Casino to sample more than 1,000 different products. I've been one of the guest chefs for the past few years, and it's a blast to meet all of these people with such a passion for spicy food and barbecue.

Although the show is a big success now, it started out small. "I got the idea for the show after attending the New Mexico Chile Conference and seeing a couple of tabletop displays of jarred salsa," Dave told me. "I'd been a show producer for years and it suddenly occurred to me that here was a large industry that was growing fast and didn't have a trade show. So Mary Jane and I launched the first show—in the wrong city at the wrong time of the year—El Paso at harvest time. We had thirty-seven exhibitors and a total attendance of two hundred people, but it was a start. Then we moved it to Albuquerque in the early spring and each year the show had more exhibitors and was better attended."

I asked Dave about the barbecue element of the show, and he told me that more and more manufacturers were spicing up their rubs and barbecue sauces. "Just a few years ago, barbecue cooks would take a barbecue sauce like KC Masterpiece and add hot sauce to it to spice it up," he said. "But that's not necessary now because there are so many brands of barbecue sauces with various chiles like jalapeño, habanero, and chipotle. We're also seeing more and more hardware manufacturers exhibiting the latest new grills and smokers at the show."

Dave and MJ also produce a contest called the Scovie Awards Competition, and he said that he had so many entries in the category American-Style Barbecue Sauce that he had to create an American Style—Hot category. He also said there was a distinct trend toward fruit-based barbecue sauces these days.

I asked Dave what was the strangest thing that ever happened at the show. "Beer and superhot sauces don't mix well," he replied. "One company was improperly tasting a superhot sauce. They're supposed to be tasted only on the end of a toothpick, but this idiot gave a half-drunk attendee a chip covered with this incredibly hot sauce. Let's just say we had a regurgitation incident, which is not a good thing at a food show."

At one of the shows I gave a demonstration about ribs and I thought that the crowd might be bored with the technical details of butchering and preparing the ribs for smoking, but they loved it and kept asking questions. As any teacher will tell you, the job gets a lot easier when they throw questions at you. Of course, you can't barbecue inside the show hall, but I had my Big Green Egg outside, and gave everyone a taste of my ribs using the recipe in my first book, and they were a big hit. The show is the first weekend in March, and if you're traveling through the Southwest, I highly recommend going. It's really a lot of fun. Here are a couple of grilling recipes from guest chefs at the show.

Jim Minion glazes the chicken as part of my team at the 2005 American Royal.

Southwestern Chile-Marinated Grilled Quail

6 quail, backbones removed

The Marinade

1 tablespoon chopped fresh sage

1 tablespoon chopped fresh parsley

1 tablespoon chopped fresh rosemary

1 teaspoon salt

1 teaspoon ground black pepper

2 teaspoons chipotle chile powder

1 fresh serrano chile, seeded and finely chopped

$\frac{1}{2}$ cup olive oil

2 cloves garlic, minced

1 tablespoon lemon zest

The Glaze

4 dried red New Mexican chiles, stemmed and seeded

$\frac{1}{2}$ cup honey

The Greens

1 tablespoon olive oil

2 cloves garlic, finely chopped

2 bunches mustard greens, washed and stemmed

This recipe was demonstrated on stage at the National Fiery Foods & Barbecue Show in 2003 by Lois Ellen Frank and Walter Whitewater, with assistance from Sam Etheridge of Ambrozia Cafe and Wine Bar in Albuquerque. Lois and Walter coauthored *Foods of the Southwest Indian Nations*. • **Yield: 6 servings as an appetizer**

Wash each quail under cold running water. Cut the wings of each quail at their joints and set aside.

To make the marinade: Combine all of the ingredients in a mixing bowl. Add the quail, making sure each quail is thoroughly coated. Cover, place in the refrigerator, and let marinate overnight.

To make the glaze: In a small saucepan heat together the dried red chiles and $\frac{1}{2}$ cup water over high heat. Bring to a boil and boil for 1 minute, then remove from the heat. Let stand for 10 minutes. Place the mixture into a blender, add the honey, and blend for 1 minute. Pour through a fine sieve to remove the chile skins and discard them. Set aside.

Heat a grill or cast-iron grill pan over medium-high heat until hot but not smoking, and then place the marinated quail on it. Grill for about 5 minutes, then remove from the heat. Reserve half of the glaze for serving. Brush the remaining glaze onto both sides of each grilled quail. Place the quail topside up in a shallow roasting pan and then place them in the oven, on broil. Broil for 3 to 4 minutes until they begin to brown, then remove from the oven.

To make the greens: Heat a skillet over high heat. Add the oil, then the garlic, and stir for about 15 seconds. Add the mustard greens and cook for 2 minutes.

Serve each quail on a bed of sautéed greens, dizzled with the reserved glaze.

Grilled Ostrich Steaks with Fiery Bourbon-Teriyaki Marinade

1 cup teriyaki sauce

¼ cup bourbon

1 tablespoon habanero hot sauce

4 ostrich steaks

Prepared and buttered pasta

John Hard of CaJohn's Fiery Foods prepared this dish on stage at the fifteenth annual National Fiery Foods & Barbecue Show. Ostrich steaks are available at upscale butcher shops and yuppie supermarkets. • **Yield: 4 servings**

Combine the teriyaki sauce, bourbon, and hot sauce in a saucepan and bring to a simmer. Remove from heat and let cool.

Cut the ostrich steaks into 1-inch strips and marinate them in the mixture in a sealed container in the refrigerator for 1½ hours. Ostrich is very lean and requires a minimum of marinating time.

Prepare a grill for direct cooking at high heat.

Remove the ostrich from the marinade and place on the hot grill. Cook to medium doneness, basting with the marinade. Ostrich meat is best served medium-rare to medium-well—do not overcook.

Place the ostrich steaks on top of the pasta and enjoy.

Barbecue in Nevada

Best of the West Nugget Rib Cookoff
John Ascuaga's Nugget Casino Resort
Sparks, Nevada

▼▼▼

By any standard, the Best of the West Nugget Rib Cookoff is a big barbecue event. With 400,000 attendees and over 100,000 pounds of ribs; it's about as big as it gets. Hosted by John Ascuaga's Nugget in Sparks, Nevada, this is a huge barbecue event held over a five-day Labor Day weekend. The event is laid out nicely over a big area, so the teams can spread out their banners and cooking equipment. It's impressive to see these showmen strutting their stuff, and the huge crowd loves it. This is not a typical sanctioned cookoff, but a combination of a cookoff and a big-time barbecue selling event, and the teams are there to sell prepared meals to the public. Picnic tables and beer stands are almost as prevalent as the barbecue vendors. Add the constant live music, and you've got a heck of a party. Of course, there is the resort and casino right there as well if you're feeling lucky.

The Nugget is a family-run casino-hotel complex, and while hospitality and getting the guests fed is important, judging is high on their list of priorities, too. I am proud to have been invited to judge at this event, and it was great fun. Michonne Ascuaga, the CEO of the company, and her brother Stephen, the senior executive VP, were with us at every turn. They hosted a wonderful judges' dinner on Saturday night at Trader Dick's, one of the many fine restaurants within the Nugget, and were still with us at the awards ceremony on Monday. They really want this to be a premier event for everyone involved, and it is. The chief judge is a clear indication of that. They have recruited Chef Jim Heywood, a longtime instructor at the Culinary Institute of America in Hyde Park, New York. Jim is a great guy and a big fan of barbecue, but he's also a big-time competition chili cook. Jim is a regular winner at sanctioned cookoffs in the Northeast and has been invited to the World Championship Chili cookoff on many occasions. The judging pool that's recruited for Chef Heywood is also very impressive. In 2005 it included a few of Chef Heywood's former students who are now successful chefs themselves, Rick O'Fallon from The Pork Board, some big-name food writers and editors such as Dave DeWitt, and even a Food Network personality, Mark Silverstein from *The Best of . . .* The executive chef Jimmy Chan was there to cut the ribs for us as needed, and the tallying was done by the Nugget's financial department. They couldn't possibly have been more organized.

There are trophies and a serious amount of money ($7,500 to the winner) for the cooking teams, but the big attraction for the guests is eating the ribs. You can get a brisket sandwich or great sausage, but the ribs are king here. I saw many people who were there to sample ribs from as many vendors as they could. Some even had their own personal judging sessions, with notes from past years. They do it mainly for fun, but it also dictates whose ribs they'll sample first the following year. This is also a very good reason for the teams to put their best effort into winning. The past champions have the longest lines of customers. This event started in 1989, and there are cooking teams, judges, and guests who have been to every one.

The Best of the West brings out the big boys of the rib-selling circuit. On a good weekend the teams will sell upward of 5,000 slabs of ribs! Multiply that times twenty-five teams, and you'll see the grand scale of this event. My friend Tommy Houston drives his Checkered Pig team (the 2004 champs) with all the needed equipment from Martinsville, Virginia, to Sparks for this one. Yahoo tells me that's a 5,340-mile round-trip. Here are some other very impressive numbers from the event.

- 75 tons of pork ribs will be cooked and eaten.

- Over 6,500 gallons of beer will be consumed.

- 200 cases of lemons will be used to make lemonade (apparently they don't know about sweet tea in Nevada).

- 35,000 ears of corn will be buttered up.

- 65 dumpsters will carry away the garbage.

- One-half mile of extension cords will power everything.

- 75 Port-a-Potties will do their thing.

So, what recipes go with this story? For starters, I'll offer the navy grog that I enjoyed with fellow judge Tad Dunbar at Trader Dick's after the judging. Tad is a local news anchor and a longtime judge of this event. He says this is his traditional finish to the judging, and I think I'll make it mine as well.

Next, of course, is a great rib recipe, and what better recipe to feature than the one from the head judge, Chef Jim Heywood. He calls them Jim's Hog Breath Ribs, and they are fabulous. This event is a foodie's dream weekend that I give a serious thumbs-up.

Dr. BBQ's Navy Grog

1 ounce dark rum

1 ounce white rum

1 ounce 151-proof rum

1 ounce Cointreau

1 ounce grapefruit juice

1 ounce pineapple juice

1 ounce orange juice

You'd better give up your keys before you drink one of these. • Yield: 1 or 2 servings

Combine all the ingredients in a small pitcher. Add ice and stir. Serve in highball glasses on the rocks.

Big Jim's Hog Breath Ribs

2 slabs loin back ribs, about 2 pounds each

Big Jim's Hog Breath Basting Sauce, as needed (recipe follows)

Big Jim's Hog Breath Dry Rub, as needed (recipe follows)

Big Jim's Hog Breath Barbecue Sauce, as needed (recipe follows)

- Yield: 2 to 4 servings

Prepare the ribs 6 to 12 hours before you plan to cook. Peel the membrane from the back of the ribs. Paint both sides with the basting sauce. Sprinkle the dry rub lightly on both sides of the ribs. Wrap in plastic wrap and refrigerate for 6 to 12 hours.

Prepare the cooker for indirect cooking at 275°F, using apple wood for flavor.

Cook the ribs for 1½ hours, turning every 20 minutes. Paint the ribs again on both sides. Cook for 1 more hour, continuing to turn every 20 minutes. Discard the used basting sauce. Lower the temperature of the cooker to 250°F. Baste with the barbecue sauce and cook for 1 more hour, flipping and basting with the barbecue sauce every 15 minutes. Check for tenderness, and if they aren't quite done cook for an additional 30 minutes.

Serve with extra barbecue sauce on the side.

Big Jim's Hog Breath Basting Sauce

Two 5-ounce bottles Pickapeppa sauce

One 5-ounce bottle Worcestershire sauce

One 5-ounce bottle A-1 sauce

¼ cup maple syrup

1 tablespoon Liquid Smoke (optional)

Combine all the ingredients in a bowl and mix well. This can be made the day before and refrigerated. Bring to room temperature before using.

Big Jim's Hog Breath Dry Rub

2 cups salt

1/4 cup mild chili powder

2 tablespoons granulated onion

2 tablespoons Spanish paprika

1 tablespoon granulated garlic

2 teaspoons ground cumin

2 teaspoons ground allspice

1 teaspoon Mexican oregano

Combine all the ingredients in a bowl. Store in an airtight container in a cool, dry place.

Big Jim's Hog Breath Barbecue Sauce

3/4 cup frozen orange juice concentrate, thawed

1/4 cup prepared chili sauce (can be found in the grocery store near the ketchup)

1/2 cup chicken broth

1/3 cup molasses

3 tablespoons soy sauce

2 tablespoons lemon juice

1 clove garlic, finely mashed

1 tablespoon prepared dark brown mustard

2 teaspoons Worcestershire sauce

1 teaspoon Tabasco sauce

1 teaspoon salt

Combine all the ingredients in a bowl and mix well. Transfer to a saucepan and simmer for 15 minutes. This can be made a day ahead and kept in the refrigerator. Bring to room temperature before using.

Barbecue in Colorado

BBQ at the Summit

Dillon, Colorado

www.bbqatthesummit.com

▼▼▼

This is the World's Highest Barbecue cookoff. Just an hour or so west of Denver, Dillon is 9,087 feet above sea level, and it is the host to a great barbecue cookoff. It all started in 1996 when a member of the Summit County Rotary club attended a cookoff and brought the idea back to the club. Up stepped Rotary member Brenda Cameron, who now admits that she didn't really think she liked barbecue back then, but thought it was a good idea to have the cookoff. So she went to Stillwater, Oklahoma, and judged a cookoff. Then she went to Kansas City, where she met me and a few thousand of my friends at the American Royal, and she was hooked. Brenda has been the "Head Hog" at the Summit County Rotary cookoff since the beginning, and she now tells me she will soon become the "Head Hog Emeritus," but if I know Brenda she'll still be around helping out quite a bit. This is a true success story about how to have a great barbecue event. Brenda works tirelessly on the Dillon cookoff and has the great support of the Rotary and the town. She goes to all the big barbecue events around the country to promote Summit County, and the teams have responded. The folks in Dillon regularly host about seventy-five of the best teams in the country and thirteen teams have cooked every year. The cookoff in Dillon has become a good fundraiser and a fun event for the people of Summit County. Dillon is one of the few cookoffs around the country where all the teams sell food. The teams know it and the people of Summit County know it. The teams bring as much food as they can cook and the guests come hungry. It all starts at noon on Friday and it's a blast. You'll see plenty of the typical barbecue fare for sale, but you'll also see teams selling just about anything you can cook on a grill. Sausages, burgers, wild game, and even desserts. BBQ at the Summit also hosts a Kids-Q contest and a People's Choice contest, and in 2006 they hosted their first ever Elvis Impersonator contest. I haven't been to the Summit County Rotary barbecue in a few years, but the new Elvis thing has me looking at my schedule for next year. Maybe I can win the title of the Highest Barbecue Champion.

1-2-BBQ Jalapeño Poppers

12 jalapeño peppers

12 slices thin bacon, cut in half

1 cup cream cheese

24 toothpicks, soaked in water 15 to 30 minutes

This recipe comes from Del Anderson of 1-2-BBQ. Del's team has competed in the World's Highest Barbecue Cookoff every year since it started. I met him at his first cookoff many years ago in Kansas City. Thanks, Del. • **Yield: 24 poppers**

Prepare the cooker for indirect cooking at 225°F, using apple wood for flavor.

Remove the stems from the peppers and cut them in half lengthwise. Remove the seeds and veins in each half-pepper with a spoon. Fill each half level with cream cheese. Wrap each cream cheese–filled pepper with half a strip of thin bacon, using a toothpick to hold it together. Put the poppers in the cooker for 2 to 3 hours, or until the bacon is crispy

Barbecue in Washington State

Ranch House BBQ

Olympia, Washington
www.ranchhousebbq.net

▼▼

Amy Anderson may be a small woman, but by any other measure she is a big barbecue star. Amy has been winning major barbecue and chili cooking awards since she first got started in the mid-1990s, and now she serves the same recipes up for all the world to eat. Amazingly though, this world-class barbecue joint is in Olympia, Washington. It's a beautiful part of the country and they're on the road that heads to the beach. When I was there a man came in to make a reservation so he could eat barbecue on his way back from a trip there. I've known Amy and her partner, Melanie Tapia, for quite a few years, so I'm not surprised at the quality of the food here, but I was impressed when I realized that everything was homemade here to Amy's exact specifications. No shortcuts are used for anything! They make the slaw from scratch, as well as the beans, chili, french fries, rub, and even the barbecue sauce. I can tell you that not many places make everything from scratch, and that's why these girls and their restaurant are so popular. You'll see the big black pig mascot named Penny when you walk in the door, and then you'll notice the trophies that are everywhere. These are no run-of-the-mill trophies, though. You'll see awards from Terlingua, Texas, to Lynchburg, Tennessee, to Vancouver, British Columbia, and all points in between. It's a great place and be sure to tell the girls I said hi.

Ranch House Beef Barley

6 tablespoons butter

1 cup barley

½ cup onion, diced

¼ cup finely chopped fresh parsley

½ cup almonds, sliced

Salt and black pepper

Two 14.5-ounce cans beef broth

I asked Amy and Melanie for a recipe and this is what they sent. Wow! This is a great idea and a great side dish to go with barbecue. I love barley and never thought of something like this. I predict this will become a staple at my house. • **Yield: About 6 servings**

Preheat the oven to 375°F.

In a saucepan, melt the butter and sauté the barley, diced onion, parsley, and almonds over low to medium heat. Add salt and pepper to taste.

Spoon into an ungreased casserole dish. Stir in the broth. Cover and bake for approximately 70 minutes. Remove the lid. Stir gently and serve. Enjoy!

Melanie Tapia and Amy Anderson, the proprietors at Ranch House BBQ, pose with a great spread of their food shortly before I ate it.

The Western BBQ Association

Bellevue, Washington

www.wbbqa.com

▼▼▼

It's a long way from any of the alleged barbecue capitals of the world to Seattle, Washington. Frankly it's a long way to anywhere from Seattle, with the exception of Portland, Oregon, but then Portland isn't close to anything either. You get the picture. So it's really amazing how popular real barbecue is up there. The folks really do know about it and care about it. Don't get me wrong, they like salmon and the other indigenous seafood better, they like those little storefront teriyaki shops better, and they certainly like coffee better. My friend Jack Rogers once told me that "You can't hardly swing a dead cat in Seattle without hitting a coffee stand." You are right, Jack. Those things are everywhere. If you've never been to Seattle, they aren't all fancy little quaint cafés like I see here in Florida. These places are for caffeine junkies. They are just wooden sheds in a parking lot where you can get a fix of latte. In my experience there's always a cute young girl doing the enabling. You can't help but get caught up in it when you're there. Not that I would know about any of that kind of addictive behavior. Back to the barbecue. They've been having barbecue contests in Seattle for years. These days the group putting on the good ones is the Western BBQ Association, led by my old friend Jim Minion. Jim is most famous for having a method of lighting charcoal after him. It's a simple but effective way to get your cooker going. He says he didn't think it was a big deal, but the Minion Method has become legend on the Internet.

The Minion Method

Fill your grill or firebox up with charcoal. In a starter chimney, light about 30 briquettes. When the 30 briquettes are white and ashed over, spread them evenly over the top of the unlit charcoal. Proceed per the needs of your cooker.

I've hung out with Chris Lilly and Jim at a cookoff, and Jim got more attention than Chris did because of it. The folks didn't even notice me. But Jim has many other qualities besides being able to light charcoal. He's an excellent cook, having won many awards cooking with the above mentioned Jack Rogers as the Car Dogs; he's organized many great events in the Pacific Northwest including some fun cooking classes with yours truly; and he and his lovely wife, Angel, have been catering in the Seattle area for years. These days Jim is doing business with a partner as Two Loose Screws, and they're busy as can be. They're vending barbecue, catering barbecue, hosting barbecue cookoffs, and just all around living the life of a barbecue man. By the time you read this his real job should be old news, and I wish him all the luck in the world.

Two Loose Screws
Barbecued Salmon

1½ pounds king salmon fillet, skin on

½ cup dry white wine

½ cup tamari (substitute soy sauce if you must)

¼ cup water

3 tablespoons light brown sugar

1 small white onion, minced

¼ teaspoon cayenne pepper or 1 teaspoon chili oil

½ teaspoon freshly ground black pepper

Fresh rosemary sprigs

Vegetable oil for the grill

The folks in Seattle get a quality of salmon that some places never see. The difference is amazing. Look for the best quality you can find in your area.

- Yield: 4 servings

Debone the salmon fillet and trim it into four 6-ounce strips, leaving the skin on.

In a nonreactive bowl combine all the remaining ingredients except the rosemary and oil for the grill, mixing until the sugar is dissolved. Submerse the salmon fillets skin side up for 4 to 5 hours, but no longer since the fish picks up the flavors very well.

Prepare the grill for direct cooking at medium heat, using cherry wood for flavor.

Clean the grill and then brush lightly with the oil. Place the marinated fillets on the cooker (reserve the marinade) skin side down with about 2 inches of space between the pieces. Add the sprigs of fresh rosemary to the grill in between the fillets. Cover and cook 20 to 30 minutes, or until the internal temperature reaches 130 degrees, basting occasionally with the remaining marinade. Discard the marinade when 5 minutes are left in the cooking time.

Remove the fillets to a platter and serve.

Barbecue in California

Tex Wasabi's—Guy Fieri

Santa Rosa, California
www.texwasabis.com

▼▼

Southwestern barbecue and California-style sushi have tied the knot in California. That's what they serve at Tex Wasabi's. "Tex" is for the barbecue and "Wasabi" is for the sushi. Now this may seem like a bit of a wacky idea, but first of all it's in California and second of all it's the brainchild of Guy "Guido" Fieri and his partner, Steve Gruber. I don't know Steve, but if he's anything like Guido, the barbecue and sushi combo seems perfectly normal. I asked if many people ordered some raw fish and some ribs at the same meal and the answer is yes. But I also learned about Gringo Sushi. You see, in Japanese the word "sushi" refers to the rice (raw fish is sashimi), and in Japan your sushi may very well include some cooked meat. So Guy took some pulled pork, added it to some rice, rolled it up in a tortilla, and Gringo Sushi was born.

The popularity of Gringo Sushi has grown, and they now also use the tapioca sheets that are common in Vietnamese cooking to wrap the Gringo Rolls, and their fillings have become a little more interesting. Guy mentioned french fries and avocado. Sounds good to me. They serve plenty of traditional California sushi, too, but the Gringo Sushi is going strong. Then there's the barbecue. It's served in Northern California, where they don't have a great barbecue tradition, so it's really a morphed version of all the styles Guy has seen in his travels. It's a good combination and the food there is excellent.

So now I have to talk about Guido. He's been in the restaurant business since 1996 and Tex Wasabi's has been open since 1998. He's an interesting guy who regularly cooked at the American Royal with some friends as the Motley Q Crew. Guy wears his hair kind of bright and spiked and is never at a loss for words, so he's well liked around the cast of characters who make up the barbecue circuit. Then one day he tried out for a spot on *The Next Food Network Star.* He was chosen to be part of the show and he did a great job all the way through the reality-based competition. When the smoke cleared Guy Fieri was the winner and was given a contract to do a new show, *Guy's Big Bite* for the Food Network. Guy is a talented chef and a charismatic speaker and everyone who knows him is really happy for him. He remains well-grounded and doesn't speak for very long without mentioning his sons, Hunter and Ryder. He's also still a restaurant guy at heart, and I don't think that will change any time soon.

Note: By the time this book comes out I expect that Guy's career will have gone much further and I'll be proud to say "I knew him when. . . ."

Tex Wasabi's Short Ribs

1 cup sherry

1 cup rice vinegar

1 cup sesame oil

³/₄ cup grated ginger

¹/₄ cup minced garlic

¹/₂ cup honey

¹/₄ cup brown sugar

2 cups soy sauce

1 cup sesame seeds

10 pounds beef short ribs, sliced across the bones about ¹/₄ inch thick

1 cup chopped scallions for garnish

This is the recipe right from Guido. You'll need to either have a party or cut it down. I'd suggest the party. • **Yield: 20 servings**

Mix all ingredients except the meat and the scallions. Let sit for up to 12 hours.

Add the short ribs, making sure to separate them for full marination effectiveness. Marinate for up to 48 hours.

Prepare a grill for direct cooking at high heat.

Place ribs on the grill, shaking off excess marinade first to reduce flare-up. Grill on both sides until cooked to medium doneness, 5 to 8 minutes.

Guy Fieri of Tex Wasabi's is a dedicated father, and often cooks with his sons Hunter (pictured) and Ryder.

Santa Maria–Style Tri-Tip Barbecue

▼▼

The tri-tip barbecue popularized in Santa Maria is a California tradition that originated with the vaqueros, Mexican cowboys who ran cattle on the huge ranchos in the Santa Maria Valley during the early days. After the cattle roundup, the vaqueros threw large beef barbecues beneath the red oak trees on the ranchos.

In the modern era, Santa Maria–style barbecue began around 1950 in Santa Maria, California, and its invention is credited to a meat market manager named Bob Shutz. He didn't want to waste the cut that was left after the sirloin was trimmed, so he sprinkled some garlic, salt, and pepper on the cut, placed it on a rotisserie, and cooked it for about 45 minutes. His friends predicted that it would be tough, but it was amazingly tender and delicious. Word got out and a "new" barbecue dish was born. These days, the meat, averaging a little over two pounds, is cooked until medium-rare over a very hot fire built with red oak. It should be charred and crusty on the outside but still juicy on the inside. Santa Maria–style barbecue is real simple, with few seasonings, minimal preparations, and quick cooking, but delicious. It's become a staple at festivals all over California. If you head to Santa Maria, California, any weekend you will probably find someone selling tri-tip cooked over red oak on the street. This is where it all began. Nowadays everyone in California cooks tri-tip. That's the main reason it's scarce in other places, they're eating it all.

Tri-tips are now a category in many California barbecue cookoffs, and if I ever enter one of those, here's how I would do it.

Dr. BBQ's Tri-Tip

1 choice-grade tri-tip, approximately 2 ½ pounds, fat untrimmed

2 tablespoons olive oil

Dr. BBQ's Tri-Tip Rub (recipe follows)

If you absolutely can't find a tri-tip, use a very thick sirloin steak. • **Yield: 6 servings**

Rub the tri-tip all over with the olive oil and rub, and let it marinate, preferably overnight in the refrigerator. About 2 hours before you plan to grill it, remove the roast from the refrigerator and let it come to room temperature.

Build a hot oak wood or charcoal fire in your grill.

Place the tri-tip on the grill and cook it for approximately 25 minutes, turning often so that all sides cook evenly. The outside of the meat should be well blackened. The internal temp should be 130°F for rare, 145°F for medium, and 160°F for well done.

Remove from the heat and tent loosely with foil. Let it rest for 5 minutes, and then slice it as thinly as possible.

Dr. BBQ's Tri-Tip Rub

1 tablespoon salt

1 tablespoon finely ground black pepper

1 tablespoon granulated garlic

½ tablespoon granulated onion

½ tablespoon mild red chile powder

In a bowl, combine all the ingredients and mix well.

APPENDIX

Kansas City, KS / Kansas City, Mo

Arthur Bryant's—The Original
1727 Brooklyn Avenue
Kansas City, MO
Ph: 816-231-1123
www.arthurbryantsbbq.com

The American Royal Barbecue
1701 American Royal Court
Kansas City, MO 64102
Ph: 816-221-9800
www.americanroyal.com

The Kansas City Barbeque Society
11514 Hickman Mills Drive
Kansas City, MO 64134
Ph: 816-765-5891
www.kcbs.us

Bichelmeyer's Meats
706 Cheyenne
Kansas City, KS 66105
Ph. 913-342-5945

Oklahoma Joe's
3002 W. 47th Avenue
Kansas City, KS 66203
Ph: 913-722-3366
   or
11950 South Strang Line Road
Olathe, KS 66063
Ph: 913-782-6858
www.oklahomajoesbbq.com

Jones Bar-B-Q
609 North 6th Street
Kansas City, KS 66101
Ph: 913-281-4148

Smokin' Guns BBQ
1218 Swift Street
North Kansas City, MO 64116
Ph: 816-221-2535
www.smokingunsbbq.com

Rosedale Barbeque
600 Southwest Boulevard
Kansas City, KS 66103
Ph: 913-262-0343

Fiorella's Jack Stack
135th Street & Holmes Street
Kansas City, MO 64145
Ph: 816-942-9141
www.jackstackbbq.com

Culinary Center of Kansas City
7917 Foster Street
Overland Park, KS 66024
Ph: 913-341-4455
www.kcculinary.com

Kansas City Barbecue Society
11514 Hickman Mills Drive
Kansas City, MO 64134
Ph: 816-765-5891
www.kcbs.us

North Carolina

Bill's Barbecue
Bill Ellis Barbecue
3007 Downing Street
Wilson, NC 27893
Ph: 1-800-68-BILLS
www.bills-bbq.com

Barbecue Center
900 N. Main Street
Lexington, NC 27292
Ph: 336-248-4633
www.barbecuecenter.com

Hursey's Bar-B-Q
1834 S. Church Street
Burlington, NC 27215
Ph: 336-226-1694
www.hurseysbarbq.com

Parker's Barbecue
2514 US Highway 301 S.
Wilson, NC 27893
Ph: 252-237-0972

Log Cabin Bar-B-Que
2322 US Highway 52 N.
Albemarle, NC 28001
Ph: 704-982-5257

King's Barbecue
910 W. Vernon Avenue
Kinston, NC 28501
Ph: 252-527-1661
www.kingsbbq.com

Wilber's Barbecue
4172 US Highway 70 E.
Goldsboro, NC 27534
Ph: 919-778-5218

The Skylight Inn
4617 Lee Street
Ayden, NC 28513
Ph: 252-746-4113

Southern Barbecue Too
10361 NC Highway 8
Lexington, NC 27292
Ph: 336-798-2300

B's Barbecue
751 B's Barbecue Road
Greenville, NC 27834
Ph: 252-758-7126
www.bsbarbecue.com

Pig-N-Out
5954 University Parkway
Winston-Salem, NC 21705
Ph: 336-377-3215

Blue Mist Barbecue Restaurant
3409 US Highway 64 E.
Asheboro, NC 27203
Ph: 336-625-3980

Smithfield's Chicken 'N Bar-B-Q
7911 Fayetteville Road
Raleigh, NC 27603
Ph: 919-661-9151
www.smithfieldschicken.com

McCall's Barbecue and Seafood
139 Millers Chapel Road
Hwy 70 E. & 111 Intersection
Goldsboro, NC 27534
Ph: 919-751-0196
www.mccallsbbq.com/index.htm

Smokey Joe's Barbecue
1101 South Main Street
Lexington, NC 27292
Ph: 336-249-0315

Jimmy's Barbecue
1703 Cotton Grove Road
Lexington, NC 27292
Ph: 336-357-2311

Lexington Barbecue
Business Loop I-85
Lexington, NC 27292
Ph: 336-249-9814

BBQ & Ribs Co.
522 St. Mary's Street
Raleigh, NC 27605
Ph: 919-755-3366
www.bbqandribs.com

Stamey's Barbecue
2206 High Point Road
Greensboro, NC 27403
Ph: 336-299-9888
www.stameys.com

Whispering Pines
1421 US Highway 52 N.
Albemarle, NC 28001
Ph: 704-982-6184

Clark's Bar-B-Q
1331 Highway 66 S.
Kernersville, NC 27284
Ph: 910-996-8644

Bubba's Barbecue
4400 Sunset Road
Charlotte, NC 28216
Ph: 704-393-2000
www.bubbasbbq.com

Kings Mountain Firehouse BBQ Cookoff
Kings Mountain, NC
www.kcbs.us

Nahunta Pork Center
200 Bertie Pierce Road
Pikeville, NC 27863
Ph: 919-242-4735
or

Nahunta Pork Center Outlet
North Carolina State Farmers Market
Raleigh, NC 27603
Ph: 919-831-1848
www.nahuntaporkcenter.com

Tennessee

**World Championship Barbecue
Cooking Contest**
Memphis in May International Festival
88 Union Avenue, Suite 301
Memphis, TN 38103
Ph: 901-525-4611
www.memphisinmay.org

Corky's Bar-B-Q
5259 Poplar Avenue (White Station)
Memphis, TN 38119
Ph: 901-685-9744
www.corkysbbq.com

The Bar-B-Q Shop
1782 Madison Avenue
Memphis, TN 38104
Ph: 901-272-1277
www.barbqshop.com

Leonard's Pit Barbecue
5465 Fox Plaza Drive
Memphis, TN 38115
Ph: 901-360-1963
www.leonardsbarbecue.com

Cozy Corner
745 N. Parkway
Memphis, TN 38105
Ph: 901-527-9158

The Rendezvous
52 South Second Street
(General Washburn Alley)
Memphis, TN 38103
Ph: 901-523-2746

Interstate Bar-B-Q
2265 S. Third Street
Memphis, TN 38109
Ph: 901-775-2304

Paradise Ridge Grille
3736 Annex Avenue
Nashville, TN 37209
Ph: 615-356-6750

Amazin' Blazin' BBQ Cookoff
Wilson County Fair
James E. Ward Agricultural Center
945 Baddour Parkway
Lebanon, TN 37088
tnamazinblazin@aol.com
www.wilsoncountyfair.net

**Jack Daniel's World Championship
Invitational Barbecue**
Every October in Lynchburg, Tennessee
Ph: 931-759-6930
www.jackdaniels.com

Texas

Obie Obermark
Trader's Village
2602 Mayfield Road
Grand Prairie, TX 75052
Ph: 972-641-2660
www.obiecue.com

International Barbecue Cookers
Association
Arlington, TX 76007
Ph: 817-469-1579
www.ibcabbq.org

BBQ Pits by Dave Klose
2216 West 34th Street
Houston, TX 77018
Ph: 1-800-487-7487
www.bbqpits.com

Bill and Barbara Milroy,
Texas Rib Rangers
2402 Sherwood Street
Denton, TX 76209
Ph: 940-565-1983
www.texasribrangers.com

Railhead Smokehouse
2900 Montgomery Street
Fort Worth, TX 76107
Ph: 817-738-9808

Burn's Bar-B-Q
8307 De Priest Street
Houston, TX 77088
Ph: 281-445-7574

Goode Company
5109 Kirby Drive
Houston, TX 77098
Ph: 713-522-2530
www.goodecompany.com

Meyer's Elgin Smokehouse
188 Highway 290
Elgin, TX 78621
Ph: 512-281-5546
www.meyerselginsausage.com

Black's BBQ
215 N. Main Street
Lockhart, TX 78644
Ph: 512-398-2712
www.blacksbbq.com

Smitty's Market
208 South Commerce Street
Lockhart, TX 78644
Ph: 512-398-9344
www.smittysmarket.com

Southside Market & BBQ
1212 Highway 290 E.
Elgin, TX 78621
Ph: 512-285-3407
www.southsidemarket.com

House Park Bar-B-Que
900 West 12th Street
Austin, TX 78703
Ph: 512-472-9621

Kreuz Market
619 N. Colorado Street
Lockhart, TX 78644
Ph: 512-398-2361
www.kreuzmarket.com

The Salt Lick
18001 FM 1826
Driftwood, TX 78619
512-858-4959
www.saltlickbbq.com

Louie Mueller Barbecue
206 W. Second Street
Taylor, TX 76574
Ph: 512-352-6206

Clem Mikeska's
1217 South 57th Street
Temple, TX 76504
Ph: 254-778-5481
www.clembbq.com

The North

Robinson's #1 Ribs
225 S. Canal Street
Chicago, IL 60606
Ph: 312-258-8477
www.rib1.com

The Illinois State BBQ Championships
Shannon, IL 61078
Ph: 815-864-2679
www.ilstatebbqchampionship.com

Sprecher Brewery
701 W. Glendale Avenue
Glendale, WI 53209
Ph: 414-964-7837
www.sprecherbrewery.com

The Great Pork BarbeQlossal
National Pork Board
1776 NW 114th Street
Des Moines, IA 50325
Ph: 1-800-456-PORK
www.pork.org

Hawgeyes BBQ
1313 SW Ordnance Road
Ankeny, IA 50021
Ph: 877-841-7192
www.hawgeyesbbq.com

City BBQ
Upper Arlington City Barbeque
2111 W. Henderson Road
Columbus, OH 43220
Ph: 614-538-8890
www.citybbq.com

The Canadian Barbecue Championship
Canadian Barbecue Association
Barrie, Ontario
Ph: 705-792-6814
www.canadianbarbecueassociation.com

The South

Big Bob Gibson Bar-B-Q
1715 Sixth Avenue, SE
Decatur, AL 35601
Ph: 256-350-6969
www.bigbobgibsonbbq.com

Dreamland Bar-B-Que Ribs
5535 15th Avenue E.
Tuscaloosa, AL 35405
Ph: 205-758-8135
www.dreamlandbbq.com

The National Barbecue Festival
373 Phelps Road
Douglas, GA 31533
Ph: 912-384-8917
www.nationalbbqfestival.com

Jack's Old South
120 N. 3rd Street
Vienna, GA 31092
Ph: 229-268-1500
www.jacksoldsouth.com

Sonny's Real Pit Bar-B-Q
150 locations throughout the Southeast
Main number: 407-660-8888
www.sonnysbbq.com

Peeble's Barbecue
503 Old Dixie Highway
Auburndale, FL 33823
Ph: 863-967-3085

First Choice Southern Bar-B-Q
10113 Adamo Drive
Tampa, FL 33619
Ph: 813-621-7434
www.firstchoicebbq.com

Moonlite Bar-B-Q Inn
2840 West Parrish Avenue
Owensboro, KY 42301
Ph: 270-004-0143
www.moonlite.com

Old Hickory Pit Bar-B-Q
338 Washington Avenue
Owensboro, KY 42301
Ph: 270-926-9000

Precious Blood Parish Barbecue Picnic
Precious Blood Parish
3306 Fenmore Street
Owensboro, KY 42301
Ph: 270-684-6888

The East

Daisy May's BBQ USA
623 11th Avenue
New York, NY 10036
Ph: 212-977-1500
www.daisymaysbbq.com

Blue Smoke
116 E. 27th Street
New York, NY 10016
Ph: 212-447-7733
www.bluesmoke.com

Dinosaur Bar-B-Que
646 W. 131st Street
New York, NY 10027
Ph: 212-694-1777
www.dinosaurbarbque.com

Grill Kings Long Island BBQ Cookoff
Belmort Park
Long Island, NY
www.grillkings.com

Peppers
Tanger Factory Outlet at Rehoboth Beach
36445 Seaside Outlet Drive
Rehoboth Beach, DE 19971
Ph: 302-227-4608
www.peppers.com

The New England Barbecue Society
Forestdale, MA 02644
www.nebs.org

Chap's Pit Beef
5801 Pulaski Highway
Baltimore, MD 21205
Ph: 410-483-2379

Big Al's Pit Beef
7926 Pulaski Highway
Rosedale, MD 21237
Ph: 410-574-3030

Waldorf Eggfest
Seasonal Distributors
12050 Trade Zone Court
Waldorf, MD 20601
www.seasonaldistributors.com

The West

Mr. Powdrell's Barbeque House
11309 Central Avenue NE
Albuquerque, NM 87107
Ph: 505-298-6766
www.mrpowdrellsbbq.com

Robb's Ribbs
3000-C San Pedro NE
Albuquerque, NM 87110
Ph: 505-884-7422
www.robbsribbs.com

Rudy's Country Store and BBQ
10136 Coors, NW
Albuquerque, NM 87114
Ph: 505-890-7113
www.rudys.com

The National Fiery Foods & Barbecue Show
3825 Beall Court, SW
Albuquerque, NM 87105
Ph: 505-873-8680
www.fiery-foods.com

Best of the West Nugget Rib Cookoff
John's Ascuaga's Nugget Casino Resort
1100 Nugget Avenue
Sparks, NV 89431
Ph: 800-648-1177

BBQ at the Summit
Frisco, CO 80443
Ph: 888-499-4499
www.bbqatthesummit.com

Tex Wasabi's
515 4th Street
Santa Rosa, CA 95401
Ph: 707-544-TEXX
www.texwasabis.com

Ranch House BBQ
10841 Kennedy Creek Road, SW
Olympia, WA 98512
Ph: 360-866-8704
www.ranchhousebbq.net

The Western Barbecue Association
Bellevue, WA 98015
www.wbbqa.com

Index

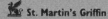

Made in the USA
Lexington, KY
10 December 2014